Evaluating Criminology and Criminal Justice

Recent Titles in
Contributions in Criminology and Penology

Coca and Cocaine: An Andean Perspective
Felipe E. Mac Gregor, editor

Police Under Pressure: Resolving Disputes
Robert Coulson

Punishing Criminals: Developing Community-Based Intermediate Sanctions
Malcolm Davies

Crack and the Evolution of Anti-Drug Policy
Steven R. Belenko

In Defense of Prisons
Richard A. Wright

Police in Contradiction: The Evolution of the Police Function in Society
Cyril D. Robinson, Richard Scaglion, with J. Michael Olivero

Drug Abuse Treatment: The Implementation of Innovative Approaches
Bennett W. Fletcher, James A. Inciardi, and Arthur M. Horton

State Police in the United States: A Socio-Historical Analysis
H. Kenneth Bechtel

Academic Politics and the History of Criminal Justice Education
Frank Morn

Crime History and Histories of Crime: Studies in the Historiography of Crime and
Criminal Justice in Modern History
Clive Emsley and Louis A. Knafla, editors

The Effectiveness of Innovative Approaches in the Treatment of Drug Abuse
*Frank M. Tims, James A. Inciardi, Bennett W. Fletcher, and Arthur MacNeill Horton, Jr.,
editors*

Tradition of the Law and Law of the Tradition: Law, State, and Social
Control in China
Xin Ren

Evaluating Criminology and Criminal Justice

Ellen G. Cohn, David P. Farrington, and Richard A. Wright

Contributions in Criminology and Penology, Number 51
Marvin Wolfgang, *Series Adviser*

GREENWOOD PRESS
Westport, Connecticut • London

Library of Congress Cataloging-in-Publication Data

Cohn, Ellen G.
    Evaluating criminology and criminal justice / Ellen G. Cohn, David
P. Farrington, and Richard A. Wright.
        p.   cm.—(Contributions in criminology and penology, ISSN
0732–4464 ; no. 51)
    Includes bibliographical references and index.
    ISBN 0–313–30153–0 (alk. paper)
    1. Criminology—Research—Evaluation.   2. Criminal justice,
Administration of—Research—Evaluation.   3. Bibliographical
citations—Evaluation.   I. Farrington, David P.   II. Wright,
Richard A. (Richard Alan), 1953–   .   III. Title.   IV. Series.
HV6024.5.C6315   1998
364′.072—DC21   97–37969

British Library Cataloguing in Publication Data is available.

Library of Congress Catalog Card Number: 97–37969
ISBN: 0–313–30153–0
ISSN: 0732–4464

First published in 1998

Greenwood Press, 88 Post Road West, Westport, CT 06881
An imprint of Greenwood Publishing Group, Inc.

Printed in the United States of America

The paper used in this book complies with the
Permanent Paper Standard issued by the National
Information Standards Organization (Z39.48–1984).

10 9 8 7 6 5 4 3 2 1

Contents

List of Tables   vii

Foreword by Marvin E. Wolfgang   ix

Preface   xi

1. Citation Analysis in Criminology and Criminal Justice   1

2. The Most-Cited Scholars and Works in Major American and International Criminology and Criminal Justice Journals, 1986–1990 and 1991–1995   23

3. Topics Covered in Nine Major Criminology and Criminal Justice Journals, 1986–1990 and 1991–1995   55

4. The Most-Cited Scholars and Works in Twenty Major Criminology and Criminal Justice Journals in 1990   65

5. The Most-Cited Scholars in Criminology and Criminal Justice Since 1945: A Longitudinal Analysis of Four Data Sets   81

6. Who Lands the Luminaries? Rating the Prestige of Criminology and Criminal Justice Journals Through an Analysis of Where Scholars Publish   91

7. A Page-Coverage Analysis of the Most Influential Scholars in Criminology Textbooks   103

8. Finis for the Convergence Controversy? A Citation Analysis
    of the Complementarity Between Criminology and Criminal Justice   113

9. The Way Forward   123

Bibliography   125

Index   137

List of Tables

2.1	Most-Cited Scholars in *Criminology*	28
2.2	Most-Cited Scholars in *Journal of Quantitative Criminology*	30
2.3	Most-Cited Scholars in *Journal of Research in Crime and Delinquency*	32
2.4	Most-Cited Scholars in Three Criminology Journals	34
2.5	Most-Cited Scholars in *Justice Quarterly*	35
2.6	Most-Cited Scholars in *Journal of Criminal Justice*	37
2.7	Most-Cited Scholars in *Criminal Justice and Behavior*	39
2.8	Most-Cited Scholars in Three Criminal Justice Journals	41
2.9	Most-Cited Scholars in *British Journal of Criminology*	43
2.10	Most-Cited Scholars in *Canadian Journal of Criminology*	45
2.11	Most-Cited Scholars in *Australian and New Zealand Journal of Criminology*	46
2.12	Most-Cited Scholars in Three International Journals	48
2.13	Most-Cited Scholars in Nine Journals, 1991–1995	49
2.14	Most-Cited Scholars in Nine Journals, 1986–1990	51
3.1	Topics Covered in Nine Journals, 1986–1995	58
3.2	More Detailed Topics Covered	59
3.3	Topics Covered, 1986–1990 and 1991–1995	60
3.4	Quantitativeness in Nine Journals	62
3.5	Quantitativeness, 1986–1990 and 1991–1995	63
4.1	Journals Included in the Analysis	68
4.2	Most-Cited Scholars in Each Journal in 1990	69
4.3	Scores in Five American Criminology Journals	70
4.4	Scores in Five American Criminal Justice Journals	71
4.5	Scores in Five International Criminology Journals	72
4.6	Scores in Five International Criminal Justice Journals	73

4.7   Scores in All Ten Criminology Journals   74
4.8   Scores in All Ten Criminal Justice Journals   75
4.9   Scores in All Ten American Journals   76
4.10   Scores in All Ten International Journals   77
4.11   Scores in All Twenty Journals   78
4.12   The Most-Cited Works of the Most-Cited Scholars   79
5.1   The Most-Cited Scholars in Criminology and Criminal Justice
       Publications, 1945–1995   83
5.2   Correlations among the Most-Cited Scholars in Four Data Sets   85
6.1   Ranking of Journals in Criminology and Criminal Justice,
       1990–1994, by the Percentage of Articles/Research Notes Written
       by Luminaries (Most-Cited Scholars)   97
6.2   A Comparison of Journal Rankings in Four Studies   99
6.3   Correlations of Journal Rankings in Four Studies   100
7.1   The 100 Most Influential Scholars in 23 Criminology Textbooks,
       1989–1993, Measured in Page-Coverage   106
7.2   A Comparison of the 47 Most Influential Scholars in Criminology
       Textbooks, 1989–1993, as Measured Through Citation Analysis
       and Page-Coverage Analysis   109
8.1   The Most-Cited Scholars in Criminology and Criminal Justice
       Textbooks, 1989–1993   118
8.2   The Most-Cited Scholars in Criminology and Criminal Justice
       Journals, 1986–1990   119
8.3   The Most-Cited Scholars in Criminology and Criminal Justice
       Journals, 1991–1995   120

Foreword

This volume is surely the most comprehensive literature review of citation analysis in general and the most thorough examination and exploration of research on this topic in criminology and criminal justice.

Having been involved in evaluating criminology through citation analysis 20 years ago, I can write such a statement with some experience. Robert Figlio, Terence Thornberry, and I are pleased to know that our study (*Evaluating Criminology*, 1978) was an inspiration for this current research. That Ellen Cohn, David Farrington, and Richard Wright have produced this superb analysis without specific grant funding has been a continuous amazement to me. The prodigious labor, time, energy, and accumulated knowledge necessary to perform the tasks they have undertaken far exceed those characteristics normally associated with most research projects in criminology. That they performed them so well is a further tribute to their scholarship.

I am gratified, of course, that my own works have appeared with some prominence in their citation analysis. Readers of this volume will not fail to notice that I am also the adviser of the criminology series of the Greenwood Press. Hence, I wish to assure the same readers that there has been no connection between these two situations. The initial contacts with the publisher, the review of the manuscript, and the decision to publish were entirely free of my involvement. I am pleased that the publisher with whom I am associated recognized the fine merits of this volume.

As can be readily noted from the table of contents, the authors have done a true service with their critical examination of citation analysis and yet find such analysis most useful in evaluating prestige and influence as well as the convergence of quantity and quality of research. They have given the field a review not only of as many as 20 journals but also of textbooks in criminology and criminal justice. The longitudinal review is uncommon, as is their analysis of topics of research and of university programs in these fields.

If you are a publishing author in criminology and feel a bit disappointed that your name does not appear in some tables, take heart by looking at Table 7.1 in Chapter 7. Your name may appear there.

I hope the final chapter on the topics for future research in evaluating criminology is not ignored by funding agencies. The more we understand what is perceived as important in our field and where the legacies of luminaries (the authors' term) are formed, the further we can advance the theories and empiricism of the increasingly significant discipline of criminology and criminal justice.

Marvin E. Wolfgang

Preface

This book is primarily concerned with the analysis of citations in journals and books in criminology and criminal justice. The assumption underlying citation analysis is that, in general, scholars in a given field who are the most-cited tend also to be the most influential in that field. Citation analysis can be used to analyze the influence of scholars, works, journals, departments, and universities. It is an objective, quantitative, replicable technique. Its use in criminology was pioneered by Wolfgang, Figlio, and Thornberry (1978) in a book entitled *Evaluating Criminology*. This book is inspired by that volume.

The raw data for citation analysis (names in the text and lists of references) are readily available to anyone who wishes to replicate our work. However, good citation analysis is extremely laborious, because it entails a great deal of checking and searching to resolve ambiguities in references. Chapter 1 reviews the advantages and problems of citation analysis in detail. While there are undoubtedly difficulties, citation analysis generally is a valid measure of prestige and influence.

Unlike the pioneering work of Wolfgang, Figlio, and Thornberry (1978), our research was carried out with no funding. We did it because we were interested in the results. We were also interested in tracing patterns of influence over time. Hence, many of our analyses are explicitly longitudinal in nature.

Unfortunately, citation analysis can arouse strong emotional reactions in scholars. A few people (those who are highly cited) are pleased with the results. Many others (those who are not highly cited) are annoyed. Many scholars find citation analysis threatening because of their concern that the results might affect their promotion prospects, salaries, or even the survival of their departments. Some scholars may feel that citations, unlike publications or grants, cannot be significantly affected by their own efforts. On the other hand, as scholars become more aware of citation analysis, we have heard about some undesirable developments such as scholars selectively citing friends and departmental colleagues and deliberately avoiding citations of works written by rivals and members of rival departments. Some scholars may agree to cite each other as part of a "you scratch my back, I'll scratch yours" bargain. These developments constitute a challenge to the validity of future citation analysis.

We have found it difficult to publish papers on citation analysis in major criminology and criminal justice journals. Some reviewers have said explicitly that papers on this topic, however interesting or competently executed, should not be published in major journals. And yet many scholars find the results fascinating and often beseech us to send them the results of our latest analyses. We believe that our results contribute to the field. For example, they have been cited as a partial justification for scholars receiving major awards from the American Society of Criminology and as part of dossiers prepared for promotion applications.

And so we are left with a conundrum. Many scholars find the results of citation analysis riveting, and our impression is that, when published, our articles are noticed and discussed more than journal articles on more conventional topics within criminology and criminal justice. Many other scholars are hostile to the entire approach and do their best to prevent the publication of articles on citation analysis. We leave our readers to make up their own minds, and hope that they will find this book informative and thought-provoking, at the very least.

We would like to acknowledge the invaluable assistance of several graduate students, who devoted untold hours to helping us compile the data for this research. Our thanks and gratitude are due to Kristina Lu, Michael Malia, and Jeffrey Morton. We would also like to thank Maureen Brown and Judy Lestansky for typing sections of this manuscript, and our families and friends for their willingness to put up with our obviously masochistic tendencies.

1

Citation Analysis in Criminology and Criminal Justice

INTRODUCTION

Citation analysis is a well-known and widely used technique for evaluating the impact and prestige of scholars, journals, and university departments in a discipline. It is also useful for determining the impact of a given article or book on subsequently published research in the field, has been used to study communication networks among scholars, has identified new research fronts and the linkages among them, and may indicate links between two highly interrelated journals or topics ("co-citation analysis").

Citation analysis research is found in such diverse fields as medicine (e.g., Logan and Shaw 1991), economics (e.g., Ferber 1986), biochemistry (e.g., Cano and Lind 1991), physics (e.g., Cole and Cole 1971), organizational science (e.g., Blackburn and Mitchell 1981), psychology (e.g., Bagby, Parker, and Bury 1990), sociology (e.g., Bott and Hargens 1991), and of course criminology (e.g., Cohn and Farrington 1996). Probably the best known example in criminology is the research by Wolfgang, Figlio, and Thornberry (1978), which employed citation analysis to determine the most-cited American books and articles from 1945 to 1972.

Citation analysis provides a quantitative method of determining the impact of a scholar, a journal, or a department on the field. It is based on the concept that "good work is work that others find useful and consequently cite in their own work" (Christenson and Sigelman 1985: 965). Citations act as a measure of the importance of a scholar's work; citations to a work suggest that colleagues in one's field find the work important and valuable. Similarly, a large number of citations to a given journal suggest that the journal enjoys high stature and prestige within the field. Although there is some debate as to whether citation counts accurately measure the quality of a work (e.g., Ferber 1986), they are commonly employed as a measure of the prestige or influence of that work on the field as a whole.

According to Meadows (1974), there are two main assumptions in citation analysis. First, that the most-cited works are those that were important in the research, and second, that citations indicate influence (so that several researchers working independently on the same problem would cite the same material).

Another use of citations is in the area of "co-citation analysis," the study of pairs of documents that are commonly cited together in a research paper (Mullens et al. 1977). The assumption behind co-citation analysis is that the two co-cited works are related. Co-citation analysis is intended to locate interacting groups of works.

There are two main methods of gathering citation data. The first, and most common, is to use the publications of the Institute for Scientific Information (ISI), which include the *Science Citation Index* (*SCI*), *Social Sciences Citation Index* (*SSCI*), and the *Arts and Humanities Citation Index* (*AHCI*). These indexes include information on millions of citations in thousands of journals. The second is to examine reference lists of journals, scholarly books, textbooks, and the like in a given field and count the number of citations to a given scholar, work, or journal. This method, while somewhat time-consuming and tedious, avoids the problems inherent in the use of the *SSCI* (discussed below) and has been developed successfully in our prior research (e.g., Cohn and Farrington 1990, 1994a, 1994b, 1996; Wright 1995a; Wright and Cohn 1996; and Wright and Soma 1996).

USES AND ADVANTAGES OF CITATION ANALYSIS

Unlike most measures of influence and prestige, such as peer rankings or professional awards, citation analysis provides an objective, quantitative index, which is much less influenced by personal bias or special interest. Rushton (1984: 33) clearly explains the rationale for using citation counts as a measure of prestige: "If psychologist A's work has been cited 50 times in the world's literature that year, and psychologist B's only 5, A's work is assumed to have had more impact than B's, thereby making A the more eminent."

There is currently a substantial body of research that supports the strong relationship between citation counts and other measures of a scholar's influence, professional prestige, intellectual reputation, and scientific quality. Myers (1970) found that citation counts were highly correlated with peer ratings of professional eminence in psychology and the receipt of scholarly prizes and appointments in psychology (such as the Distinguished Scientific Contribution Award and the Presidency of the American Psychological Association). Rushton and Endler (1979) cite Garfield's (1977a, 1977b, 1977c) findings which also show a clear relationship between citations and scholarly recognition (such as election to the National Academy of Science and/or the Royal Society of London). Cole and Cole (1971) found a significant relationship between citation counts and receiving a Nobel Prize in physics. Gordon and Vicari (1992) have demonstrated that citations are also highly correlated with scholarly productivity (i.e., publication rates). Both Hamermesh, Johnson, and Weisbrod (1982) and Diamond (1986) have shown that a scholar's citation frequency may significantly influence his or her salary.

A number of researchers (e.g., Roche and Smith 1978; Doerner, DeZee, and Lab

1982; Rushton et al. 1983) have found correlations between citation counts and ratings of the prestige of university departments. Rushton et al. (1983) found a significant relationship between departmental citation counts and the number of graduate students. Research into the prestige and eminence of doctoral programs (e.g., DeZee 1980) has also regularly found correlations between citations, peer rankings, and journal publications. For example, Endler, Rushton, and Roediger (1978) found Pearson correlations of .60 or greater between peer rankings of psychology departments in the United States, Canada, and the United Kingdom, and citation counts of departmental faculty.

Rushton and Endler (1979) and Rushton (1984) discussed in some detail the question of the reliability and validity of citation counts. Rushton (1984: 34) stated that "it is fair to say that citation measures meet all the psychometric criteria for reliability." For example, Myers (1970) found a rank order correlation of .91 between his citation index (based on all references in 14 respected psychology journals) and the number of citations in *SCI*. Rushton and Endler (1977) demonstrated the year-to-year stability of citation counts in psychology, showing a correlation of .98 between the number of citations to the top 25 British psychologists in 1974 and in 1975. Similarly, based on the large body of evidence that shows that citation counts correlate strongly with a variety of other indicators, Rushton (1984: 34) has stated that "citation counts are highly valid indices of 'quality.'"

There are several other measures of prestige and influence; however, most of these are directly subject to some form of personal bias. One of the most common methods of measuring prestige is through peer review. For example, Fabianic (1979) ranked criminal justice Ph.D. programs based on a survey of members of the Academy of Criminal Justice Sciences and other criminal justice educators and Mijares and Blackburn (1990) ranked four-year undergraduate criminal justice programs by surveying program directors to obtain their list of the top ten programs in the United States. The receipt of scholarly awards and/or prizes is effectively another form of peer review, as the recipients are generally chosen by members of the given field. These measures of prestige are clearly subjective, open to influence, and not truly quantitative. Regardless of one's desire to be objective, it is easy to be influenced by one's personal likes or dislikes for the individuals being reviewed, or one's knowledge (or lack of knowledge) of the individual, department, or scholarly work under consideration.

Another method of assessing prestige involves counts of journal publications by individuals or departmental faculty. This may be enhanced by weighting the journals according to some system, so that articles published in more prestigious journals (those that are refereed, for example) are considered to be more significant than articles published in less important journals. However, while a publication count is a more objective and quantitative method than peer review, it is a measure of institutional and/or faculty activity or productivity and does not provide an indicator of the impact, influence, or significance of the published research in the field. Publishing an article does not ensure that it will be read or referred to, or that other scholars will consider it to be of significance. In addition, ranking or weighting journals is again a subjective process. Finally, as Wolfgang, Figlio, and Thornberry (1978: 21) pointed out, "the explosion of scientific information inflates rates of publication, hence deflating the validity of publication rates as a measure of scientific productivity."

It appears that of these methods, only citation analysis provides a straightforward, objective, quantitative measure of influence and prestige. While citation analysis also has its shortcomings, it appears to be more valid and more reliable than any other method. The overwhelming body of evidence clearly supports the use of citation analysis as a measure of scholarly eminence, influence, and prestige, or as a way of determining "how many scientists are contributing through their published research to the movement of science" (Cole and Cole 1972: 369).

PROBLEMS OF CITATION ANALYSIS

Citation analysis, as a method of measuring influence, is not perfect; it has a number of problems. Some of these are specific to *SSCI/SCI* and others are more general in nature.

Problems Specific to *SSCI/SCI*

SSCI, and its scientific counterpart *SCI*, list all bibliographic references made in an extremely large number of journals. They do not include citations *in* books and book chapters but do include citations *to* books and book chapters. *SSCI/SCI* are extremely useful and important tools for bibliometric research in general; however, there are several problems with their use for citation analysis research.

First of all, *SSCI/SCI* use only the initials and surnames of cited authors, which may cause confusion when several individuals share the same surname and initial. Cohn and Farrington (1996) pointed out the difficulty, for example, of determining which of the many citations under the heading "J. Cohen" belonged to Jacqueline Cohen and which to other individuals (such as Joseph Cohen or Jacob Cohen) with the same first initial and surname. Other problems include the difficulties of distinguishing between the various R. Berks and P. Brantinghams. Endler, Rushton, and Roediger (1978) used an *SSCI*-based citation count to determine the top 100 psychologists and listed Milton J. Rosenberg as number 47. When Rosenberg (1979) attempted to check this, he found that his citations had been combined with those of Morris Rosenberg, thus inflating his citation count. Garfield (1979) has acknowledged this to be a significant concern. He found that, in the 1974 *SCI*, 137 works were listed under "J. Cohen." When the cited and source journals were examined, it was found that there were eight different individuals included under that heading. Additionally, citations may include or omit the author's middle initial or may use a "nickname" first initial. For example, Chapman (1989) found his citations distributed between A. Chapman, A.J. Chapman, and T. Chapman (the "T" presumably standing for "Tony," an abbreviation for Chapman's first name of Antony).

Chapman also pointed out that citation counts using *SSCI/SCI* may result in a bias against some married women as it may not be known that one person may be cited under more than one surname (e.g., Ilene Nagel, Ilene Bernstein, Ilene Nagel-Bernstein). Other individuals with hyphenated names, or who change their surnames, will create similar difficulties for the citation analyst.

Another problem with *SSCI/SCI* is that all citations to a work are listed only under the name of the first author. This penalizes junior authors in collaborative work. Thus, "if a scientist writes numerous papers, but is never the first author, his name will not be found in *SCI*" (Long, McGinnis, and Allison 1980: 127). Geis and Meier's (1978) examination of Wolfgang, Figlio, and Thornberry's (1978) research found that this practice penalized wives as well, as the 44 most-cited authors found in this research included Sheldon Glueck (but not Eleanor) and William McCord (but not Joan). In addition, as there is some tendency for authors to be listed alphabetically, the listing of first authors favors scholars with surnames near the beginning of the alphabet (Lindsey 1980). Interestingly, Long, McGinnis, and Allison (1980) have found that, for older scholars in biochemistry, the proportion of a scholar's works that were first authored decreased with age, and concluded that the practice of listing only first authors was more likely to exclude professionally older scholars than younger ones.

Another problem is that clerical or other errors in the original reference lists or bibliographies are repeated in *SSCI/SCI*. As Sweetland (1989: 292) points out, "whether one considers bibliographic references from the point of view of the author or the reader, the assumption is that the citations are accurate. Unfortunately, considerable evidence exists that suggests such an assumption is questionable." Farrington, for example, is frequently misspelled as Farringdon, and Hirschi as Hirsch, Hirsh, or Hirshi. Hirschi's citations have also been found under "P. Hirschi" and "L. Hirschi," as well as the more appropriate "T. Hirschi" (Cohn and Farrington 1996). Dates of articles are also frequently incorrect in the original bibliography, and thus are entered in *SSCI/SCI* under the incorrect year. Sweetland (1989) provides numerous examples of such errors, which have caused difficulty, embarrassment, and annoyance over the years. These errors have included misspelling the author's surname, incorrect author initials, omitting journal titles, incorrect journal titles, page numbers, volume numbers, dates, and so forth. In their study of ten major American medical journals published in 1975, Goodrich and Roland (1977) found that, over all journals, an average of 29 percent of all citations contained errors. Other studies of citation accuracy have found similar results (e.g., DeLacy, Record, and Wade 1985; Poyer 1979).

Of course this concern over errors does not include those errors that may be made by the staff at ISI, who put together *SSCI/SCI*. Smith (1989) has pointed out that there are in fact three different *SSCI/SCI*s. The first is an annual publication, the second a five-year cumulative set, and the third an on-line database. According to Smith, these products are not identical in their coverage. First, errors that are detected in the annual volumes may be corrected in the cumulation but these corrections are generally not incorporated into the online database. Second, the cumulation includes more references than the annual volumes. Smith found that the 1980 to 1984 cumulative set of *SCI* contained almost 500,000 more references than the original annual volumes.

Another problem is that *SSCI/SCI* include self-citations. Self-citations are, of course, perfectly justifiable as authors commonly build on their own prior work. However, a study of citations as a measure of influence on others in a field reasonably should omit self-citations. The practice of listing only the first author of a coauthored work makes it extremely difficult to exclude self-citations when using *SSCI/SCI* to obtain a citation count.

In addition, *SSCI/SCI* do not include *all* published works. *SSCI* includes over 300 psychology journals, approximately 100 law journals, about 75 sociology journals, about 75 psychiatry journals, and 16 crime and justice journals. Most of the important criminology and criminal justice journals are covered by *SSCI/SCI* but several key journals, such as *Justice Quarterly* are not yet included. In addition, *SSCI/SCI* does not index works cited in books or book chapters. It is possible that this omission may produce a bias. Cohn and Farrington (1994b) postulated that the relative significance of books and journal articles may vary among disciplines. Their research suggested that books are highly significant in criminology and criminal justice; the most-cited works of the most-cited authors were all books, rather than articles. Smith (1989: 5) pointed out that "important results may be published, and cited, in journals not widely read outside a particular discipline, and therefore excluded from *SCI*."

General Problems of Citation Analysis

In addition to those problems discussed above, which are specific to the use of *SSCI/SCI*, there are also some more general issues related to citation analysis. One of the most common objections to citation analysis is that it is a crude and inaccurate measure of influence, focusing more on the quantity of citations than on the quality. However, as discussed above, citation counts correlate highly with almost all other measures of influence and scholarly prestige. It has also been suggested that high citation counts may indicate a past contribution to knowledge rather than a present or ongoing contribution (Travis 1987). However, in general, authors tend to cite more recent papers rather than older ones. Cohn and Farrington (1994a) suggested that the influence of a scholarly work decays, rather like a radioactive substance. In the social sciences, Courtney, Kawchuk, and Spafford (1987) estimated that research works had a half-life of approximately six years, while Cole and Cole (1971) found that physics papers had a half-life of no more than five years.

Another issue is a possible bias against individuals working in a narrow specialty. As Chapman (1989: 340) stated, "researchers in sparsely-populated topic areas have relatively few colleagues who can cite them and few to cite. One consequence is likely to be that they are not frequently cited." Similarly, Cole and Cole (1971) have pointed out that extremely influential research may not be recognized as such during the researcher's lifetime; it may be resisted or ignored (and not cited), thus depriving the researcher of proper recognition. However, they also feel that this problem may be decreasing with the increase of modern communication and evaluation systems. Garfield (1979) termed this the "Mendel syndrome," as he claimed that these critics of citation analysis inevitably point to the research of Gregor Mendel, whose research was ridiculed and ignored until well after his death, although he is now hailed as the founder of the modern science of genetics.

Smith (1989: 5) claimed that "methods or recipe papers are particularly often cited and have spuriously heavy 'impact' ratings." Peritz (1983) found that methodological papers were more highly cited in sociology than theoretical or empirical articles. In psychology, Douglas (1992: 405) suggested that, if one wishes to write a highly cited article, "your best bet would be to devise or revise a paper-and-pencil test of personality or motivation, improve on a commonly used method, coin a snappy new word or phrase, or think of a new way to apply statistics." However, Garfield (1979: 363) pointed out that "methods papers do not inevitably draw a large number of references." Of the 100 most-cited works in chemistry, as compiled from *SCI*, he found that approximately 73 percent did not deal primarily with experimental methodology (Garfield 1977d). Similarly, Cohn and Farrington's (1994a, 1994b) research into the most-cited scholars in criminology and criminal justice journals did not find that authors of "recipe books" were among the most-cited scholars.

Another objection to citation analysis is that analysts typically do not distinguish between positive, neutral, and negative citations, or, as Chapman (1989: 341) puts it, "Citation does not necessarily denote approval." However, the evidence (e.g., Garfield 1979; Cohn and Farrington 1994a) suggests that the vast majority of citations are positive or neutral, rather than negative. Cole's (1975) analysis of 533 social deviance articles published from 1950 to 1973, specifically examining reactions to Merton's "Social Structure and Anomie" (1938) article, shows that the vast majority of citations to this article comprised a positive or a neutral response; only 6 percent of citations were critical of Merton's work.

In any case, Cole and Cole (1971: 25) suggested that "these few pieces of research that stimulate wide criticism have, in fact, stimulated other research. Consequently, it must be considered mistaken but significant; it must be seen as work which has had an impact on future scientific research." Similarly, Cohn and Farrington (1994a: 530) point out that if a scholar takes the trouble to formally criticize a work, "it is arguable that the work must have been of some substance and, hence, even its refutation has made some contribution to . . . knowledge."

It also appears that citations of one work by a given author may be affected by the publication of another work. For example, Cole's (1975) study of Robert K. Merton's citations in four sociological journals found that citations of Merton (1938) were strongly affected by the publication of several other major studies which were inspired by Merton. Citations to Merton's article rose immediately following the publication of Cohen (1955) and Cloward and Ohlin (1960), but fell shortly after.

Another problem with citation analysis is that the number of citations a scholar receives may depend, at least in part, on the number of articles written by that scholar. In Cohn and Farrington's research, the most-cited scholars in criminology and criminal justice tended to be those who were older, more established, and had longer publication records. They found that a scholar's high ranking was often a function of the large number of different works cited (versatility), rather than a function of a large number of citations of one or two major works (specialization).

Chapman (1989: 341) also discussed the problem of "obliteration by incorporation"; the idea that individuals may be "so eminent and prolific in their fields that, although their names appear in the body of an article, they can elude the ordinary counting process because the writer neglects to list them in the references at the end of the text. In psychology, textual mentions of Freud, for example, are thus underrepresented in citation counts." Ferber (1986: 382) also suggested that "truly important work is no longer cited once everyone knows it." However, Garfield (1979: 365) felt that this was not a significant problem, as it only happened to works that had already made an extremely important, basic, and fundamental contribution to the field and "before the obliteration takes place, both the citation count and reputation of the scientist . . . usually reach a level that makes additional citation credits superfluous."

The selection of citations may be influenced by social factors such as personal likes and dislikes (e.g., Chapman 1989), attempts to please journal editors or editorial board members (e.g., Rushton 1984), a preference for citing same-sex authors (e.g., Ferber 1986), and so on. It is possible, for example, that faculty in a given university department may cite departmental colleagues as a way of boosting overall department citation counts, or may avoid citing faculty from a rival department to reduce that department's citation counts. Gilbert (1977) has discussed some of the additional factors that may influence the selection of works to be cited, including the use of references as a means of persuading the scientific community of the importance and value of the work being discussed.

If citation analysis becomes a common way of evaluating academic productivity, analysts must guard against deliberate attempts to inflate citation counts. While it is probably true, as Garfield (1979) maintained, that it is difficult to use self-citations to inflate one's citation count without it becoming fairly obvious, it is also true that there are other, less obvious methods, such as the "you cite me, I'll cite you" approach. However, any such attempts would still require the scholars in question to have a reasonably high publication rate in journals that are visible and of at least reasonably high quality.

Finally, there are some clear ambiguities with citation analysis that Garfield (1979) has been at pains to mention. These include the fact that, while Nobel Prize winners and other similarly honored scholars have high citation rates, there are other scholars with equally high rates who have not received these types of peer recognition. In addition, some citation analysis research may not clearly differentiate between a scholar who receives a given number of citations over a short period and one who receives the same number of citations spread out over a much longer period of time.

ASSESSING SCHOLARS AND JOURNALS USING CITATION ANALYSIS

The techniques of citation analysis have been used in a variety of fields. In this section, some of the research in areas other than criminology will be briefly discussed.

Rushton and Endler (1977) ranked 45 departments of psychology in the United Kingdom based on the total number of citations each departmental faculty member received in the 1975 *SSCI*. They found that two of the 45 universities (London and Oxford) accounted for almost half of all citations of British psychologists. They also found that the distribution of citations across the members of the universities was significantly skewed, so that a very small number of "superstar" psychologists received a very large proportion of the citations and many faculty received no citations at all during the year. Earlier research into citations to faculty of Canadian psychology departments produced similar findings (Buss 1976; Endler 1977). A follow-up to this research (Rushton et al. 1983) found a high correlation between total and mean citations to a university's psychology department and the production of first degrees and doctorates.

Roche and Smith (1978) used frequency of citations to rank departments of sociology, individual sociologists, and sociological journals. They found moderately strong correlations between citations and other subjective rankings and productivity measures, as well as a distinct relationship between the reputation of a journal and its frequency of citation.

Blackburn and Mitchell (1981) examined citations in seven organizational science journals during the years 1957, 1967, and 1977. They developed four indices to summarize the citation information. The "self-feeding index" measured the frequency with which authors publishing in a given journal cited other articles published in that journal. The "producer-consumer index" measured the extent to which authors in one journal in the sample cited articles from the other journals in the sample. The "inside-outside index" examined the frequency with which authors cited articles from journals not in the sample. Finally, the "cross-pollination index" measured the exchange of knowledge among the three disciplines that made up organizational science (psychology, social psychology, and sociology).

Ferber (1986) questioned whether researchers tended to cite members of their own sex more frequently than members of the opposite sex, hypothesizing that, in subjects where women are in the minority, they are at a disadvantage in acquiring high citation counts. She obtained a sample of articles and research notes in the area of manpower, labor, and population, published between September 1982 and June 1983, and written by male authors only (MA), by female authors only (FA), or by a collaboration of at least one male and one female author (FMA). She then matched each FA and FMA article with an MA article with an identical classification from the *Journal of Economic Literature*. The references in these articles to FA, MA, and FMA publications were then counted. Self-citations were counted separately.

Ferber found that works by women were significantly more frequently cited in articles written by women than in those by men, and that the reverse was true for articles written by men. Citations in FMA articles fell somewhere in between. When articles dealing specifically with women or sex discrimination were examined separately, to test whether the results were a function of differences in subject matter, the sex differences in citation remained. She suggested several possible explanations for these findings, including the effects of networking (which may involve some segregation by sex) and the possibility that scholars tended to have a higher opinion of work by members of their own sex, and concluded by saying that "citations . . . should not be regarded as unbiased indicators of merit" (1986: 389).

Courtney, Kawchuk, and Spafford (1987) looked at the citations of all items (articles, review articles, notes, comments, communications) published in the first ten volumes of the *Canadian Journal of Political Science/Revue canadienne de science politique* (*CJPS/Rcsp*) during the years 1968 to 1977. They obtained citation counts from the *SSCI* for each item during its year of publication and in the next seven years. They found that approximately 73 percent of all items in the journal were cited at least once during the target period, with review articles being least likely to be cited. On average, English-language items were cited four times as often as French-language items. Slightly more than half of all citations appeared in non-Canadian publications, while just over 25 percent were cited in *CJPS/Rcsp*.

Bagby, Parker, and Bury (1990) used citation analysis to compare two key social psychological theories, attribution theory and cognitive dissonance theory, to determine whether the general consensus that cognitive dissonance theory is no longer an active area of research was true. They used one key book in each area as source indicators and tabulated citations to these books over the years 1958 to 1987, using *SSCI* and *SCI*, social psychology journals, and American Psychological Association journals (with the social psychology journals omitted). They confirmed their hypothesis that research into cognitive dissonance had declined while research into attribution theory had continued at a relatively constant rate.

Garfield and Welljams-Dorof (1990) used the ISI database to study the languages in which international research was conducted. They ranked the top 15 languages in the 1984 ISI database by the total number of source items. As expected, the most common language was English; 85 percent of all source items were written in English. Similarly, the majority of first authors (42 percent) were American. In addition, they examined who wrote in which languages and who cited in which languages. Not surprisingly, they concluded that English predominated as "the primary language of international research . . . also, most major scientific nations, regardless of their native language or languages, cite the English-language literature almost exclusively" (1990: 23–24).

Richards (1991) suggested that the number of years in which a scholar is cited might serve as an alternative measure of accomplishment and influence, circumventing the problems involved when using *SSCI/SCI* to obtain total citation counts. He selected a sample of the 271 scientists listed in the 1980 membership directory of the Population Association of America and determined whether each was cited in *SSCI* in each of the five years 1981 to 1985. Attempts were made to minimize errors due to misattribution. Richards found a bimodal distribution, with 41 percent of the scholars never cited and 22 percent cited in all five years. He states that this skewed distribution is consistent with prior research into citation distribution.

Richards then studied 135 articles published in the *Journal of Fertility and Sterility* in the year 1974 and determined whether each article was cited in *SSCI* in the ten year period 1975-1984. He also noted articles that were cited two or more times in a given year and counted the total number of citations to each article over the ten-year period. Again, he found highly skewed distributions. He also found that the number of years cited and total citations were highly correlated. Richards pointed out that years cited is easier to compute and less influenced by outliers, possibly making it a better measure of influence than total citations.

Cano and Lind (1991) examined ten "citation classics" (key articles in medicine and biochemistry with high citation counts) and compared them with ten low-to-medium cited papers in the same fields, all published between 1957 and 1960. Using *SCI*, they determined annual citation counts for each paper during the period 1957 to 1983. They found two distinct life cycle patterns. Type A consisted of a rapid accumulation of citations in the first four to seven years after publication, followed by a gradual decline. This pattern applied to some of the citation classics and all the ordinary papers. Type B consisted of a moderate number of citations during the first six years, followed by a rapid increase. This pattern applied only to citation classics.

Bott and Hargens (1991) looked at citations of books, journal articles, and edited book chapters in sociology published during 1974, using the five-year compilation volumes of *SSCI*. Using a random sample of 699 documents (553 journal articles, 113 sociological books, and 33 book chapters), they determined the number of citations received by each work between 1974 and 1985. They also searched around each work to check for errors in *SSCI*. They found a highly positively skewed distribution of citations to journal articles: the mean number of citations was 14.3, the median was 5, and the mode only 1. Less than 10 percent of the articles were never cited. Chapters in edited books were much less frequently cited than journal articles. The average book received about as many citations as an average paper in a top journal.

Overall, Bott and Hargens (1991: 155) found that "the great majority of sociological publications . . . are subsequently cited." This held true even when first-author self-citations were eliminated. However the range of citation frequency was extremely large. They also found that the journal-specific average citation levels were strongly correlated with other measures of journal prestige or status.

Pardeck et al. (1991) looked at the editorial boards of five social work journals and five psychology journals during the year 1990 and counted the number of citations of works by each board member published during the years 1972 to 1974, using *SSCI*. They computed the "mean citation index" by dividing the total number of citations of all members of an editorial board by the number of board members and found that the mean citation indexes for editorial boards in psychology were generally higher than in social work. They suggested that "editorial boards of psychology journals are generally comprised of members who have higher levels of distinction and achievement within their discipline than editorial board members of social work journals" (1991: 527). However, it should be noted that this may not be a fair comparison. A more accurate method of determining the distinction of editorial board members would be to compare their citation counts to those of non-board members in the same discipline, rather than comparing across disciplines. It is distinctly possible that citation rates are higher overall in psychology than in social work, which could also account for the disparity.

Gorenflo and McConnell (1991) examined 24 introductory psychology textbooks published between 1985 and 1989 to determine the most-cited journal articles and scholars. When looking at the most-cited articles, they found 3 articles cited in 22 of the 24 texts and 76 additional articles cited in 10 or more textbooks. The median year of publication was 1968, almost 20 years before the publication of the oldest textbook examined. Of the 79 most-frequently cited articles, only 12 were from the 1980s. Gorenflo and McConnell (1991: 10) concluded that "it typically takes 20 years or so before an article is perceived as being 'classic' by most authors of introductory psychology texts."

They also listed the most-cited authors in the textbooks (including all citations, not just those to journal articles). They suggested that the differences between most frequently cited authors and most frequently cited articles was due to the fact that many of the most highly cited authors published predominantly in book form. Gorenflo and McConnell also mentioned their concern about the large number of citation errors they found in the textbooks.

Gordon and Vicari (1992) used citations in textbooks to study scientific eminence in social psychology. They inspected eight social psychology textbooks published in 1987 to 1990, counted the total number of pages in which an author was cited in each textbook (not including bibliography pages), and summed across all eight texts. Self-citations (of the textbook author) were corrected for by replacing the number of citations in the self-authored text with the mean number of citations of the author across the remaining seven textbooks. A total of 545 authors were found to have at least four citations in any one text or a total of ten or more citations in all. These data were compared with citation data obtained from the 1987 to 1989 *SSCI* and with productivity data obtained from the PsycINFO database and from a count of publications in three key social psychology journals. Comparisons were also made with findings from prior research into prestige in social psychology. Gordon and Vicari found that the most frequently cited scholars in social psychology texts had remained fairly stable over the past 15 years. They reported a significant relationship between textbook citations and *SSCI* citations, and between citations in *SSCI* and scholarly productivity measures.

Yoels (1973) studied the citations to sociology Ph.D. dissertations appearing in two leading sociology journals, *American Journal of Sociology* and *American Sociological Review*, between 1956 and 1969. He found that dissertations completed by students in the most prestigious sociology departments were far more likely to be cited than dissertations completed by students in less prestigious departments and that they were usually cited by the author (self-citations), the author's graduate-school professors, or fellow graduate students. Yoels also found that dissertations were typically cited within six years of completion and that few dissertations were cited in the two journals (only 13.1 percent of the sociology dissertations completed from 1955 to 1969 were cited at least once). Extending this analysis from 1969 to 1993, Wright and Soma (1995) found that, over time, fewer journal articles and research notes cited sociology dissertations, fewer sociology dissertations were being cited in the journals, and the average age of cited dissertations increased markedly between the two time periods (from a mean age of 6.2 years from 1969 to 1973 to 11.2 years from 1989 to 1993). They concluded that sociology Ph.D. dissertations have had a declining impact on scholarship in sociology.

Finally, Wright (1995b) used citation analysis to add quantitative evidence to the long-standing debate in sociology over whether there ever was a "golden past" for introductory sociology textbooks, when high-quality books were believed to have influenced the development of scholarship and thinking. He examined citations to introductory sociology textbooks in all articles and research notes published in three leading journals, *American Journal of Sociology*, *American Sociological Review*, and *Social Forces*, from 1960 to 1969 and from 1984 to 1993. He found that although introductory textbooks were frequently cited during the earlier period, citations to these books all but disappeared from the journals during the later period. Wright concluded that while introductory sociology textbooks once enjoyed a golden era, these books have virtually no influence on modern sociological research.

ASSESSING SCHOLARS AND JOURNALS IN CRIMINOLOGY AND CRIMINAL JUSTICE

The use of citation analysis in the field of criminology and criminal justice is less common than in some of the other social sciences, particularly psychology. However, it has enjoyed a recent resurgence and there are a number of interesting studies using citations to examine the prestige and influence of scholars, journals, and university departments in criminology and criminal justice.

Wolfgang, Figlio, and Thornberry (1978) produced what is probably the most famous citation analysis in criminology and certainly the most in-depth study we have yet come across in any subject. They studied citations in 556 American criminology books (excluding textbooks) and 3,134 journal articles published between 1945 and 1972 (a total of 3,690 works), counting the number of citations to each work in *SCI*. When examining raw frequencies of citations they discovered a characteristically skewed distribution. In other words, rather than citations being evenly distributed over the source works, a small number of works were highly cited and the rest received few or no citations. They found that "2.2 percent of all the works . . . received one-half, and 0.5 percent received one-quarter of the citations" (Wolfgang, Figlio, and Thornberry 1978: 37). Over 50 percent of all the source works were never cited.

Shichor (1982) examined citations in 20 introductory criminology textbooks published between 1976 and early 1980 to determine the most influential scholars in the field. Following a procedure used in earlier citation analyses of sociology textbooks (see Bain 1962; Oromaner 1968), Shichor first compiled a list of all the authors who were cited at least five times in 40 percent (eight or more) of the textbooks, and then counted the total number of citations received by each scholar. Using this rather arbitrary technique, the four most-cited scholars were Edwin H. Sutherland, Donald R. Cressey, Marvin E. Wolfgang, and Richard Quinney. Shichor found that, with one exception (James Q. Wilson), the 19 most-cited scholars in the textbooks were all sociologists; however, he also noted that almost all the texts analyzed were written by sociologists.

Allen (1983) criticized Shichor's (1982) work, discussing the process of textbook review and publication and suggesting that citations in textbooks may be affected by editorial policy and production factors. He suggests that "one of the latent factors in citations may be the insistence by reviewers and editors that more citations be made to major criminologists, those with substantial reputations, with recognized prominence in the field, or with substantial numbers of former students who might adopt the proposed work" (1983: 177). In reply, Shichor (1983: 197) accepted Allen's suggestions, but stated that "my contention is still that the most quoted social scientists in criminology textbooks can be seen, by and large, as the most influential . . . since their works are being communicated to the largest audience and will be used by the students."

In a recent series of studies, Wright and his associates (Wright 1995a, 1996a, 1997; Wright and Cohn 1996; Wright and Soma 1996) have extended the analysis of the most-cited scholars to recent introductory criminology and criminal justice textbooks. Using the same technique as Shichor (1982), Wright (1995a) compiled a list of the 47 most-cited scholars in 23 introductory criminology textbooks published from 1989 to 1993. Comparing these findings to those of Shichor (1982) and Cohn and Farrington (1994b), Wright (1995a) found higher correlations between the most-cited scholars in earlier and recent criminology textbooks than between the most-cited scholars in recent criminology textbooks and recent journals. He noted that scholars who were extensively cited in recent textbooks but not in journals tended to be criminological theorists whose publications appeared decades ago (e.g., Emile Durkheim, Edwin H. Sutherland, and George B. Vold); scholars who were extensively cited in recent journals but not textbooks were largely quantitative researchers whose work appeared recently (within the last 15 years; e.g., Suzanne S. Ageton, Richard A. Berk, Jacqueline Cohen, Marvin D. Krohn, and Robert J. Sampson).

Again using the same technique as Shichor (1982), Wright and Soma (1996) compiled a list of the 65 most-cited scholars in 53 introductory criminology textbooks published from 1963 to 1968, 1976 to 1980, and 1989 to 1993. They found little stability among the most-cited scholars over time; only seven names (10.8 percent) appeared among the most-cited scholars in all three time periods (Albert K. Cohen, Marshall B. Clinard, Donald R. Cressey, Thorsten J. Sellin, Edwin H. Sutherland, Gresham M. Sykes, and Marvin E. Wolfgang). Wright and

Soma (1996) concluded that prominence is ephemeral for most scholars in criminology, although they linked several career factors, including longevity, perseverance, and breadth of scholarship (i.e., making important theoretical and empirical contributions, while conducting research in several different areas) to the likelihood of enduring fame.

Once again using the same technique, Wright and Cohn (1996) identified the 22 most-cited scholars in 16 introductory criminal justice textbooks published from 1989 to 1993. Comparing these findings to those of Wright (1995a) and Cohn and Farrington (1994b), they found fairly low correlations between the most-cited scholars in recent criminal justice journals and textbooks. While the most-cited scholars in introductory criminal justice textbooks were primarily applied (or practitioner/policy-oriented) researchers, and the most-cited scholars in introductory criminology textbooks were mostly academic researchers (especially criminological theorists), those who were extensively cited in criminal justice journals included a mixture of applied and academic researchers.

In two closely related articles, Wright (1996a, 1997) used citation analysis to estimate the match between what criminology and criminal justice journals report and what textbooks discuss. By comparing the most-cited scholars in recent leading journals (see Cohn and Farrington 1994b) to the most-cited scholars in recent textbooks (Wright 1995a; Wright and Cohn 1996), Wright ranked 39 textbooks in criminology (1996a) and criminal justice (1997) by how extensively they cited the same scholars who were heavily cited in the journals. Wright (1997: 84) interpreted these rankings "as empirical estimates of the extent to which particular textbooks prominently discussed the same influential scholars and studies that were featured in the leading journals, [but] not as assessments of the overall quality of the textbooks."

Two studies have demonstrated the declining influence of criminology textbooks (Wright and Carroll 1994) and criminology textbook authors (Wright 1998) on recent scholarship. Wright and Carroll (1994) compared the citations to 45 textbooks published from 1918 to 1965 and 49 textbooks published from 1976 to 1985 in seven leading criminology, criminal justice, and sociology journals appearing from 1966 to 1972 and from 1986 to 1992. They found that the earlier textbooks were cited far more often in the journals than were the newer texts, suggesting that criminology textbooks, like introductory sociology textbooks (Wright 1995b), once enjoyed a golden era during which they substantially impacted scholarship. In a related study, Wright (1998) showed that the authors of criminology textbooks years ago were better known scholars than the authors today. When 23 authors and coauthors of criminology textbooks appearing from 1936 to 1965 were compared to 55 authors and coauthors of criminology textbooks appearing from 1984 to 1993, a far larger percentage of the former were rated among the most-cited scholars of their time.

Poole and Regoli (1981: 473) defined journal eminence or prestige by "the relative frequency with which a particular periodical is cited in the criminological literature." Using *Criminology* as the source journal, they used the frequency of citations in *Criminology* during the five year period May 1975 to November 1979 to rank 43 criminology and criminal justice journals. Poole and Regoli's citation-based rankings were found to be highly correlated with subjective peer rankings of the same journals (obtained by Shichor, O'Brien, and Decker, 1981), so that there was "an overall similarity between the rank order of the subjective ratings and the rank order of citation counts for the journals" (1981: 475).

Stack (1987a) poined out that Poole and Regoli (1981), like much of the other prior research which ranked journals, used only one source journal (*Criminology*) and failed to adjust for the age of each ranked journal or the number of articles published. In his study, which ranked 26 criminology and criminal justice journals, using citation analysis to consider their relative impact and importance, Stack employed a large number of source journals. Citation counts were obtained from *SSCI* for the years 1984 and 1985. He first obtained a raw citation count (the number of citations of articles in a given journal) in articles published in source journals in 1984 or 1985. Realizing that this method biases the results in favor of older journals, he removed the bias by computing an age-adjusted citation count (counting the number of citations in 1985 source journals of articles published in the 26 journals in 1983 and 1984). Stack found a correlation of $r = .80$ between the ratings using raw citation counts and age-standardized counts.

Finally, to control for both age and the number of articles published by each journal, Stack computed an impact factor by dividing the age-adjusted citation count by the number of articles published in the given journal in 1983 and 1984. He considered this factor to be a measure of the quality of a journal and its impact on the field. Correlations between the impact factor and the other measures were still significant (age-adjusted/impact factor $r = .72$, $p < .05$; raw count/impact factor $r = .54$, $p < .05$).

Stack also compared his rankings with those of Shichor, O'Brien, and Decker's (1981) subjective rankings and Poole and Regoli's (1981) citation counts and found significant similarities and differences. He found that his impact factor score was significantly correlated with Shichor, O'Brien, and Decker's subjective scores but not with the Poole and Regoli raw impact score (although the correlation coefficient was nearly significant).

In the first application of citation analysis to British criminology, Cohn and Farrington (1990) examined the differences between British and American criminology, using one American journal (*Criminology-CRIM*) and one British journal (*British Journal of Criminology-BJC*). They examined all articles published in each journal during 1984 to 1988 and counted all citations of articles published in the journals from 1974 to 1983. They found that articles published in *BJC* were rarely cited in *CRIM* and that the rate of citation of *BJC* articles in *CRIM* and in *SSCI* increased with the quantitativeness of the article.

Cohn and Farrington (1994a) next applied citation analysis to determine the most influential scholars in the English-speaking world. They broadened their research to include not only England and the United States but also Canada (using the *Canadian Journal of Criminology-CJC*), and Australia and New Zealand (*Australian and New Zealand Journal of Criminology-ANZ*). They determined the most-cited scholars in each journal during the five-year period 1986 to 1990 and calculated the correlations between rankings in the four journals. They found that, while those scholars highly-cited in *CRIM* tended also to be highly-cited in the other three journals, the reverse was not true. The correlations between the most highly-cited scholars in *ANZ* and in the other three journals were negative, suggesting that *ANZ* may be the most isolated journal. A combined measure of influence, which controlled for journal size and gave equal weight to citations in all journals, found that only four scholars, all Americans (Marvin E. Wolfgang, Alfred Blumstein, James Q. Wilson, and Michael J. Hindelang), were ranked among the top 50 in all four journals.

The third study (Cohn and Farrington 1994b) examined citations in six major American criminology and criminal justice journals in 1986 to 1990 and found that the most-cited authors in the journals were Wolfgang, Hindelang, and Blumstein. Cohn and Farrington also studied the most-cited works by these authors to determine in what areas and topics their influence lay during that time period. It was determined that "their influence was linked to the perceived importance of criminal career research and the longitudinal method, measuring crime and delinquency, and the prestigious National Academy of Science Reports" (1994b: 532).

Cohn and Farrington's (1996) next research focused specifically on *Crime and Justice: A Review of Research*, a serial publication, between 1979 and 1993. All 12 general volumes were examined, looking separately at the six issues published in 1979 to 1985 and the six issues published in 1986 to 1993. Cohn and Farrington found that the most-cited scholars in both time periods combined were again Hindelang, Blumstein, and Wolfgang. When citation rankings in *Crime and Justice* during the 1986 to 1993 time period were compared with the 1986 to 1990 data from Cohn and Farrington's prior research using journals, they found significant positive correlations between scores in *Crime and Justice* and scores in American criminology journals, American criminal justice journals, and international criminology journals. However, citation rankings from 1979 to 1985 in *Crime and Justice* were negatively correlated with the 1986 to 1993 data, and uncorrelated with scores in the journals, suggesting changes in influence between the two time periods.

Cohn and Farrington (1996) also examined *SSCI* to determine the most-cited works in criminology and criminal justice. They searched *SSCI* for a sample of over 350 criminology and criminal justice books and articles that were considered to be important and that they expected to be highly cited, and listed the most-cited works during 1979 to 1985 and 1986 to 1993. One interesting finding was that the most-cited works tended to be books rather than journal articles. Cohn and Farrington also attempted to develop some basic mathematical models of citation careers of works, along the lines of age-crime research. They showed citation careers of specific works, distinguishing between careers that were increasing, those that were decreasing, those that were curvilinear (increasing to a peak number of citations per year and then decreasing), and those that were stable. Quantitatively oriented research monographs were relatively more highly cited in *Crime and Justice*, while more general, qualitative, non-technical, or theoretical works were relatively more highly cited in *SSCI*.

ASSESSING UNIVERSITY PROGRAMS IN CRIMINOLOGY AND CRIMINAL JUSTICE

Citation analysis has also been used to rank university criminology programs. DeZee (1980) focused on citations to faculty in five introductory criminology and criminal justice textbooks and found that citations in texts correlated highly with peer rankings and journal publications. He found that the most-cited departments (those with faculty cited a minimum of 20 times in the five textbooks) were the University of Pennsylvania, SUNY-Albany, Florida State University, John Jay College, Portland State University, and the University of Maryland. DeZee argued that citation analysis provided information about both current and future trends in the discipline.

Thomas and Bronick (1984) identified a sample of 36 doctoral programs in criminology and criminal justice. Of these, six awarded doctoral degrees in criminology and/or criminal justice and 30 were sociology departments which employed a minimum of three or four faculty specializing in criminology. Using *SSCI* to obtain citation counts over a two-year period (1979 to 1980), Thomas and Bronick employed five different citation-based measures: total number of citations, number of citations per faculty member, number of citations per experience year, number of citations per experience year per faculty member, and overall university ranking (an average of the first four measures). According to the overall average university ranking, the top five programs were Vanderbilt University, Yale University, the University of Pennsylvania, the University of California-Berkeley, and New York University. None of the most-cited departments were independent programs of criminology or criminal justice; the highest-ranked independent program was SUNY-Albany with an overall ranking of 13.

However, Thomas and Bronick's work has been severely criticized by Travis (1987) and Sorenson, Patterson, and Widmayer (1992). In addition to a distinct concern over the use of citations as a measure of departmental quality, Travis (1987) warned against the problem of reductionism, suggesting that Thomas and Bronick (1984) used "only a single measure of quality of doctoral programs-the number of citations of the work of program faculty that appeared in the Social Science Citation Index. They then controlled for such factors as faculty size or the length of faculty academic career . . . [but] . . . only one indicator was employed–a count of citations" (Travis 1987: 160). Both Travis and Sorenson, Patterson, and Widmayer (1992) express concern over the method of sample selection; Sorenson, Patterson and Widmayer (1992: 9) felt that "Thomas and Bronick biased it in favor of sociology programs by selecting some sociology programs with three faculty members specializing in criminology and by excluding more than half of the independent criminal justice/criminology programs without sufficient rationale."

In replying to Travis' critique, Thomas (1987: 169) argued that "virtually every single development of any consequence to criminology . . . this century has come from the work of people with backgrounds in sociology." While admitting that the focus on citations as a single measure of quality was a cause for concern, Thomas (1987: 168) stated that the strong correlation between citation frequency and many other prestige-related variables had been so clearly and frequently demonstrated that "citation-based measures have far more utility than they might appear to have initially."

Sorenson, Patterson, and Widmayer (1992) measured the quality of 23 criminology and criminal justice doctoral programs. However, they were unwilling to rely on *SSCI* as a source of citations, as was done by Thomas and Bronick (1984), fearing that this would bias the results in favor of those departments "whose faculty members publish and cite others in traditional sociological journals" (Sorenson, Patterson, and Widmayer 1992: 21). Instead, they followed the lead of DeZee (1980) and focused on citations in 43 introductory textbooks. Their citation measure consisted of the number of pages on which a faculty member's name or work appeared, as opposed to the number of citations per text. Criminal justice and criminology texts were considered separately.

When the programs were ranked by the average number of citations per faculty member, the five most-cited programs in introductory criminology texts were the University of California-Berkeley, Bowling Green University, the University of Pennsylvania, Rutgers University, and the University of Tennessee-Knoxville. The five most-cited programs in introductory criminal justice texts were the University of California-Berkeley, Rutgers University, the University of Maryland, American University, and Arizona State University. Interestingly, Sorenson, Patterson, and Widmayer (1992: 23) also ranked the departments by raw number of citations (without standardizing for the number of faculty) and found that "departments with large faculties often lose rank when the average number of publications is considered."

Marenin (1993) criticized the Sorensen, Patterson, and Widmayer (1992) research, pointing out that, in the case of Washington State University (WSU), where he was the director of the criminal justice program, they had erred in estimating the number of faculty at the university. However, a brief glance at the raw data (Sorenson, Patterson, and Widmayer 1992: 26-27) clearly shows that WSU had no citations in criminal justice texts and only two citations in criminology texts during the period in question, so this is clearly a minor issue. Marenin (1993: 190) also criticized Sorenson, Patterson, and Widmayer's productivity measures (number of journal publications, number of pages published, etc.) as being "biased toward single-minded disciplines." However, as Sorenson, Patterson, and Widmayer (1993) pointed out, the data for these measures were obtained from a variety of social science indices, including *SSCI*, which covers journals in a wide variety of fields. Marenin considered the citation measures to be narrow as well; a focus on introductory textbooks limited the field to traditional criminology and criminal justice research and thus biased the results against Ph.D. programs which were multidisciplinary (such as WSU). Sorenson, Patterson, and Widmayer (1993) replied that the University of California-Berkeley, with a Ph.D. in jurisprudence and social policy (clearly multidisciplinary in nature) ranked first on average citations per faculty member in both types of textbooks (as well as ranking highly on the raw citation counts).

Cohn and Farrington (1998c) assessed the quality of 20 American doctoral programs in criminology and criminal justice, based on the citation counts of the faculty in those programs. Like Sorenson, Patterson, and Widmayer (1992), Cohn and Farrington chose not to rely on *SSCI* as the source of the citation counts. However, rather than follow their lead and use textbooks, Cohn and Farrington based their study on citations in six major American criminology and criminal justice journals during the years 1991 to 1995. Using citations per faculty member per journal, the top four programs were the University of Maryland-College Park, the University of Cincinnati, Rutgers University-Newark, and SUNY-Albany.

Because of their concern that the presence of a small number of highly-cited individuals might significantly affect the overall average citation rate, Cohn and Farrington also ranked the programs according to the percentage of faculty members with at least one citation. Again, the University of Maryland was ranked first, as every faculty member in the program was cited in at least one of the six source journals.

Finally, Cohn and Farrington also obtained another measure of program quality by counting the number of publications of faculty members in the six source journals during the 1991 to 1995 period. They found that the University of Maryland had the highest publication rate in the six journals, followed by the University of Cincinnati and the University of Missouri-St. Louis.

CONCLUSION

Despite various problems (which are more specific to *SSCI/SCI* than general), citation analysis is an extremely useful technique for assessing the influence of scholars, journals, and university departments. We hope to show this in more detail in the remainder of this book. Chapters 2 through 5 demonstrate the use of citation analysis as a procedure for rating the prestige and influence of scholars and works in criminology and criminal justice. Chapter 2 examines nine major American and international criminology and criminal justice journals, comparing the two most recent half-decades, 1986 to 1990 and 1991 to 1995, to determine the most-cited scholars and the most-cited works in these journals, and what changes have occurred in the last ten years. Chapter 3 looks at the same journals to determine the subject matter and the statistical and analytic complexity of the articles. Chapter 4 expands the field to 20 journals, to determine the most-cited scholars and works in the single year 1990. While the time period is limited, the large number of journals is significantly more representative of the field as a whole. We reverse the procedure in Chapter 5, extending the time period and focusing on the most-cited scholars in the field since 1945. This longitudinal study is conducted by comparing the most-cited scholars in four preexisting datasets.

The next three chapters consider textbooks as well as journals, and compare the use of citation analysis to other empirical ranking techniques. In Chapter 6 we propose a new method of rating the prestige of journals, the luminaries technique, which uses the publication outlets of the most-cited scholars to rate the prestige of journals in criminology and criminal justice. Using procedures developed in content analysis, the luminaries technique is compared to other systems for rating journals, including citation analysis. Chapter 7 suggests an alternative method for measuring influence, looking at the amount of page coverage that textbooks devote to particular scholars. This chapter then compares the results of this page-coverage analysis to those obtained using conventional citation analysis techniques. Finally, Chapter 8 uses citation analysis to examine the divergence/convergence controversy and consider the relationship between the disciplines of criminology and criminal justice. We conclude in Chapter 9 with a brief discussion of what we have learned and how we feel citation analysis in criminology and criminal justice needs to progress in the future.

2

The Most-Cited Scholars and Works in Major American and International Criminology and Criminal Justice Journals, 1986–1990 and 1991–1995[1]

Cohn and Farrington (1994a, 1994b) investigated the most-cited scholars in major American and international journals in criminology and criminal justice in 1986–1990. This chapter extends that research through the 1991–1995 time period (see also Cohn and Farrington 1998a, 1998b). Identifying the most-cited authors helps to identify the most influential scholars and topics during a particular time period, and hence helps to document the historical development of criminology and criminal justice.

PREVIOUS CITATION RESEARCH

As mentioned in Chapter 1, Cohn and Farrington (1994a) determined the most-cited scholars in the four major criminology journals of the major countries of the English-speaking world in 1986–1990: *Criminology-CRIM, British Journal of Criminology-BJC, Canadian Journal of Criminology-CJC,* and *Australian and New Zealand Journal of Criminology-ANZ.* Only four scholars were among the 50 most-cited authors in all four journals in this time period: Marvin E. Wolfgang, Alfred Blumstein, James Q. Wilson, and Michael J. Hindelang. Wolfgang's most-cited work was *Delinquency in a Birth Cohort* (Wolfgang, Figlio, and Sellin 1972); Blumstein's was *Criminal Careers and "Career Criminals"* (Blumstein et al. 1986); Wilson's was *Crime and Human Nature* (Wilson and Herrnstein 1985); and Hindelang's was *Measuring Delinquency* (Hindelang, Hirschi, and Weis 1981). As with "chronic offenders" in criminal career research, a small number of authors accounted for a disproportionate fraction of all citations.

Cohn and Farrington (1994b) also determined the most-cited scholars and the most-cited works in three major American criminology journals (*Criminology-CRIM, Journal of Quantitative Criminology-JQC,* and *Journal of Research in*

Crime and Delinquency-JRCD) and three major American criminal justice journals
*(Justice Quarterly-JQ, Journal of Criminal Justice-JCJ, and Criminal Justice and
Behavior-CJB*) in 1986–1990. The most-cited scholars were Marvin E. Wolfgang,
Michael J. Hindelang, and Alfred Blumstein. Wolfgang's most-cited works were
Delinquency in a Birth Cohort (Wolfgang, Figlio, and Sellin 1972) in criminology
journals and *The Subculture of Violence* (Wolfgang and Ferracuti 1967) and
Patterns in Criminal Homicide (Wolfgang 1958) in criminal justice journals.
Hindelang's most-cited work was *Measuring Delinquency* (Hindelang, Hirschi, and
Weis 1981) in both criminology and criminal justice journals. Blumstein's most-
cited works were *Criminal Careers and "Career Criminals"* (Blumstein et al.
1986) in criminology journals and *Research on Sentencing* (Blumstein et al. 1983)
in criminal justice journals.

Cohn and Farrington (1996) identified the most-cited scholars and the most-cited
works in the serial publication *Crime and Justice* (which is highly prestigious and
publishes only a limited number of articles which are subjected to careful selection
and rigorous screening) and in *SSCI* (which has a far more comprehensive but less
selective coverage). The most-cited scholars in *Crime and Justice* in 1979–1993
were Michael J. Hindelang, Alfred Blumstein, and Marvin E. Wolfgang. The most-
cited works were *Delinquency in a Birth Cohort* (Wolfgang, Figlio, and Sellin
1972) in 1979–1985 and *Criminal Careers and "Career Criminals"* (Blumstein
et al. 1986) in 1986–1993. The most-cited works in *SSCI* were *Asylums* (Goffman
1961) in 1979–1985 and *Discipline and Punish* (Foucault 1977) in 1986–1993.

Cohn and Farrington (1996) also argued that concepts developed in criminal
career research could be used to enrich citation analysis. In particular, they
distinguished between the prevalence and frequency of citations. One problem with
the common use of the total number of citations as a measure of influence is that
a large number of citations may be obtained if a scholar is either cited in many
different articles (a high prevalence) or cited many times in a few articles (a high
frequency). A high prevalence of citations may be a better measure of influence on
a large number of other scholars than a high frequency (which may reflect a great
influence on only a few other scholars).

Another distinction that can be drawn is between specialization and versatility.
Some highly cited authors had several of their works cited (versatility), whereas
others had only one or two of their works cited (specialization). Logically, a high
frequency of citation has to be associated with versatility, while a high prevalence
is frequently associated with specialization. However, a high prevalence may also
be associated with versatility, if a number of different works by a scholar were
cited in many different articles. This would also indicate that the scholar's works
were influencing a large number of other researchers.

SELECTING MAJOR JOURNALS

The aim of this chapter is to identify the most-cited scholars in three major
American criminology journals (*CRIM, JQC,* and *JRCD*), three major American
criminal justice journals (*JQ, JCJ,* and *CJB*), and three major international

criminology and criminal justice journals (*BJC*, *CJC*, and *ANZ*). The major international journals are unquestionably the leading ones in their respective countries.

Selecting the major American criminology and criminal justice journals depends to some extent on one's definitions of criminology and criminal justice (see also Chapter 8). Roughly speaking, criminology refers to the study of crime and its causes, whereas criminal justice focuses on the processing of offenders and the workings of the criminal justice system (police, courts, and corrections). The six journals that we have chosen are centrally concerned with criminology and/or criminal justice. *CRIM*, *JQC*, and *JRCD* focus somewhat more on criminology, while *JQ*, *JCJ*, and *CJB* are more concerned with criminal justice. We define American journals as those with American editors and American publishers, but we have excluded explicitly international journals with a significant international content.[2]

Criminology and criminal justice articles are also published at least occasionally in many American journals centrally concerned with other disciplines, such as sociology, psychology, psychiatry, economics, law, and statistics.[3] Many criminologists and criminal justice scholars whose initial training was in a discipline other than criminology prefer to publish some or all of their articles in mainstream journals of that discipline rather than in mainstream criminology and criminal justice journals.

Related articles may also be found in American journals centrally concerned with areas of other disciplines that border on criminology and criminal justice, including the sociology of deviance,[4] socio-legal studies,[5] legal psychology,[6] and child and adolescent psychopathology.[7] However, these types of journals are less centrally concerned with criminology and criminal justice than the six major journals that we have chosen. Similarly we did not include more specialized journals[8] as major criminology and criminal justice journals, nor have we included criminal law journals or journals in the cognate areas of alcohol and drug abuse.

There is empirical evidence in favor of our choice of these six journals (see also Chapter 6). Shichor, O'Brien, and Decker (1981) asked a sample of over 150 American criminologists to rate the importance of 42 specified American and non-American journals containing criminology and criminal justice articles.[9] *Journal of Criminal Law and Criminology* (*JCLC*) had the highest average ranking, followed by *CRIM* and *JRCD*. *Crime and Delinquency* (*CD*) ranked fourth, followed by *JCJ*. The next most highly rated American criminology and criminal justice journals were *Criminal Justice Review* (*CJR*) and *CJB*. In a much larger survey of over 1,000 American criminologists, Regoli, Poole, and Miracle (1982) found that the most prestigious criminology and criminal justice journals were *CRIM*, *JRCD*, *JCLC*, *CD*, *JCJ*, and *CJB*. Similar results were obtained in Fabianic's (1980) survey of criminal justice professionals; the most highly rated criminology and criminal justice journals were *JCLC*, *JCJ*, *CRIM*, and *JRCD*. In addition, in Parker and Goldfeder's (1979) survey of heads of graduate programs, the most highly rated criminology and criminal justice journals were *JCLC*, *CRIM*, *CD*, *JCJ*, *Federal Probation* (*FP*), *JRCD*, and *CJB*.

Poole and Regoli (1981) criticized Shichor, O'Brien, and Decker's (1981) use of subjective ratings of journals. They studied the frequency of citations of journals in *CRIM* in 1975–1979 and found a remarkably high rank correlation of 0.75 between their citation-based rankings of journals and Shichor, O'Brien, and Decker's subjective ratings of importance. According to citations, *JCLC* was first, *CRIM* second, *CD* third, *JRCD* fourth, and *FP* fifth. The next most-cited American criminology and criminal justice journals were *JCJ* and *CJB*. Similarly, Cohn and Farrington (1990) studied journals cited in *CRIM* in 1984–1988 and found that the most-cited American criminology and criminal justice journals were *CRIM*, *JCLC*, *JRCD*, *CD*, *JCJ*, and *CJB*. In addition, Stack (1987a) studied citations in *SSCI* in 1984–1985. Controlling for the number of articles available for citation (as did Cohn and Farrington 1990), Stack found that the most-cited American criminology and criminal justice journals were *CRIM*, *JRCD*, *CD*, *JCLC*, *CJB*, and *JCJ*.

Sorensen, Patterson, and Widmayer (1992) summarized the results of nine previous analyses of journal prestige. Their composite table shows that the most prestigious criminology and criminal justice journals in these studies were *JCLC*, *CRIM*, *JRCD*, *CD*, *JCJ*, *CJR*, and *CJB*. None of these projects included *JQ* or *JQC*, because they were founded relatively recently.[10] However, the most recent research on journal prestige, by Williams, McShane, and Wagoner (1992), does include *JQ* and *JQC*. On the basis of journal prestige ratings (on a scale from 0 to 10) by over 250 members of the Academy of Criminal Justice Sciences, they found that the most prestigious American criminology and criminal justice journals were *CRIM* (8.7), *JCLC* (8.2), *JQ* (8.0), *JRCD* (7.9), *CD* (7.6), *JCJ* (7.3), *JQC* (7.3), and *CJB* (6.7). Their rankings of journals correlated .76 with the composite rankings of Sorenson, Patterson, and Widmayer (1992).

Existing research suggests that *JCLC*, *CD*, and *FP* might be among the most prestigious American criminology and criminal justice journals. However, we did not choose *JCLC* because its legal style of footnoting excludes the initials of authors of articles cited and hence makes it almost impossible in practice to distinguish between different authors with the same surnames. Most of the time involved in our analyses was actually taken up in distinguishing between different authors with the same surnames and first initials and in resolving errors in citations (e.g., whether a cited R.A. Sampson was really R.J. Sampson or a different person) by consulting original sources. This checking would have taken a prohibitively long time with *JCLC*.

We have not included *FP* among our major American academic journals because it is primarily a practitioner-oriented journal. It had a lower prestige rating (5.2) than our six major journals in the Williams, McShane, and Wagoner (1992) survey. We have not included *CD* because it often publishes special issues on particular topics, involving solicited rather than unsolicited articles, and hence not subject to a rigorous refereeing process. We believe that most American researchers would regard *CJR* and other American criminology and criminal justice journals (e.g., *Journal of Crime and Justice*) as less prestigious than the six we have chosen. These other journals also received lower ratings in the Williams, McShane, and Wagoner (1992) survey.

THE PRESENT RESEARCH

We counted all authors cited in all articles in these nine journals in 1991–1995. "Articles" included research notes, comments, and rejoinders, but excluded book reviews, book review articles, editorials, letters, and obituaries. Every cited author was counted (not just first authors), except that institutional authors (e.g., National Institute of Justice) were excluded. It was not practical to restrict the count to only published books and papers; unpublished reports and conference papers were included if they were cited. All self-citations were excluded because we were interested in the influence of one scholar on other scholars. Cohn and Farrington (1996) previously identified the problem of coauthor citation. For example, if Jacqueline Cohen cites an article by Alfred Blumstein and Jacqueline Cohen, Blumstein will be counted as cited in our analysis, but not Cohen, because of the exclusion of self-citation. However, it is arguable to what degree coauthor citation measures the influence of one scholar on another, since it may essentially reflect self-citation. We did not attempt to exclude coauthor citations from our analyses.

For each journal, the reference pages were entered into the computer using an optical scanner and edited to correct typographical errors. When a reference had multiple authors, duplicate listings were made of the reference, with each coauthor listed first. Extensive checking was carried out to ensure that no references were omitted, to minimize the possibility of typographical errors, and to detect mistakes in reference lists. When the references for all five years of a journal had been entered into the computer file, they were sorted into alphabetical order and this alphabetical list was examined to determine the number of times each name occurred. Citations to scholars with multiple names (e.g., Ilene Nagel/Bernstein) were amalgamated, where these were known.

Where references did not include first names or middle initials, or merely specified "*et al.*," we spent much time checking them against the original publications to distinguish between, for example, the various J. Cohens (Jacqueline, Joseph, Jacob, etc.) and the various D. Smiths (Douglas, David D., David E., David J., etc.), not to mention the American and Australian Patrick O'Malleys. In addition, we spent a good deal of time checking and correcting errors in the original reference lists, which were depressingly common. Our knowledge of criminology and criminal justice authors was extremely important in maximizing the accuracy of the data; this was not merely a clerical task by any means. Obviously, we cannot claim to have detected every error in the reference lists, but we are confident that we located and corrected the vast majority of them, especially those involving the most-cited authors in each journal.

An advantage of citation analysis, apart from the fact that it is quantitative and objective, is that the raw data are readily available to anyone who wishes to try to replicate our conclusions. However, we should perhaps warn other researchers that our conclusions required the analysis of as many as 64,633 cited authors in nine journals in this five-year period. (These are not all different persons; the same person would be counted more than once if he or she was cited several times.) We cannot guarantee that another researcher would replicate our results exactly, because of mistakes in the spelling of authors' names and in reference lists that we may not have detected (or that other researchers may not detect), because of difficulties in distinguishing between individuals with the same initial and surname, because of possible inconsistencies in what is defined as an "article," or because of minor and infrequent clerical errors that, despite our careful checking, may have crept into our computerization of such a large number of citations. However, we are confident that our main conclusions would hold up with only marginal changes in any replication.

AMERICAN CRIMINOLOGY JOURNALS

In *CRIM* in 1991–1995, 131 articles were published by a total of 284 individual authors, 94 percent of whom (268) were American. The non-American authors were most commonly British (5), Canadian (4), or Australian (4). These articles contained a total of 10,650 cited authors, or an average of 81 cited authors per article (more than the comparable figure of 68 in 1986–1990 and the most in any journal in 1991–1995). Table 2.1 shows the 50 most-cited authors in *CRIM* in 1991–1995. Where two or more authors had the same number of citations, they were each given the average ranking.

Table 2.1
Most-Cited Scholars in *Criminology*

Rank	Rank in 1986–90	Name	Number
1	1	Travis Hirschi	153
2	9	Michael R. Gottfredson	100
3	2.5	David P. Farrington	98
4	4	Delbert S. Elliott	83
5	6	Alfred Blumstein	77
6	8	Jacqueline Cohen	66
7	26	Robert J. Sampson	65
8	20	Charles R. Tittle	63
9.5	21	David Huizinga	56
9.5	—	Raymond Paternoster	56
11.5	7	John L. Hagan	51
11.5	5	Michael J. Hindelang	51
13	—	Harold G. Grasmick	47
14	22	Lawrence E. Cohen	43
15	15.5	Ronald L. Akers	42
16.5	15.5	Suzanne S. Ageton	41
16.5	—	Robert J. Bursik	41
18	2.5	Marvin E. Wolfgang	39
20	14	Marvin D. Krohn	38
20	—	Daniel S. Nagin	38
20	24	Douglas A. Smith	38
22	24	James Q. Wilson	37
23.5	—	John H. Laub	36

23.5	32.5	Rolf Loeber	36
25.5	18.5	Edwin H. Sutherland	33
25.5	29	Christy A. Visher	33
27.5	—	Lloyd E. Ohlin	32
27.5	35.5	Gerald R. Patterson	32
29	49.5	David F. Greenberg	31
30	24	Albert J. Reiss, Jr.	30
31.5	32.5	Jack P. Gibbs	29
31.5	—	Gary F. Jensen	29
33	—	Ross Matsueda	28
34.5	—	Theodore G. Chiricos	27
34.5	—	Kenneth C. Land	27
36.5	49.5	Marcus Felson	26
36.5	—	Gordon P. Waldo	26
39	—	John Braithwaite	25
39	—	Richard A. Cloward	25
39	—	Lee N. Robins	25
41.5	—	Ronald V.G. Clarke	24
41.5	18.5	Donald J. West	24
45	—	Francis T. Cullen	23
45	12	Robert M. Figlio	23
45	—	James F. Short, Jr.	23
45	—	Cathy S. Widom	23
45	—	William J. Wilson	23
48.5	38.5	Donald J. Black	22
48.5	—	Jeffrey Fagan	22

The most-cited scholar, Travis Hirschi, was cited 153 times, excluding self-citations. Hirschi's most-cited works in *CRIM* were *A General Theory of Crime* (Gottfredson and Hirschi 1990) cited in 35 articles, and *Causes of Delinquency* (Hirschi 1969) cited in 33 articles. These works were cited much more than the next most-cited works, "Age and the Explanation of Crime" (Hirschi and Gottfredson 1983, cited in 15 articles) and *Measuring Delinquency* (Hindelang, Hirschi, and Weis 1981, cited in 11 articles). In total, Hirschi was cited in 65 articles (50 percent of all articles, excluding those authored by Hirschi). Hence, he had a very high prevalence of citations as well as a high frequency, and his citations showed both specialization (two highly-cited works) and versatility (25 different works cited).

Table 2.1 also shows the comparable rankings of these scholars in *CRIM* in 1986–1990. Twenty-nine scholars (59 percent) were also ranked in the top 50 in the earlier period. Hirschi was also the most-cited scholar then, with 123 citations, and he was then cited in 34 percent of all articles. Hence, his influence on *CRIM* authors increased between the two time periods. His most-cited work in the earlier time period was *Causes of Delinquency* (Hirschi 1969), cited in 38 articles. New entrants in the ten most-cited scholars in *CRIM* in 1991–1995 were Robert J. Sampson, Charles R. Tittle (editor of *CRIM* in 1992–1996), David Huizinga, and

Raymond Paternoster. The highest-ranked scholars in the earlier period to drop out of the later table were Thorsten J. Sellin (ranked 10) and Sheldon E. Glueck (ranked 11), and Eleanor T. Glueck (ranked 13), all deceased.

In *JQC* in 1991–1995, 85 articles were published by a total of 177 authors, 84 percent of whom (149) were American. The non-American authors were most commonly Australian (13) or Dutch (8), due to two special issues on quantitative criminology in Australia and the Netherlands. These articles contained a total of 5,839 cited authors, or an average of 69 per article (more than the comparable figure of 47 in 1986–1990). Table 2.2 shows that the most-cited author in *JQC* was Travis Hirschi, with 74 citations. In total, Hirschi was cited in 24 *JQC* articles (28 percent of all articles). His most-cited works were *Causes of Delinquency* (Hirschi 1969), cited in 13 articles, and "Age and the Explanation of Crime" (Hirschi and Gottfredson 1983) and *A General Theory of Crime* (Gottfredson and Hirschi 1990), each cited in 10 articles. However, David P. Farrington had the highest prevalence of citations in *JQC*, cited in 28 articles (33 percent). His most-cited works were "Criminal Career Research: Its Value for Criminology" (Blumstein, Cohen, and Farrington 1988a) and "Age and Crime" (Farrington 1986).

Table 2.2
Most-Cited Scholars in *Journal of Quantitative Criminology*

Rank	Rank in 1986–90	Name	Number
1	8	Travis Hirschi	74
2	9.5	David P. Farrington	70
3	2	Alfred Blumstein	66
4	5.5	Jacqueline Cohen	63
5	4	Michael R. Gottfredson	49
6	—	Robert J. Sampson	42
7	25	Delbert S. Elliott	38
8	22.5	Christy A. Visher	33
9	31.5	David Huizinga	32
10	16.5	David F. Greenberg	31
11	49	Philip J. Cook	29
12.5	3	Lawrence E. Cohen	28
12.5	—	Daniel S. Nagin	28
14	13.5	Ann D. Witte	25
15.5	—	Terence P. Thornberry	24
15.5	1	Marvin E. Wolfgang	24
18	5.5	Michael J. Hindelang	23
18	—	John H. Laub	23
18	—	Darrell J. Steffensmeier	23
21	31.5	Suzanne S. Ageton	22
21	—	Marvin D. Krohn	22
21	49	Kenneth C. Land	22
23	18	Richard A. Berk	20
25.5	7	Robert M. Figlio	19
25.5	36.5	Joan Petersilia	19

25.5	31.5	Peter Schmidt	19
25.5	43	Wesley G. Skogan	19
28.5	—	Rolf Loeber	18
28.5	—	David McDowall	18
32	—	Ronald L. Akers	17
32	—	Walter R. Gove	17
32	—	Douglas A. Smith	17
32	—	Cathy Streifel	17
32	—	Joseph G. Weis	17
35	—	Lawrence W. Sherman	16
39	—	Jan M. Chaiken	15
39	19.5	John L. Hagan	15
39	—	Alan J. Lizotte	15
39	49	Richard B. McCleary	15
39	—	Steven F. Messner	15
39	26	Jeffrey A. Roth	15
39	43	James Q. Wilson	15
44.5	11.5	Marcus Felson	14
44.5	—	Miles D. Harer	14
44.5	36.5	Michael D. Maltz	14
44.5	—	Raymond Paternoster	14

Table 2.2 shows that 27 of the most-cited scholars in *JQC* in 1991–1995 (60 percent) were also ranked in the top 50 in 1986–1990. In the earlier period, Marvin E. Wolfgang was the most-cited scholar, cited in 36 percent of all *JQC* articles. His most-cited work then was *Delinquency in a Birth Cohort* (Wolfgang, Figlio, and Sellin 1972), cited in 20 articles. The highest new entrants in the ten most-cited scholars in *JQC* in 1991–1995 were Robert J. Sampson, Delbert S. Elliott, Christy A. Visher, and David Huizinga. The highest-ranking scholars in the earlier period to drop out of the table were Thorsten J. Sellin (ranked 9.5), William H. McGlothlin (ranked 11.5), and David N. Nurco (ranked 13.5)

In *JRCD* in 1991–1995, 104 articles were published by a total of 214 authors, 91 percent of whom (195) were American. The non-American authors were most commonly Canadian (9), British (3), or Australian (3). These articles contained a total of 7,121 cited authors, or an average of 68 per article (similar to the comparable figure of 67 in 1986–1990). Table 2.3 shows that Travis Hirschi was the most-cited author in *JRCD*, cited in 36 articles (35 percent). His most-cited works were *Causes of Delinquency* (Hirschi 1969), cited in 19 articles, and *A General Theory of Crime* (Gottfredson and Hirschi 1990) cited in 18 articles.

Table 2.3 shows that 25 of the most-cited scholars in 1991–1995 (51 percent) were also ranked in the top 50 in 1986–1990. In the earlier period, Hirschi was again the most-cited author, cited in 33 percent of all articles. His most-cited work was again *Causes of Delinquency* (Hirschi 1969), cited in 20 articles. The highest new entrants in the ten most-cited scholars in *JRCD* in 1991–1995 were Delbert S. Elliott, David Huizinga, David P. Farrington, and Robert J. Sampson. The highest-ranked scholars in the earlier period to drop out of the later table were Theodore

G. Chiricos (ranked 7), Richard A. Cloward (ranked 11.5), and Gary F. Jensen (ranked 11.5).

Table 2.3
Most-Cited Scholars in *Journal of Research in Crime and Delinquency*

Rank	Rank in 1986–90	Name	Number
1	1	Travis Hirschi	73
2	11.5	Delbert S. Elliott	65
3	—	David Huizinga	54
4	6	Michael R. Gottfredson	50
5	—	David P. Farrington	49
6	20.5	Robert J. Sampson	44
7	14	Raymond Paternoster	40
8	4	Lawrence E. Cohen	37
9	—	Robert J. Bursik	36
11	25	Suzanne S. Ageton	31
11	38.5	Marcus Felson	31
11	9	Marvin E. Wolfgang	31
13	29.5	Ronald L. Akers	30
15	18	Alfred Blumstein	29
15	3	John L. Hagan	29
15	8	Charles R. Tittle	29
17.5	—	Jeffrey Fagan	28
17.5	—	D.L. Murphy	28
19	34.5	Harold G. Grasmick	27
20.5	11.5	Marvin D. Krohn	26
20.5	—	L. Oreland	26
22.5	—	Richard A. Berk	25
22.5	—	Lawrence W. Sherman	25
24	2	Michael J. Hindelang	24
27	29.5	Jacqueline Cohen	23
27	43	Albert J. Reiss, Jr.	23
27	—	Murray A. Straus	23
27	29.5	Edwin H. Sutherland	23
27	15.5	James Q. Wilson	23
31	—	Kenneth C. Land	21
31	18	Lloyd E. Ohlin	21
31	—	Douglas A. Smith	21
35	—	Ronald V.G. Clarke	20
35	—	Francis T. Cullen	20
35	—	Daniel S. Nagin	20
35	43	Joan Petersilia	20
35	—	Kirk R. Williams	20
39	20.5	Albert K. Cohen	19
39	—	Rolf Loeber	19
39	—	Thorsten J. Sellin	19
42.5	—	Jerald G. Bachman	18

42.5	—	John Braithwaite	18
42.5	—	Jeffrey A. Roth	18
42.5	—	Christy A. Visher	18
45.5	38.5	Donald R. Cressey	17
45.5	—	Steven F. Messner	17
48	—	Robert M. Figlio	16
48	—	Patrick M. O'Malley	16
48	5	Gordon P. Waldo	16

There was considerable agreement between the three criminology journals on the most-cited scholars in 1991–1995. Travis Hirschi, Michael R. Gottfredson, and David P. Farrington were among the five most-cited scholars in all three journals. Additionally, Delbert S. Elliott, Robert J. Sampson, and David Huizinga were among the ten most-cited scholars in all three journals. Compared with the earlier period, Robert J. Sampson and David Huizinga were increasingly cited.

In order to produce a combined measure of influence based on all three criminology journals, each cited author was given a score of 51 minus his or her rank on citations in each journal. Thus, the most-cited author in each journal was scored 50, and all authors ranked outside the top 50 in a journal were scored zero. The scores on all three journals were then added for each author, to yield a total score out of a theoretical maximum of 150. This measure gives equal weight to all three journals. If we had merely added all citations, authors cited in journals with a relatively high number of citations (e.g., *CRIM*) would have dominated.

Table 2.4 shows the 30 most-cited authors in criminology journals according to this combined measure. All were ranked in the top 50 in at least two journals, and the top 17 authors were ranked in the top 50 in all three journals. The most-cited authors (Travis Hirschi, David P. Farrington, Michael R. Gottfredson, Delbert S. Elliott, and Robert J. Sampson) were very highly cited (in the top seven) in all three journals. Their most cited works in the three journals were *Causes of Delinquency* (Hirschi 1969, cited in 65 articles), "Criminal Career Research: Its Value for Criminology" (Blumstein, Cohen, and Farrington 1988a, cited in 23 articles), *A General Theory of Crime* (Gottfredson and Hirschi 1990, cited in 60 articles), *Explaining Delinquency and Drug Use* (Elliott, Huizinga, and Ageton 1985, cited in 46 articles), and *Crime in the Making* (Sampson and Laub 1993, cited in 21 articles).

Table 2.4 also shows the comparable rankings of these scholars in 1986–1990. Twenty-one scholars (70 percent) were also ranked in the top 30 then. Eight of the ten most-cited scholars in the earlier period survived to be among the ten most-cited scholars in 1991–1995 (all except Michael J. Hindelang and John L. Hagan). The only new entrants in the top ten in the later period were Robert J. Sampson and David Huizinga. The highest new entrants in the top 30 were David Huizinga, Raymond Paternoster, and Daniel S. Nagin. The highest-ranked scholars in the earlier period to drop out of the later table were Robert M. Figlio (ranked 11), Thorsten J. Sellin (ranked 12), and Joseph G. Weis (ranked 17).[11]

Table 2.4
Most-Cited Scholars in Three Criminology Journals

Rank	Rank in 1986–90	Name	CRIM	SCORE JQC	JRCD	TOTAL
1	1	Travis Hirschi	50	50	50	150
2	10	David P. Farrington	48	49	46	143
3	4	Michael R. Gottfredson	49	46	47	142
4	8	Delbert S. Elliott	47	44	49	140
5	21	Robert J. Sampson	44	45	45	134
6	—	David Huizinga	41.5	42	48	131.5
7	5	Alfred Blumstein	46	48	36	130
8	6	Lawrence E. Cohen	37	38.5	43	118.5
9	9	Jacqueline Cohen	45	47	24	116
10	2.5	Marvin E. Wolfgang	33	35.5	40	108.5
11	13	Suzanne S. Ageton	34.5	30	40	104.5
12	2.5	Michael J. Hindelang	39.5	33	27	99.5
13	20	Ronald L. Akers	36	19	38	93
14	—	Raymond Paternoster	41.5	6.5	44	92
15	14	Marvin D. Krohn	31	30	30.5	91.5
16	7	John L. Hagan	39.5	12	36	87.5
17	—	Daniel S. Nagin	31	38.5	16	85.5
18	15	Charles R. Tittle	43	0	36	79
19	28	Christy A. Visher	25.5	43	8.5	77
20	—	Robert J. Bursik	34.5	0	42	76.5
21.5	—	Douglas A. Smith	31	19	20	70
21.5	—	Harold G. Grasmick	38	0	32	70
23	—	Kenneth C. Land	16.5	30	20	66.5
24	16	James Q. Wilson	29	12	24	65
25	18.5	David F. Greenberg	22	41	0	63
26	—	Rolf Loeber	27.5	22.5	12	62
27	25	Marcus Felson	14.5	6.5	40	61
28	—	John H. Laub	27.5	33	0	60.5
29	22	Richard A. Berk	0	28	28.5	56.5
30	23.5	Edwin H. Sutherland	25.5	0	24	49.5

AMERICAN CRIMINAL JUSTICE JOURNALS

In *JQ* in 1991–1995, 137 articles were published by a total of 255 authors, 99 percent of whom (252) were American. These articles contained a total of 9,188 cited authors, or an average of 67 cited authors per article (similar to the comparable figure of 68 in the earlier time period). Table 2.5 shows that the most-cited author in *JQ* was Lawrence W. Sherman. His most-cited work was "Hot Spots of Predatory Crime" (Sherman, Gartin, and Buerger 1989), but this was cited in only six articles. No other work by Sherman was cited in more than three articles. Hence, Sherman's large number of citations was mainly a function of his large number of different works cited (35), so that his citations showed versatility rather than specialization. He was cited in 19 articles (14 percent). However, Francis T.

Cullen and James Q. Wilson had the highest prevalence of citations in *JQ*; both were cited in 26 articles (19 percent). Cullen's most-cited work was *Reaffirming Rehabilitation* (Cullen and Gilbert 1982), while Wilson's most-cited work was *Varieties of Police Behavior* (Wilson 1968).

Table 2.5
Most-Cited Scholars in *Justice Quarterly*

Rank	Rank in 1986–90	Name	Number
1	18	Lawrence W. Sherman	49
2	9.5	John L. Hagan	47
3	1	Francis T. Cullen	45
4.5	3	Travis Hirschi	37
4.5	2	James Q. Wilson	37
6	7.5	Michael R. Gottfredson	29
8.5	—	Delbert S. Elliott	27
8.5	22.5	Timothy J. Flanagan	27
8.5	—	David Huizinga	27
8.5	—	Murray A. Straus	27
11	41	Joan Petersilia	25
12.5	33	Lawrence E. Cohen	24
12.5	—	Robert J. Sampson	24
14	—	Marcus Felson	23
15	5	Wesley G. Skogan	22
16.5	41	Richard A. Berk	21
16.5	—	Meda Chesney-Lind	21
19.5	15	Ronald L. Akers	20
19.5	4	Alfred Blumstein	20
19.5	28	David P. Farrington	20
19.5	—	Paul Gendreau	20
23.5	—	James J. Fyfe	19
23.5	—	Douglas A. Smith	19
23.5	—	Michael H. Tonry	19
23.5	—	Kirk R. Williams	19
27.5	7.5	Jacqueline Cohen	18
27.5	—	Jeffrey Fagan	18
27.5	—	Martha A. Myers	18
27.5	6	Marvin E. Wolfgang	18
32.5	48.5	Suzanne S. Ageton	17
32.5	—	Kathleen Daly	17
32.5	—	Herman Goldstein	17
32.5	11	Michael J. Hindelang	17
32.5	33	Albert J. Reiss, Jr.	17
32.5	—	Jerome H. Skolnick	17
38	—	Gary F. Jensen	16
38	—	Marvin D. Krohn	16
38	—	Robert J. Langworthy	16
38	—	Rolf Loeber	16

38	48.5	Christy A. Visher	16
45	—	Todd R. Clear	15
45	—	Richard J. Gelles	15
45	—	Richard Hawkins	15
45	—	Mary P. Koss	15
45	—	Michael G. Maxfield	15
45	—	Joan McCord	15
45	28	Raymond Paternoster	15
45	—	Darrell J. Steffensmeier	15
45	28	Franklin E. Zimring	15

Table 2.5 shows that 22 of the most-cited authors in 1991–1995 (45 percent) were also ranked in the top 50 in 1986–1990. In the earlier period, the most-cited author in *JQ* was Francis T. Cullen,[12] cited in 18 percent of all articles. His most-cited work was *Reaffirming Rehabilitation* (Cullen and Gilbert 1982), but this was cited in only eight articles. Cullen's large number of citations, therefore, were mainly a function of his large number of different works cited (versatility). The highest new entrants in the ten most-cited scholars in *JQ* in 1991–1995 were Lawrence W. Sherman and Travis Hirschi. The highest-ranked scholars in 1986–1990 to drop out of the later table were Eric D. Poole (ranked 8.5), Richard Quinney (ranked 11), and Robert M. Regoli (ranked 13).

In *JCJ* in 1991–1995, 196 articles were published by a total of 363 authors, 93 percent of whom (337) were American. (*JCJ* published 30 issues in this five-year period, whereas the other eight journals each published 21 or fewer issues.) The non-American authors were most commonly from Australia (13), Canada (4), or Israel (4). These articles contained a total of 9,716 cited authors, or an average of 50 per article (more than the comparable figure of 40 in the earlier time period). Table 2.6 shows that John L. Hagan was the most-cited author in *JCJ*. However, his most-cited work, "Extra-Legal Attributes and Criminal Sentencing: An Assessment of a Sociological Viewpoint" (Hagan 1974), was only cited in six articles. Thus, Hagan's large number of citations was mainly a function of his large number of different works cited (25), or the versatility of his citations. He was cited in 24 articles (12 percent). However, the next most-cited author, Francis T. Cullen, had the highest prevalence of citations in *JCJ*, being cited in 30 articles (15 percent). His most-cited work was "The Social Dimensions of Correctional Officer Stress" (Cullen et al. 1985), cited in nine articles.

Table 2.6 shows that 19 of the most-cited scholars in *JCJ* in 1991–1995 (35 percent) were also ranked in the top 50 in 1986–1990. In the earlier period, Robert M. Regoli was the most-cited scholar in *JCJ*, but he was cited in only 7 percent of all articles. His most-cited work, "Police Cynicism and Professionalism" (Lotz and Regoli 1977), was cited in only four articles. In the earlier period, Regoli's large number of citations was mainly a function of the large number of his different works that were cited in a relatively small number of articles. Hence, he had high frequency and versatility and low prevalence and specialization. The highest new entrants in the ten most-cited scholars in *JCJ* in 1991–1995 were Francis T. Cullen,

Travis Hirschi, and James Q. Wilson. The highest-ranked scholars in the earlier period to drop out of the later table were Andrew von Hirsch (ranked 9.5), Richard A. Berk (ranked 11.5), Robert M. Martinson (ranked 13.5 and now deceased), and Christine Maslach (ranked 13.5).

Table 2.6
Most-Cited Scholars in *Journal of Criminal Justice*

Rank	Rank in 1986–90	Name	Number
1	7	John L. Hagan	48
2	17.5	Francis T. Cullen	39
3.5	—	Travis Hirschi	36
3.5	4.5	Marvin E. Wolfgang	36
5	11.5	James Q. Wilson	33
6	22.5	Joan Petersilia	32
7.5	1	Robert M. Regoli	30
7.5	3	Lawrence W. Sherman	30
9	31	Michael R. Gottfredson	28
10.5	2	Eric D. Poole	26
10.5	—	Lawrence E. Cohen	26
12.5	—	Richard S. Lazarus	23
12.5	—	John T. Whitehead	23
14.5	4.5	Alfred Blumstein	22
14.5	—	Douglas A. Smith	22
16.5	—	Jurgen Habermas	21
16.5	—	Charles W. Thomas	21
18.5	17.5	Michael J. Hindelang	19
18.5	7	Jacqueline Cohen	19
20	—	Rolando V. del Carmen	18
23	—	George L. Kelling	17
23	—	Robert J. Sampson	17
23	17.5	Wesley G. Skogan	17
23	—	Terence P. Thornberry	17
23	—	Susan F. Turner	17
28	—	Geoffrey P. Alpert	16
28	—	Bruce G. Link	16
28	—	Martha A. Myers	16
28	—	Michael H. Tonry	16
28	—	Samuel Walker	16
34	—	David P. Farrington	15
34	—	S. Folkman	15
34	7	Don M. Gottfredson	15
34	49	David Huizinga	15
34	—	Nancy C. Jurik	15
34	9.5	Hans Toch	15
34	—	Christy A. Visher	15
39.5	—	Todd R. Clear	14
39.5	—	Marcus Felson	14

39.5	31	James J. Fyfe	14
39.5	—	William H. Kroes	14
48	—	Don A. Andrews	13
48	—	David H. Bayley	13
48	—	Jacques-Pierre Brissot	13
48	31	Donald R. Cressey	13
48	—	Delbert S. Elliott	13
48	—	Robert M. Figlio	13
48	—	Paul Gendreau	13
48	—	Victor E. Kappeler	13
48	—	Kenneth C. Land	13
48	—	Peter K. Manning	13
48	—	Belinda R. McCarthy	13
48	31	Albert J. Reiss, Jr.	13
48	—	Charles R. Tittle	13

In *CJB* in 1991–1995, 134 articles were published by a total of 290 authors, 78 percent of whom (226) were American. The non-American authors were most commonly from Canada (45), the United Kingdom (7), or Israel (5). These articles contained a total of 7,442 cited authors, or an average of 55 per article (more than the comparable figure of 46 in 1986–1990). Table 2.7 shows that William L. Marshall was the most-cited author in *CJB*. His most-cited works were "The Long-Term Evaluation of a Behavioral Treatment Program for Child Molesters" (Marshall and Barbaree 1988) and "Erectile Responses among Heterosexual Child Molesters, Father-Daughter Incest Offenders and Matched Nonoffenders" (Barbaree and Marshall 1989), each cited in only four articles. Thus, Marshall's large number of citations was mainly a function of the large number of his different works that were cited (25), or versatility. He was cited in 13 articles (10 percent); however, Judith V. Becker had the highest prevalence of citations in *CJB* (14 articles, or 11 percent). Her most-cited work was "Predicting Child Molesters' Response to Treatment" (Abel et al. 1988).

Table 2.7 shows that there was very little consistency in *CJB* between citation rankings in the two time periods. Only 11 of the most-cited authors in 1991–1995 (21 percent) were also ranked in the top 50 in 1986–1990. In the earlier time period, Edwin I. Megargee was the most-cited scholar, cited in 17 percent of all *CJB* articles. His most-cited work then was *Classifying Criminal Offenders* (Megargee and Bohn 1979), cited in 23 articles. Every one of the top ten most-cited scholars in *CJB* in 1991–1995 was a new entrant and eight were new entrants to the top 50. The highest-ranked scholars in the earlier period to drop out of the later table were Martin J. Bohn (ranked 2), Lawrence Kohlberg (ranked 4 and now deceased), and Robert R. Ross (ranked 5).

A combined measure of influence based on all three criminal justice journals was then calculated, on the same basis as before. There was considerable agreement between *JQ* and *JCJ* on the most-cited scholars, but the most-cited scholars in *CJB* did not, in general, tend to be among the most-cited in *JQ* or *JCJ*. This is probably

Table 2.7
Most-Cited Scholars in *Criminal Justice and Behavior*

Rank	Rank in 1986–90	Name	Number
1	40.5	William L. Marshall	41
2	—	Don A. Andrews	34
3	28.5	Vernon L. Quinsey	33
4	—	Howard E. Barbaree	32
5	—	Judith V. Becker	25
6.5	—	Gene G. Abel	23
6.5	—	Dante V. Cicchetti	23
8	—	James L. Bonta	21
10.5	—	Byron R. Egeland	19
10.5	7.5	John T. Monahan	19
10.5	—	Frank J. Porporino	19
10.5	—	Robert D. Rogers	19
15	—	Terry C. Chaplin	17
15	6	Robert D. Hare	17
15	—	Grant T. Harris	17
15	—	David A. Wolfe	17
15	—	J. Stephen Wormith	17
19	1	Edwin I. Megargee	16
19	—	Larry L. Motiuk	16
19	—	Marnie E. Rice	16
23	—	David Finkelhor	15
23	—	Kurt Freund	15
23	19.5	Herbert C. Quay	15
23	7.5	Hans Toch	15
23	—	C.T. Twentyman	15
27.5	16.5	Francis T. Cullen	14
27.5	—	G.C.N. Hall	14
27.5	—	J.R. Lutzker	14
27.5	—	Murray A. Straus	14
30.5	—	M.S. Kaplan	13
30.5	33.5	David D. Robinson	13
33	—	Patricia M. Crittenden	12
33	—	Martha F. Erickson	12
33	—	Gary L. Wells	12
38	—	Jacob Cohen	11
38	—	C.M. Earles	11
38	3	Paul Gendreau	11
38	—	D. Richard Laws	11
38	—	Bruce G. Link	11
38	—	N.A. Polansky	11
38	—	W.C. Proctor	11
47	—	D. Daro	10
47	—	Graham M. Davies	10
47	—	David P. Farrington	10
47	16.5	Travis Hirschi	10

47	—	Carl F. Jesness	10
47	—	Mary P. Koss	10
47	—	Joan McCord	10
47	—	M.S. Mittelman	10
47	—	W.D. Murphy	10
47	—	Charles D. Spielberger	10
47	—	Mark R. Weinrott	10

because *CJB* has a distinctively psychological focus on criminal justice. Table 2.8 shows the 30 most-cited authors on this combined measure. The five most-cited authors in criminal justice journals were Francis T. Cullen, John L. Hagan, Travis Hirschi, Lawrence W. Sherman, and James Q. Wilson. All were among the top eight scholars in both *JQ* and *JCJ*. Cullen's most-cited works in the three journals were "Does Correctional Treatment Work? A Clinically Relevant and Psychologically Informed Meta-Analysis" (Andrews et al. 1990) and "The Social Dimensions of Correctional Officer Stress" (Cullen et al. 1985), both cited in 12 articles. The most-cited works of the next four scholars were "Extra-Legal Attributes and Criminal Sentencing: An Assessment of a Sociological Viewpoint" (Hagan 1974, cited in 12 articles), *Causes of Delinquency* (Hirschi 1969, cited in 24 articles), "Hot Spots of Predatory Crime" (Sherman, Gartin, and Buerger 1989, cited in 10 articles), and *Varieties of Police Behavior* (Wilson 1968, cited in 23 articles).

Table 2.8 also shows the comparable rankings of these scholars in 1986–1990. Only 14 scholars (45 percent) were also ranked in the top 30 then. Only one of the top five scholars from the earlier time period (Francis T. Cullen) was still in the top five in 1991–1995, although four others from the top ten in 1986–1990 were still in the top ten in the later period (John L. Hagan, James Q. Wilson, Marvin E. Wolfgang, and Alfred Blumstein). Travis Hirschi, Lawrence W. Sherman, and Michael R. Gottfredson were the highest new entrants in the top 10 in 1991–1995. The highest-ranked scholars in the earlier period to drop out of the later table were Eric D. Poole (ranked 1), Robert M. Regoli (ranked 2), and Timothy J. Flanagan (ranked 11). Only three scholars (Francis T. Cullen, Travis Hirschi, and David P. Farrington) were ranked among the most-cited 50 scholars in all three journals. Four of the five most-cited scholars in *CJB* (William L. Marshall, Vernon L. Quinsey, Howard E. Barbaree, and Judith V. Becker) were not ranked among the top 50 scholars in either *JQ* or *JCJ*.

MOST-CITED WORKS

The most-cited works of the most-cited scholars in American criminology and criminal justice journals were primarily theoretical or on longitudinal/criminal career research (Cohn and Farrington, 1998a). Ten of the 20 most-cited scholars were most-cited for primarily theoretical works in either criminology or criminal justice journals or both (unless otherwise specified, the following works were most-cited in both). Travis Hirschi's most-cited work was *Causes of Delinquency* (Hirschi 1969), while Michael R. Gottfredson's most-cited work was *A General*

Theory of Crime (Gottfredson and Hirschi 1990). Robert J. Sampson's most-cited work (in criminology journals only) was *Crime in the Making* (Sampson and Laub 1993), while John L. Hagan's most-cited work (in criminology journals only) was "Class in the Household: A Power-Control Theory of Gender and Delinquency" (Hagan, Gillis, and Simpson 1987). The most-cited work of Delbert S. Elliott, David Huizinga, and Suzanne S. Ageton was *Explaining Delinquency and Drug Use* (Elliott, Huizinga, and Ageton 1985), while the most-cited work of Lawrence E. Cohen and Marcus Felson was "Social Change and Crime Rate Trends: A Routine Activity Approach" (Cohen and Felson 1979). Ronald L. Akers was most-cited for *Deviant Behavior* (Akers 1985).

Table 2.8
Most-Cited Scholars in Three Criminal Justice Journals

Rank	Rank in 1986–90	Name	JQ	JCJ	CJB	TOTAL
1	4	Francis T. Cullen	48	49	23.5	120.5
2	10	John L. Hagan	49	50	0	99
3	16	Travis Hirschi	46.5	47.5	4	98
4	13	Lawrence W. Sherman	50	43.5	0	93.5
5	7.5	James Q. Wilson	46.5	46	0	92.5
6	12	Michael R. Gottfredson	45	42	0	87
7	23.5	Joan Petersilia	40	45	0	85
8	—	Lawrence E. Cohen	38.5	40.5	0	79
9	3	Marvin E. Wolfgang	23.5	47.5	0	71
10	6	Alfred Blumstein	31.5	36.5	0	68
11	—	Robert J. Sampson	38.5	28	0	66.5
12	—	Murray A. Straus	42.5	0	23.5	66
13.5	14	Wesley G. Skogan	36	28	0	64
13.5	—	Douglas A. Smith	27.5	36.5	0	64
15	—	David Huizinga	42.5	17	0	59.5
16	7.5	Jacqueline Cohen	23.5	32.5	0	56
17	—	David P. Farrington	31.5	17	4	52.5
18	—	Don A. Andrews	0	3	49	52
19	5	Michael J. Hindelang	18.5	32.5	0	51
20	—	Michael H. Tonry	27.5	23	0	50.5
21	—	William L. Marshall	0	0	50	50
22	—	Marcus Felson	37	11.5	0	48.5
23	—	Vernon L. Quinsey	0	0	48	48
24	25	Paul Gendreau	31.5	3	13	47.5
25	—	Howard E. Barbaree	0	0	47	47
26	—	Martha A. Myers	23.5	23	0	46.5
27	—	Judith V. Becker	0	0	46	46
28	—	Delbert S. Elliott	42.5	3	0	45.5
29	9	Hans Toch	0	17	28	45
30.5	—	Gene G. Abel	0	0	44.5	44.5
30.5	—	Dante V. Cicchetti	0	0	44.5	44.5

Ten of the 20 most-cited scholars were most-cited for longitudinal/criminal career works. These include the works of Robert J. Sampson, Delbert S. Elliott, David Huizinga, and Suzanne S. Ageton already mentioned, which were concerned with both theoretical and longitudinal/criminal career issues. The most-cited work of Alfred Blumstein and Jacqueline Cohen was *Criminal Careers and "Career Criminals"* (Blumstein et al. 1986), while David P. Farrington's most-cited works were "Criminal Career Research: Its Value for Criminology" (Blumstein, Cohen, and Farrington 1988a) in criminology journals and *Who Becomes Delinquent?* (West and Farrington 1973) in criminal justice journals. Marvin E. Wolfgang's most-cited work was *Delinquency in a Birth Cohort* (Wolfgang, Figlio, and Sellin 1972) in criminology journals, while Joan Petersilia's most-cited work was "Criminal Career Research: A Review of Recent Evidence" (Petersilia 1980) in criminology journals. Douglas A. Smith's most-cited works in criminology journals were "Participation in and Frequency of Delinquent Behavior" (Nagin and Smith 1990) and "Dimensions of Delinquency: Estimating the Correlates of Participation, Frequency, and Persistence of Delinquent Behavior" (Smith, Visher, and Jarjoura 1991).

Nine of the 20 most-cited scholars were most-cited in criminology or criminal justice journals for works on a variety of other topics. Robert J. Sampson was most-cited in criminal justice journals for "Urban Black Violence: The Effect of Male Joblessness and Family Disruption" (Sampson 1987), and John L. Hagan was most-cited in criminal justice journals for "Extra-Legal Attributes and Criminal Sentencing: An Assessment of a Sociological Viewpoint" (Hagan 1974). Marvin E. Wolfgang was most-cited in criminal justice journals for *Patterns in Criminal Homicide* (Wolfgang 1958), while James Q. Wilson was most-cited for *Crime and Human Nature* (Wilson and Herrnstein 1985) in criminology journals and for *Varieties of Police Behavior* (Wilson 1968) in criminal justice journals. Michael J. Hindelang was most-cited for *Measuring Delinquency* (Hindelang, Hirschi, and Weis 1981), and Francis T. Cullen was most-cited for "Does Correctional Treatment Work? A Clinically Relevant and Psychologically Informed Meta-Analysis" (Andrews et al. 1990). Lawrence W. Sherman's most-cited works were "The Specific Deterrent Effects of Arrest for Domestic Assault" (Sherman and Berk 1984) and *Policing Domestic Violence* (Sherman 1992) in criminology journals and "Hot Spots of Predatory Crime: Routine Activities and the Criminology of Place" (Sherman, Gartin, and Buerger 1989) in criminal justice journals. Joan Petersilia's most-cited work in criminal justice journals was *Granting Felons Probation* (Petersilia et al. 1985), while Douglas A. Smith had no clearly most-cited works in criminal justice journals.

INTERNATIONAL JOURNALS

In *BJC* in 1991–1995, 145 articles were published by a total of 247 individual authors, 64 percent of whom (157) were from the United Kingdom. The foreign authors were most frequently from the United States (22), Canada (17), the Netherlands (9), Australia (7), and Sweden (5). *BJC* is the most "international" journal of those studied here. These 145 articles contained a total of 6,771 cited authors, or an average of 47 cited authors per article (similar to the comparable figure of 44 in 1986–1990). Table 2.9 shows that Patricia M. Mayhew was the most-cited author in *BJC* in 1991–1995, cited in 30 articles. This was the highest prevalence of citations in *BJC*. Her most-cited works all related to the British Crime Survey; *The 1988 British Crime Survey* (Mayhew, Elliott, and Dowds 1989) and *The British Crime Survey* (Hough and Mayhew 1983), each cited in nine articles, and *Taking Account of Crime* (Hough and Mayhew 1985), cited in eight articles. The second most-cited author, J. Michael Hough, is also best-known for his work on the British Crime Survey.

Table 2.9 shows that 28 of the most-cited scholars in *BJC* in 1991–1995 (60 percent) were also ranked in the top 50 in 1986–1990. In the earlier period, Stanley Cohen was the most-cited author, cited in 19 percent of all articles. His most-cited work then was *Visions of Social Control* (Cohen 1985), cited in 17 articles. There were three new entrants in the ten most-cited scholars in *BJC* in the later period: Alfred Blumstein, Travis Hirschi, and John Braithwaite. Conversely, the highest-ranked scholars in the earlier period to drop out of the later table were John Lea (ranked 7), David M. Downes[13] (ranked 10), and Steven Box, now deceased (ranked 11.5).

Table 2.9
Most-Cited Scholars in *British Journal of Criminology*

Rank	Rank in 1986–90	Name	Number
1	5	Patricia M. Mayhew	45
2	3.5	J. Michael Hough	41
3.5	8	Kenneth Pease	40
3.5	2	Jock Young	40
5.5	9	Ronald V.G. Clarke	35
5.5	3.5	David P. Farrington	35
8	38.5	Alfred Blumstein	26
8	6	Anthony E. Bottoms	26
8	16.5	Travis Hirschi	26
10	19	John Braithwaite	25
11	30	David J. Smith	24
12	1	Stanley Cohen	23
13.5	—	Michael R. Gottfredson	21
13.5	33.5	Michael McConville	21
17	16.5	Delbert S. Elliott	20
17	24	Michel Foucault	20
17	44.5	Tony Jefferson	20
17	—	Mike Maguire	20
17	—	Wesley G. Skogan	20
21	24	Rod Morgan	19
21	45.5	Geoffrey Pearson	19
21	11.5	Donald J. West	19

23.5	16.5	John Baldwin	18
23.5	—	Jacqueline Cohen	18
26.5	14	David Garland	17
26.5	38.5	Robert Reiner	17
26.5	24	Joanna M. Shapland	17
26.5	—	Nigel D. Walker	17
29	—	Lawrence W. Sherman	16
30.5	24	Trevor Jones	15
30.5	45.5	Roger Matthews	15
32.5	—	Barrie L. Irving	14
32.5	—	Kathleen McDermott	14
35	—	Pat Carlen	13
35	—	Nicholas Dorn	13
35	—	Nigel South	13
39	—	Trevor H. Bennett	12
39	—	Egon Bittner	12
39	38.5	Howard Parker	12
39	24	James Q. Wilson	12
39	45.5	Marvin E. Wolfgang	12
44.5	—	Timothy J. Hope	11
44.5	—	Rolf Loeber	11
44.5	—	Peter K. Manning	11
44.5	—	Michael G. Maxfield	11
44.5	—	Robert J. Sampson	11
44.5	—	Paul N.P. Wiles	11

In *CJC* in 1991–1995, 123 articles were published by a total of 198 authors, 93 percent of whom (185) were Canadian.[14] The non-Canadian authors most commonly came from the United States (5). These 123 articles contained a total of 4,184 cited authors, or an average of 34 cited authors per article (similar to the comparable figure of 30 in 1986–1990 and the fewest in 1991–1995 of all journals studied). Table 2.10 shows that Murray A. Straus was the most-cited author in *CJC*. However, Straus was cited in only seven articles (6 percent); one article (Lenton 1995) accounted for more than half of his citations, citing him 17 times. While a total of 21 different articles by Straus were cited, his most-cited work, *Behind Closed Doors* (Straus, Gelles, and Steinmetz 1980), was cited in only four articles. Hence, Straus had high frequency and versatility but low prevalence and specialization. Anthony N. Doob (cited in 15 articles) had the highest prevalence of citations in *CJC*. His most-cited work was "Trends in the Use of Custodial Dispositions for Young Offenders" (Doob 1992), cited in five articles.

Table 2.10 shows that 17 of the most-cited scholars in *CJC* in 1991–1995 (35 percent) were also ranked in the top 50 in 1986–1990. In the earlier period, Anthony N. Doob was the most-cited scholar, cited in 9 percent of all articles. His most-cited work then was *Sentencing* (Doob and Roberts 1983), cited in only four articles. Of the ten most-cited scholars in *CJC* in the earlier period, only Doob survived to be among the ten most-cited scholars in 1991–1995. The highest-ranked scholars in 1986–1990 to drop out of the later table were Robert R. Ross (ranked 3), Francis T. Cullen (ranked 4.5) and Ronald V.G. Clarke (ranked 7).

Table 2.10
Most-Cited Scholars in *Canadian Journal of Criminology*

Rank	Rank in 1986–90	Name	Number
1	—	Murray A. Straus	33
2.5	1	Anthony N. Doob	29
2.5	16	Peter G. Jaffe	29
4.5	—	Alan W. Leschied	23
4.5	—	Alan E. Markwart	23
6	—	Raymond R. Corrado	21
7	47.5	Nicholas Bala	20
8	—	Travis Hirschi	19
9	47.5	Wesley G. Skogan	16
13	9	Don A. Andrews	15
13	—	Lucien A. Beaulieu	15
13	—	R. Emerson Dobash	15
13	—	Russell P. Dobash	15
13	22	Marcel Frechette	15
13	—	Chris Murphy	15
13	—	Robert A. Silverman	15
18.5	—	Leslie W. Kennedy	14
18.5	—	Carol P. LaPrairie	14
18.5	—	Sharon Moyer	14
18.5	—	Vincent F. Sacco	14
23	—	Aaron Caplan	13
23	36	Michael R. Gottfredson	13
23	36	Michael J. Hindelang	13
23	4.5	Marc LeBlanc	13
23	16	Julian V. Roberts	13
26.5	—	Richard J. Gelles	12
26.5	—	Michael D. Smith	12
31	—	David H. Bayley	11
31	22	Alfred Blumstein	11
31	—	Donald G. Dutton	11
31	—	David P. Farrington	11
31	—	James C. Hackler	11
31	—	George L. Kelling	11
31	12.5	Andre Normandeau	11
37.5	2	Paul Gendreau	10
37.5	47.5	Robert D. Hoge	10
37.5	—	Rick Linden	10
37.5	—	Rolf Loeber	10
37.5	16	Dennis P. Rosenbaum	10
37.5	6	Marvin E. Wolfgang	10
44.5	—	Delbert S. Elliott	9
44.5	—	Richard V. Ericson	9

44.5	—	Curt T. Griffiths	9
44.5	—	Michael G. Maxfield	9
44.5	—	Lawrence W. Sherman	9
44.5	—	Jerome H. Skolnick	9
44.5	—	Elizabeth A. Stanko	9
44.5	9	James Q. Wilson	9

Finally, in *ANZ* in 1991–1995, 98 articles were published by a total of 136 authors, 76 percent of whom (103) were from Australia and 10 percent of whom (14) were from New Zealand. The foreign authors were most commonly from the United Kingdom (7), Canada (5), and the United States (4). These 98 articles contained a total of 3,833 cited authors, or an average of 39 cited authors per article, slightly more than *CJC* (similar to the comparable figure of 43 in 1986–1990). Table 2.11 shows that John Braithwaite was by far the most-cited author in *ANZ*, with 58 citations. In total, Braithwaite was cited in 24 different articles (24 percent), which was the highest prevalence of citations in *ANZ*. His most-cited works were *Crime, Shame and Reintegration* (Braithwaite 1989) cited in 11 articles, and *Of Manners Gentle* (Grabosky and Braithwaite 1986) cited in six articles. None of his other works were cited in more than three articles.

Table 2.11 shows that only 20 of the most-cited scholars in *ANZ* in 1991–1995 (37 percent) were also ranked among the top 50 in 1986–1990. Richard G. Fox was the most-cited scholar in the earlier period, cited in 16 percent of all articles. His most-cited work was *Sentencing* (Fox and Freiberg 1985), cited in 13 articles. Of the ten most-cited scholars in *ANZ* in the earlier period, only five (John Braithwaite, John Walker, Paul R. Wilson, David Biles, and Stanley Cohen) survived to be among the top ten scholars in 1991–1995. The highest-ranked scholars in 1986–1990 to drop out of the later table were Gordon J. Hawkins (ranked 9), Gilbert Geis, Richard Quinney, and Peter H. Rossi (all ranked 15).

Table 2.11
Most-Cited Scholars in *Australian and New Zealand Journal of Criminology*

Rank	Rank in 1986–90	Name	Number
1	3.5	John Braithwaite	58
2	2	John Walker	26
3	6.5	Paul R. Wilson	25
4	—	Pat O'Malley	24
5	32.5	Peter Grabosky	23
6.5	6.5	David Biles	22
6.5	32.5	Jock Young	22
8	3.5	Stanley Cohen	21
9.5	—	Chris Cunneen	19
9.5	—	Brent Fisse	19
11	—	Jocelynne A. Scutt	18
12	—	David Garland	15

13.5	—	Michel Foucault	14
13.5	6.5	Kenneth Polk	14
15	6.5	Arie Freiberg	13
17.5	21	Duncan Chappell	12
17.5	—	Clifford Shearing	12
17.5	—	Lawrence W. Sherman	12
17.5	43	Grant Wardlaw	12
20.5	—	Richard V. Ericson	11
20.5	—	Nigel D. Walker	11
24	—	Roderic G. Broadhurst	10
24	1	Richard G. Fox	10
24	—	John Lea	10
24	—	Ian O'Connor	10
24	21	Ian R. Taylor	10
29.5	—	Christine Alder	9
29.5	—	Judith Allen	9
29.5	43	David P. Farrington	9
29.5	12.5	Satyanshu K. Mukherjee	9
29.5	—	Ngaire Naffine	9
29.5	12.5	Marvin E. Wolfgang	9
35.5	—	Chris Corns	8
35.5	—	Stephen K. Mugford	8
35.5	—	David J. Neal	8
35.5	—	John Pratt	8
35.5	—	Adam Sutton	8
35.5	—	Joy Wundersitz	8
45.5	—	Michael Bersten	7
45.5	32.5	Anthony E. Bottoms	7
45.5	—	Michael Brogden	7
45.5	10.5	David Brown	7
45.5	21	Janet Chan	7
45.5	—	Marshall B. Clinard	7
45.5	—	Mona Jackson	7
45.5	—	Tony Jefferson	7
45.5	—	Peter K. Manning	7
45.5	—	David Matza	7
45.5	—	Greg Newbold	7
45.5	—	Leon Radzinowicz	7
45.5	—	Carol Smart	7
45.5	10.5	George Zdenkowski	7

A combined measure of influence based on all three international journals was calculated on the same basis as before (see also Cohn and Farrington, 1998b.) Table 2.12 shows the 30 most-cited authors on this combined measure. The five most-cited scholars were Jock Young, John Braithwaite, David P. Farrington, Travis Hirschi, and Stanley Cohen; of these, only Farrington was ranked among the top 50 in all three journals. Young's most-cited works in the three journals were *The Islington Crime Survey* (Jones, MacLean, and Young 1986), *The Second*

Islington Crime Survey (Crawford et al. 1990) and *The New Criminology* (Taylor, Walton, and Young 1973), each cited in eight articles. The most-cited works of the next four scholars were *Crime, Shame and Reintegration* (Braithwaite 1989, cited

Table 2.12
Most-Cited Scholars in Three International Journals

| Rank | Rank in 1986–90 | Name | SCORE | | | |
			BJC	CJC	ANZ	TOTAL
1	7	Jock Young	47.5	0	44.5	92
2	4	John Braithwaite	41	0	50	91
3	12	David P. Farrington	45.5	20	21.5	87
4	29	Travis Hirschi	43	43	0	86
5	1	Stanley Cohen	39	0	43	82
6	—	Wesley G. Skogan	34	42	0	76
7	—	Michel Foucault	34	0	37.5	71.5
8	—	Michael R. Gottfredson	37.5	28	0	65.5
9	42.5	David Garland	24.5	0	39	63.5
10	10	Alfred Blumstein	43	20	0	63
11	—	Lawrence W. Sherman	22	6.5	33.5	62
12	—	Nigel D. Walker	24.5	0	30.5	55
13.5	6	Patricia M. Mayhew	50	0	0	50
13.5	—	Murray A. Straus	0	50	0	50
15.5	19	J. Michael Hough	49	0	0	49
15.5	16.5	John Walker	0	0	49	49
18	9	Anthony E. Bottoms	43	0	5.5	48.5
18	14.5	Anthony N. Doob	0	48.5	0	48.5
18	48	Peter G. Jaffe	0	48.5	0	48.5
20	24.5	Paul R. Wilson	0	0	48	48
21	28	Kenneth Pease	47.5	0	0	47.5
22.5	2	Marvin E. Wolfgang	12	13.5	21.5	47
22.5	—	Pat O'Malley	0	0	47	47
24.5	—	Alan W. Leschied	0	46.5	0	46.5
24.5	—	Alan E. Markwart	0	46.5	0	46.5
26	—	Peter Grabosky	0	0	46	46
27	3	Ronald V.G. Clarke	45.5	0	0	45.5
28	—	Raymond R. Corrado	0	45	0	45
29	24.5	David Biles	0	0	44.5	44.5
30	—	Nicholas Bala	0	44	0	44

in 20 articles), "Age and Crime" (Farrington 1986, cited in six articles), *A General Theory of Crime* (Gottfredson and Hirschi 1990, cited in 12 articles), and *Visions of Social Control* (Cohen 1985, cited in 20 articles). Table 2.12 also shows the comparable rankings of these scholars in 1986–1990. Eighteen scholars (60 percent) were also ranked in the top 30 then. Only four scholars who were in the top ten in the earlier time period survived to be in the top ten in the later period (Jock Young, John Braithwaite, Stanley Cohen, and Alfred Blumstein). David P.

Farrington, Travis Hirschi, and Wesley G. Skogan were the highest new entrants in the top ten in 1991–1995. The highest ranked scholars in 1986–1990 to drop out of the later table were James Q. Wilson (ranked 5), Peter H. Rossi (ranked 8), and Andrew von Hirsch (ranked 11).

MOST-CITED AUTHORS IN NINE JOURNALS

Table 2.13 identifies the most-cited scholars in all nine journals by adding the scores in criminology, criminal justice, and international journals. These were Travis Hirschi, Michael R. Gottfredson, David P. Farrington, Alfred Blumstein, and Marvin E. Wolfgang. Only Farrington was among the most-cited 50 scholars in every journal, although Hirschi and Wolfgang were among the most-cited 50 scholars in eight out of nine journals.

Table 2.14 shows the comparable table for the 1986–1990 time period. The top six scholars in 1991–1995 also were among the top ten scholars in the earlier period. The highest new entrants in the 1991–1995 table were Robert J. Sampson, David Huizinga, and Murray A. Straus. The highest-ranked scholars in 1986–1990 to drop out of the later table were Andrew von Hirsch (ranked 13), Eric D. Poole (ranked 14), and Peter H. Rossi (ranked 16). Remarkably, all the top 12 scholars in the earlier table survived to be in the top 16 in the 1991–1995 table.

Table 2.13
Most-Cited Scholars in Nine Journals, 1991–1995

Rank	Rank in 1986–90	Name	CRIM	CJ	INT	TOTAL
1	4	Travis Hirschi	150	98	86	334
2	7	Michael R. Gottfredson	142	87	65.5	294.5
3	10	David P. Farrington	143	52.5	87	282.5
4	3	Alfred Blumstein	130	68	63	261
5	1	Marvin E. Wolfgang	108.5	71	47	226.5
6	9	Delbert S. Elliott	140	45.5	39.5	225
7	—	Robert J. Sampson	134	66.5	6.5	207
8	36.5	Lawrence W. Sherman	44.5	93.5	62	200
9	12	Lawrence E. Cohen	118.5	79	0	197.5
10	8	Jacqueline Cohen	116	56	22.5	194.5
11	—	David Huizinga	131.5	59.5	0	191
12	5	John L. Hagan	87.5	99	0	186.5
13	2	Michael J. Hindelang	99.5	51	27	177.5
14	6	James Q. Wilson	65	92.5	17.5	175
15	31	Wesley G. Skogan	25.5	64	76	165.5
16	11	Francis T. Cullen	22	120.5	0	142.5
17	—	Murray A. Straus	24	66	50	140
18	—	Douglas A. Smith	70	64	0	134
19	42	Joan Petersilia	41.5	85	0	126.5
20	30	Ronald L. Akers	93	32	0	125
21	36.5	Suzanne S. Ageton	104.5	18.5	0	123
22	—	John Braithwaite	20.5	0	91	111.5

23	—	Marcus Felson	61	48.5	0	109.5
24	—	Christy A. Visher	77	30	0	107
25	38	Marvin D. Krohn	91.5	13	0	104.5
26	49	Raymond Paternoster	92	6	0	98
27	—	Rolf Loeber	62	13	19	94
28	—	Jock Young	0	0	92	92
29	—	Don A. Andrews	0	52	38	90
30	—	Daniel S. Nagin	85.5	0	0	85.5
31	40	Albert J. Reiss, Jr.	48	21.5	0	69.5
32	—	Terence P. Thornberry	35.5	28	0	63.5
33	26	Paul Gendreau	0	47.5	13.5	61
34	—	Jeffrey A. Fagan	36	23.5	0	59.5
35	—	Michael H. Tonry	0	50.5	0	50.5
36	—	William L. Marshall	0	50	0	50
37.5	—	George L. Kelling	0	28	20	48
37.5	—	Vernon L. Quinsey	0	48	0	48
39	—	Howard E. Barbaree	0	47	0	47
40	—	Martha A. Myers	0	46.5	0	46.5
41	—	Judith V. Becker	0	46	0	46
42	32	Hans Toch	0	45	0	45
43.5	—	Gene G. Abel	0	44.5	0	44.5
43.5	—	Dante V. Cicchetti	0	44.5	0	44.5
46	34	Lloyd E. Ohlin	43.5	0	0	43.5
46	15	Robert M. Regoli	0	43.5	0	43.5
46	—	Kirk R. Williams	16	27.5	0	43.5
48	—	James L. Bonta	0	43	0	43
49	23	Timothy J. Flanagan	0	42.5	0	42.5

Note: CRIM=3 criminology journals; CJ=3 criminal justice journals; INT=3 international journals.

CONCLUSION

The most-cited scholar in the three criminology journals was Travis Hirschi, and he had the highest prevalence of citations in *CRIM* and *JRCD*. David P. Farrington had the highest prevalence of citations in *JQC*. Twenty-three scholars were ranked in the top 50 in all three journals. Generally, the three journals agreed quite well in identifying the most-cited scholars, who were Travis Hirschi, David P. Farrington, Michael R. Gottfredson, Delbert S. Elliott, and Robert J. Sampson. In all three journals, more than half of the 50 most-cited scholars in 1986–1990 survived to be in the top 50 in 1991–1995, and the citations of Robert J. Sampson and David Huizinga had markedly increased. The most-cited works of the most-cited scholars were mainly theoretical or on longititudinal/criminal career research. The three criminology journals had the largest number of cited authors per article.

In the three criminal justice journals, the most-cited scholars were Lawrence W. Sherman (*JQ*), John L. Hagan (*JCJ*), and William L. Marshall (*CJB*). However, the prevalence of citations was greatest for Francis T. Cullen and James Q. Wilson (*JQ*), Francis T. Cullen (*JCJ*), and Judith V. Becker (*CJB*). *JQ* and *JCJ* generally agreed on the most-cited scholars, but the most-cited scholars in *CJB* were not often among the most-cited in the other two journals. Only three scholars were ranked among the top 50 in all three journals. There was little consistency in the 50 most-cited scholars between the two time periods, especially for *CJB*. The most-cited scholars overall were Francis T. Cullen, John L. Hagan, Travis Hirschi, Lawrence W. Sherman, and James Q. Wilson, and the citations of Hirschi and Sherman increased markedly between the two time periods. The most-cited works of the most-cited scholars were extremely diverse, covering police behavior, sentencing, and the effectiveness of correctional treatment.

In the three international journals, the most-cited scholars were Patricia M. Mayhew (*BJC*), Murray A. Straus (*CJC*), and John Braithwaite (*ANZ*). However, the prevalence of citations in *CJC* was greatest for Anthony N. Doob. There was little agreement on the most-cited scholar among these journals, and only three scholars were ranked among the top 50 in all three journals. Between the two time periods, the most-cited scholars were very consistent in *BJC*, but not in *CJC* or *ANZ*. Overall, the most-cited scholars were Jock Young, John Braithwaite, David P. Farrington, Travis Hirschi, and Stanley Cohen. The most-cited works of the most-cited scholars were quite diverse. The three international journals had the fewest cited authors per article.

Table 2.14
Most-Cited Scholars in Nine Journals, 1986–1990

| Rank | Name | SCORE | | | |
		CRIM	CJ	INT	TOTAL
1	Marvin E. Wolfgang	140.5	124	89	353.5
2	Michael J. Hindelang	140.5	101.5	51	293
3	Alfred Blumstein	127	94.5	60	281.5
4	Travis Hirschi	143	74.5	42.5	260
5	John L. Hagan	123.5	86.5	37	247
6	James Q. Wilson	70.5	88.5	77	236
7	Michael R. Gottfredson	135	82	15	232
8	Jacqueline Cohen	110	88.5	30	228.5
9	Delbert S. Elliott	112.5	37.5	34.5	184.5
10	David P. Farrington	90	23	55.5	168.5
11	Francis T. Cullen	0	118	46.5	164.5
12	Lawrence E. Cohen	124	18	15	157
13	Andrew Von Hirsch	0	78.5	59	137.5
14	Eric D. Poole	0	132.5	0	132.5
15	Robert M. Regoli	0	125.5	0	125.5
16	Peter H. Rossi	28.5	28.5	65	122
17	Thorsten J. Sellin	82.5	0	33.5	116
18	Robert M. Martinson	0	65.5	46.5	112
19	Donald R. Cressey	36.5	53	18.5	108
20.5	Richard A. Berk	55	49.5	0	104.5
20.5	Richard Quinney	28.5	40	36	104.5
22	Ronald V.G. Clarke	14.5	0	86	100.5

23	Timothy J. Flanagan	16.5	83	0	99.5
24	David F. Greenberg	62	18	18.5	98.5
25	Stanley Cohen	0	0	97.5	97.5
26	Paul Gendreau	0	48	49	97
27	Patricia M. Mayhew	28.5	0	68	96.5
28	Jack P. Gibbs	62	33	0	95
29	Robert R. Ross	0	46	48	94
30	Ronald L. Akers	57	36	0	93
31	Wesley G. Skogan	8	80.5	0	88.5
32	Hans Toch	0	88	0	88
33	Robert M. Figlio	83	3	0	86
34	Lloyd E. Ohlin	47.5	38	0	85.5
35	Edwin H. Sutherland	54	10	18.5	82.5
36.5	Suzanne S. Ageton	81	0	0	81
36.5	Lawrence W. Sherman	0	81	0	81
38	John Braithwaite	0	0	79.5	79.5
39	Marvin D. Krohn	76.5	0	0	76.5
40	Charles R. Tittle	74	0	0	74
41	Albert J. Reiss, Jr.	35	38	0	73
42	Donald J. West	32.5	0	39.5	72
43	Joan Petersilia	22.5	49	0	71.5
44	Henry J. Steadman	0	41	29	70
45	Peter M. Bentler	36	31.5	0	67.5
46.5	J. Michael Hough	19.5	0	47.5	67
46.5	Joseph G. Weis	67	0	0	67
48	Gilbert Geis	0	28.5	36	64.5
49	James B. Jacobs	0	61.5	0	61.5
50	Raymond Paternoster	37	23	0	60

Note: CRIM=3 criminology journals; CJ=3 criminal justice journals; INT=3 international journals.

Over all nine journals, Travis Hirschi was the most-cited scholar, and he was the only scholar to be ranked in the top five in all three categories of criminology, criminal justice, and international journals. His pre-eminence was mainly based on his theoretical books *Causes of Delinquency* (Hirschi 1969) and *A General Theory of Crime* (Gottfredson and Hirschi 1990). We conclude that, in 1991–1995, the most-cited works were either theoretical or on longitudinal and criminal career research or on a variety of disparate topics.

NOTES

1. Portions of this material have appeared in Cohn and Farrington (1998a, 1998b). They appear here with the kind permission of Oxford University Press and Elsevier Science Ltd. We are very grateful to the *British Journal of Criminology* and the *Journal of Criminal Justice* for giving us permission to reproduce this material.

2. For example, *International Journal of Comparative and Applied Criminal Justice, International Journal of Offender Therapy and Comparative Criminology*, and *Crime, Law and Social Change*.

3. For an extremely valuable list of 133 major journals, see Vaughn and del Carmen (1992).

4. For example, *Social Problems*, *Social Justice*, and *Deviant Behavior*.

5. For example, *Law and Society Review*.

6. For example, *Law and Human Behavior*.

7. For example, *Journal of Abnormal Child Psychology*, *Developmental Psychopathology*, and *Journal of the American Academy of Child and Adolescent Psychiatry*.

8. For example, *Violence and Victims*, *Journal of Interpersonal Violence*, *Journal of Police Science and Administration*, and *Juvenile and Family Court Journal*.

9. Not all the journals were centrally concerned with criminology and criminal justice.

10. *JQ* began publishing in 1984 and *JQC* in 1985.

11. Joseph G. Weis was the editor of *CRIM* from 1985–1987.

12. Francis T. Cullen was the editor of *JQ* from 1987–1989.

13. David Downes was the editor of *BJC* from 1985–1989.

14. *CJC* has an editorial policy that favors Canadian authors.

3

Topics Covered in Nine Major Criminology and Criminal Justice Journals, 1986–1990 and 1991–1995

CLASSIFICATION OF ARTICLES

It is clear that the selection of works and individuals cited in a journal article will depend to some extent on the topic of the paper. Consequently, the explanation of changes in citations over time will be enhanced by an investigation of the changes in topics covered during that same period of time.

Cohn and Farrington (1990) developed a simple system of classifying topics of articles, using seven basic subject categories. Category 1 included articles that examined explanations or theories of delinquency or crime, male or female, using individual or aggregate data. Category 2 covered those articles that dealt with measurement, methodology, criminal careers, crime trends and patterns, crime rates, victim studies, or fear of crime. Category 3 contained articles on general criminology, crime control and prevention, criminal justice systems, and attitudes/perceptions of criminal justice. Category 4 included political crime, organized crime, corporate crime, professional/white collar crime, and radical and Marxist studies. Category 5 focused on articles dealing with police, police diversion, vigilantes, private police, and arrests. Category 6 contained articles examining the areas of sentencing, law, courts, bail, juvenile justice, prosecution, deterrence, and the death penalty. Finally, category 7 focused on correctional issues, including prisons, juvenile facilities, mental health, treatment, probation, parole, predicting recidivism, rehabilitation, correctional officers, jails, private prisons, and inmate behavior.

Cohn and Farrington (1990) analyzed the topics covered by articles in *Criminology* (*CRIM*) and the *British Journal of Criminology* (*BJC*) during the years 1974–1983 and investigated how these were related to their probability of being cited in *CRIM*, *BJC*, and *SSCI* in 1984–1988. The majority of *BJC* articles (60 percent) were on criminal justice topics (police, sentencing, prisons), compared with only 44 percent of *CRIM* articles. *BJC* articles that were concerned with explanations of crime and delinquency were most likely to be cited in *CRIM*, while

BJC articles on the police were most likely to be cited in *SSCI*. *CRIM* articles concerned with explanations of delinquency were most likely to be cited in *BJC* and *SSCI*.

In the same paper Cohn and Farrington developed a simple system of classifying the level of quantitativeness of articles. Articles classified as level 1 contained no data presented by the author (this includes reproducing data from earlier research in a literature review). Level 2 articles contained raw data and/or summary statistics only, such as frequencies, percentages, means, and standard deviations. Articles classified as level 3 included two-way comparisons such as chi-square, correlations, one-way ANOVA and Student's *t* tests for differences between groups. Finally, level 4 included articles which contained multivariate analysis, factor analysis, time series analysis, multiple regression/discriminant function analysis, loglinear/logistic models, causal modeling/LISREL, and other mathematical models.

In 1974–1983, very few *BJC* articles (9 percent) contained multivariate analyses, compared with 29 percent of *CRIM* articles. However, for both journals, the likelihood of articles being cited showed a tendency to increase with the degree of quantitativeness, and both *BJC* and *CRIM* articles containing multivariate analyses were more likely to be cited than less quantitative articles.

The aim of the present analysis was to classify the topics and quantitativeness of nine journals in 1986–1990 and 1991–1995 (the same nine journals discussed in Chapter 2). The articles were coded for quantitativeness and subject matter by one of the authors (E.G.C.) A second author (D.P.F.) independently coded a randomly selected issue of each journal to provide a reliability check. The quantitativeness ranking is relatively objective and the coding agreed for 47 of the 51 articles coded by both authors (92 percent). The errors centered on whether articles should be classified as level 3 or 4. For example, a complicated economic analysis of crime rates was classified as 3 by one rater and as 4 by the other. A detailed inspection of the article by both raters led them to agree that the correct classification was 3.

The classification of articles by topic was less reliable. In the above analysis, the raters agreed on 35 of the 51 articles (69 percent). After extensive discussions between them, a second independent coding of another issue of each journal was carried out. However, the results were almost identical: the raters agreed on 34 of the 50 articles (68 percent).

An examination of the disagreements revealed that the basic problem was that many articles fall into multiple subject categories. For example, an article on deterring corporate crime was classified as category 4 (corporate crime) by one rater and as category 6 (deterrence) by the other. Quite a number of articles contained information both on delinquency careers (category 2) and on correlates of delinquency (category 1). Articles on police collaboration with lawyers could be classified as either category 5 or 6. And so on.

The only way to increase the reliability of the coding process would be to develop explicit rules about how to categorize such bridging articles. For example, any article that could be classified as 1 or 2 might always be classified as 1. However, this would be an arbitrary rule and an undesirable level of complexity.

The main rater (E.G.C.) classified articles according to what was considered to be the major thrust of the article. Thus, an article on deterring corporate crime would be classified as falling into category 4 if it was considered to be primarily about corporate crime and as category 6 if it was considered to be primarily about deterrence. This seems a better solution to the problem than adopting arbitrary rules. While the ratings do not have high reliability, the fact that they were all made by the same person means that they have strong internal consistency.

ARTICLE TOPICS

Table 3.1 shows the topics covered in the nine journals in the ten-year period, 1986–1995. The most common topics overall were theories of delinquency (16.7 percent), measurement/crime trends/criminal careers/victims (16.7 percent), general criminology/attitudes to criminal justice/crime control (16.6 percent), sentencing/law/juvenile justice/deterrence (18.6 percent), and corrections (18.8 percent). Relatively few articles were concerned with the police (9.6 percent), and fewer still with radical/corporate crime/white collar topics (3.0 percent).

Not surprisingly, the most common category of articles in *CRIM* and *JRCD* was theories of delinquency, while the most common category in *JQC* was measurement/crime trends/criminal careers/victims. The most common categories in *JQ* and *JCJ* were sentencing/law/juvenile justice/deterrence and corrections. As expected (given its sponsorship by the American Association of Correctional Psychologists), the most common category in *CJB* was corrections. More surprisingly, the most common category in *BJC* was general criminology/attitudes to criminal justice/crime control, while the most common categories in *CJC* and *ANZ* were sentencing/law/juvenile justice/deterrence and general criminology/attitudes to criminal justice/crime control.

Table 3.2 divides up the topic categories in more detail and relates them to the three categories of journals (criminology, criminal justice, and international). Categories 1 (theories and explanations of delinquency), 4 (mainly white collar/corporate crime), and 5 (police studies) were not subdivided further, because they were already relatively homogeneous.

The most common topics contained in category 2 were measurement/methodology (especially in *CJB*, *JCJ*, and *JQC*), crime rates/trends/patterns (especially in *JQC*, *CJC*, and *CRIM*), victims/victimology (especially in *BJC* and *JCJ*), and criminal careers (virtually all in *CRIM* and *JQC*). The most common topics in category 3 were general criminology (especially in *BJC*, *JCJ*, *CJC*, and *ANZ*), attitudes to the criminal justice system (especially in *JCJ*, *CJC*, and *JQ*), and crime control/prevention (mostly in the three international journals).

The most common topics within category 6 were sentencing (especially in *JQ*, *CJC*, *JCJ*, and *ANZ*), law (especially in *ANZ*, *JCJ*, and *CJC*), juvenile justice (especially in *CJC* and *JCJ*), and deterrence (especially in *CRIM* and *JQ*). Finally, the most common topics contained in category 7 were prisons/jails/juvenile facilities (especially in *JQ*, *JCJ*, *CJB*, and *BJC*), rehabilitation and treatment

Table 3.1
Topics Covered in Nine Journals, 1986–1995

TOPIC	CRIM	JQC	JRCD	JQ	JCJ	CJB	BJC	CJC	ANZ	TOTAL
1	100 (33.6)	50 (27.0)	62 (33.5)	43 (15.6)	25 (6.6)	43 (16.0)	28 (10.2)	20 (7.8)	13 (7.2)	384 (16.7)
2	67 (22.5)	69 (37.3)	29 (15.7)	27 (9.8)	50 (13.2)	51 (19.0)	44 (16.1)	38 (14.8)	10 (5.5)	385 (16.7)
3	22 (7.4)	17 (9.2)	27 (14.6)	42 (15.2)	70 (18.5)	29 (10.8)	72 (26.3)	63 (24.5)	41 (22.7)	383 (16.6)
4	15 (5.0)	1 (0.5)	7 (3.8)	12 (4.3)	12 (3.2)	0 (0)	10 (3.6)	2 (0.8)	11 (6.1)	70 (3.0)
5	18 (6.0)	3 (1.6)	5 (2.7)	34 (12.3)	61 (16.1)	18 (6.7)	35 (12.8)	28 (10.9)	18 (9.9)	220 (9.6)
6	53 (17.8)	24 (13.0)	33 (17.8)	63 (22.8)	74 (19.6)	22 (8.2)	30 (10.9)	70 (27.2)	59 (32.6)	428 (18.6)
7	23 (7.7)	21 (11.4)	22 (11.9)	55 (19.9)	86 (22.8)	105 (39.2)	55 (20.1)	36 (14.0)	29 (16.0)	432 (18.8)
TOTAL	298	185	185	276	378	268	274	257	181	2302

Note: Column percentages in parentheses

CRIM = Criminology
JQC = Journal of Quantitative Criminology
JRCD = Journal of Research in Crime and Delinquency
JQ = Justice Quarterly
JCJ = Journal of Criminal Justice
CJB = Criminal Justice and Behavior
BJC = British Journal of Criminology
CJC = Canadian Journal of Criminology
ANZ = Australian and New Zealand Journal of Criminology

1=Theories of delinquency and crime
2=Measurement/crime trends/criminal careers/victims
3=General criminology/attitudes to criminal justice/crime prevention
4=White collar crime/organized crime/corporate crime
5=Police
6=Sentencing/law/juvenile justice/deterrence
7=Prison/rehabilitation/recidivism/probation/parole

(especially in *CJB*), recidivism and prediction (especially in *CJB*), and probation and parole (especially in *JCJ*).

Table 3.2
More Detailed Topics Covered

	CR	CJ	INT	TOTAL
TOPIC 2:				
Measurement/methodology	53	71	18	142
Crime trends/rates/patterns	47	23	34	104
Victims/victimology	14	24	21	59
Criminal careers	41	4	4	49
Fear of crime	10	6	15	31
TOTAL	165	128	92	385
TOPIC 3:				
General criminology	37	77	97	211
Attitudes towards criminal justice	19	35	22	76
Crime control/prevention	7	12	43	62
Criminal justice system	3	17	14	34
TOTAL	66	141	176	383
TOPIC 6:				
Sentencing/bail/death penalty	34	57	55	146
Law	9	28	44	81
Juvenile justice	14	20	35	69
Deterrence	37	21	6	64
Courts	12	20	11	43
Prosecution	4	13	8	25
TOTAL	110	159	159	428
TOPIC 7:				
Prisons/jails/juvenile facilities	34	127	73	234
Rehabilitation/treatment	10	38	13	61
Recidivism/prediction	14	23	14	51
Probation/parole	6	32	10	48
Mental health	2	26	10	38
TOTAL	66	246	120	432

Note: CR = 3 criminology journals; CJ = 3 criminal justice journals; INT = 3 international journals

Table 3.3 shows the distribution of topics within the three major categories of journals (criminology, criminal justice, and international) during the two time periods (1986–1990 and 1991–1995). It is clear from this table that there was very little change between the two time periods in the distribution of articles over categories. The biggest change was an increase in the percentage of articles on police topics in international journals in 1991–1995 compared with the earlier time period, and a corresponding decrease in articles on sentencing/law/juvenile justice/deterrence and corrections. The percentage of articles on theories and explanations of delinquency increased in criminology and criminal justice journals. The largest corresponding decreases were in articles on corrections in criminology

Table 3.3
Topics Covered, 1986–1990 and 1991–1995

TOPIC	CR 1986–90	CR 1991–95	CJ 1986–90	CJ 1991–95	INT 1986–90	INT 1991–95	TOTAL 1986–90	TOTAL 1991–95
1	97 (27.9)	115 (35.9)	45 (9.9)	66 (14.2)	30 (8.7)	31 (8.5)	172 (15.0)	212 (18.4)
2	90 (25.9)	75 (23.4)	66 (14.5)	62 (13.3)	39 (11.3)	53 (14.5)	195 (17.0)	190 (16.5)
3	37 (10.6)	29 (9.1)	79 (17.3)	62 (13.3)	82 (23.7)	94 (25.7)	198 (17.2)	185 (16.1)
4	15 (4.3)	8 (2.5)	14 (3.1)	10 (2.1)	17 (4.9)	6 (1.6)	46 (4.0)	24 (2.1)
5	16 (4.6)	10 (3.1)	53 (11.6)	60 (12.9)	21 (6.1)	60 (16.4)	90 (7.8)	130 (11.3)
6	50 (14.4)	60 (18.8)	76 (16.7)	83 (17.8)	88 (25.4)	71 (19.4)	214 (18.6)	214 (18.6)
7	43 (12.4)	23 (7.2)	123 (27.0)	123 (26.4)	69 (19.9)	51 (13.9)	235 (20.4)	197 (17.1)
TOTAL	348	320	456	466	346	366	1150	1152

Note: Column percentages in parentheses
CR = 3 criminology journals; CJ = 3 criminal justice journals; INT = 3 international journals

1 = Theories of delinquency and crime
2 = Measurement/crime trends/criminal careers/victims
3 = General criminology/attitudes to criminal justice/crime prevention
4 = White collar crime/organized crime/corporate crime
5 = Police
6 = Sentencing/law/juvenile justice/deterrence
7 = Prison/rehabilitation/recidivism/probation/parole

journals and on general criminology/attitudes to criminal justice/crime control in criminal justice journals.

ARTICLE QUANTITATIVENESS

Table 3.4 shows the ratings of quantitativeness of articles in the nine journals. Overall, 30.2 percent of articles contained no data, while at the other extreme 35.3 percent contained multivariate analyses. Articles that employed multivariate techniques were most common in the three criminology journals and least common in the three international journals.

Table 3.5 shows changes in quantitativeness over the two time periods in the three categories of journals. Overall, it is clear that over time an increasing percentage of articles contained multivariate analyses, and a decreasing percentage contained no data. However, these trends were marked only in the criminology and criminal justice journals. There was no change in quantitativeness in the international journals between the two time periods.

CONCLUSION

The investigation of the topics covered in the nine journals is useful in interpreting the results presented in Chapter 2. For example, the most common topic of articles in *CRIM* and *JRCD* was theories and explanations of delinquency and crime. This might explain why Travis Hirschi, Michael R. Gottfredson, Delbert S. Elliott, and David Huizinga were highly cited in these journals. The fact that articles in *JQC* were most commonly on the topic of measurement/criminal careers/crime trends might explain why David P. Farrington, Alfred Blumstein, and Jacqueline Cohen were highly cited in this journal. The most common topics of articles published in *JQ* and *JCJ* were sentencing/law/juvenile justice/deterrence and corrections, possibly explaining why John L. Hagan, Francis T. Cullen, and James Q. Wilson were highly cited in these journals. Similarly, the most-cited scholars in *CJB* tended to work in the prison/rehabilitation/recidivism areas, and the most-cited scholars in *BJC* tended to work on victim surveys and crime prevention.

It would clearly be desirable to devote more time to the development of an improved typology of topics for the classification of journal articles. Such a typology would make it possible to classify both articles cited and articles citing, and to determine for what types of articles each scholar was most-cited. For the moment, however, this analysis provides some initial indications about the topics covered in different journals, changes over time in these topics, and why certain scholars were most-cited in certain journals.

Table 3.4
Quantitativeness in Nine Journals

TOPIC	CRIM	JQC	JRCD	JQ	JCJ	CJB	BJC	CJC	ANZ	TOTAL
1	52 (17.4)	10 (5.4)	50 (27.0)	85 (30.8)	94 (24.9)	65 (24.2)	121 (44.2)	122 (47.5)	99 (54.7)	698 (30.2)
2	23 (7.7)	18 (9.7)	17 (9.2)	45 (16.3)	56 (14.8)	21 (7.8)	71 (25.6)	58 (22.6)	52 (28.7)	361 (15.5)
3	39 (13.1)	16 (8.6)	30 (16.2)	38 (13.8)	104 (27.5)	100 (37.3)	52 (19.0)	40 (15.6)	16 (8.8)	435 (19.0)
4	184 (61.7)	141 (76.2)	88 (47.6)	108 (39.1)	124 (32.8)	82 (30.6)	30 (10.9)	37 (14.4)	14 (7.7)	808 (35.3)
TOTAL	298	185	185	276	378	268	274	257	181	2302

Note: Column percentages in parentheses

CRIM	= Criminology	1 = No data
JQC	= Journal of Quantitative Criminology	2 = Summary statistics
JRCD	= Journal of Research in Crime and Delinquency	3 = Two-way comparisons
JQ	= Justice Quarterly	4 = Multivariate analyses
JCJ	= Journal of Criminal Justice	
CJB	= Criminal Justice and Behavior	
BJC	= British Journal of Criminology	
CJC	= Canadian Journal of Criminology	
ANZ	= Australian and New Zealand Journal of Criminology	

Table 3.5
Quantitativeness, 1986–1990 and 1991–1995

TOPIC	CR		CJ		INT		TOTAL	
	1986–90	1991–95	1986–90	1991–95	1986–90	1991–95	1986–90	1991–95
1	67 (19.3)	45 (14.1)	142 (31.1)	102 (21.9)	173 (50.0)	169 (46.2)	382 (33.2)	316 (27.4)
2	39 (11.2)	19 (5.9)	62 (13.6)	60 (12.9)	80 (23.1)	101 (27.6)	181 (15.7)	180 (15.6)
3	51 (14.8)	34 (10.6)	126 (27.6)	116 (24.9)	56 (16.2)	52 (14.2)	233 (20.3)	202 (17.5)
4	191 (54.9)	222 (69.4)	126 (27.6)	188 (40.3)	37 (10.7)	44 (12.0)	354 (30.8)	454 (39.4)
TOTAL	348	320	456	466	346	366	1150	1152

Note: Column percentages in parentheses
CR = 3 criminology journals; CJ = 3 criminal justice journals; INT = 3 international journals

1 = No data
2 = Summary statistics
3 = Two-way comparisons
4 = Multivariate analyses

The Most-Cited Scholars and Works in Twenty Major Criminology and Criminal Justice Journals in 1990

The majority of research using citations in journals to study prestige of scholars and works has focused on a small number of well-known peer reviewed journals over a period of years. For example, Cohn and Farrington (1994b) considered six major criminology and criminal justice journals and Blackburn and Mitchell (1981) examined seven key organizational science journals. However, these analyses are clearly vulnerable to the criticism that the limited number of journals studied possibly created a bias against scholars who publish in less mainstream journals. It could be argued that the most-cited scholars are, at least to some extent, specific to particular journals and that the results would differ if different journals were analyzed. While researchers such as Cohn and Farrington (1994a, 1994b, 1996) have, arguably, analyzed the major mainstream criminology and criminal justice journals, they did not study journals covering more specific topics such as violence or critical criminology.

To avoid such criticisms, we decided to increase the range of our investigation and consider the question of the most-cited scholars in a much larger number of criminology and criminal justice journals of the United States and the other major countries of the English-speaking world (Great Britain, Canada, Australia, and New Zealand). This chapter considers citations in 20 journals published during the year 1990. Citations from five American criminology journals, five American criminal justice journals, five international criminology journals, and five international criminal justice journals were studied.

SELECTING THE MAJOR CRIMINOLOGY AND CRIMINAL JUSTICE JOURNALS

Cohn and Farrington (1994a, 1994b, 1996) previously counted citations in ten journals or serial publications: *Criminology* (*CRIM*), *Journal of Quantitative Criminology* (*JQC*), *Journal of Research in Crime and Delinquency* (*JRCD*),

Justice Quarterly (JQ), *Journal of Criminal Justice (JCJ)*, *Criminal Justice and Behavior (CJB)*, *British Journal of Criminology (BJC)*, *Canadian Journal of Criminology (CJC)*, *Australian and New Zealand Journal of Criminology (ANZ)*, and *Crime and Justice (CJ)*. They justified the choice of these as the major criminology and criminal justice journals on the basis of prior research on the rated prestige of journals (Shichor, O'Brien, and Decker 1981; Regoli, Poole, and Miracle 1982; Sorenson, Patterson, and Widmayer 1992; Williams, McShane, and Wagoner 1992). One highly prestigious criminology and criminal justice journal that they could not include was the *Journal of Criminal Law and Criminology*, because its legal style of footnotes excludes the initials of authors of articles cited and hence makes it difficult, if not impossible, in practice to distinguish between different authors with the same surnames.

For the present analysis the number of criminology and criminal justice journals covered was increased to 20 by adding ten important and mainstream criminology and criminal justice journals. Because of the number of citations and the amount of work involved, citations in the ten additional journals were only counted for the end-of-decade year of 1990. Our goal was to compare American and international journals, and criminology and criminal justice journals; thus, we planned to cover five journals in each of the four possible categories (American criminology, American criminal justice, international criminology, international criminal justice). However, it was not easy to achieve this design.

We first added the following eight criminology and criminal justice journals: *Crime and Delinquency (CD)*, *Criminal Justice Review (CJR)*, *Federal Probation (FP)*, *Criminologie (CRGE)*, *Contemporary Crises (CC*; now renamed *Crime, Law and Social Change)*, *International Journal of Comparative and Applied Criminal Justice (IJCA)*, *International Journal of Offender Therapy and Comparative Criminology (IJOT)*, and *Social Justice (SJ)*.[1] As we had too few American criminology journals, we also added two journals focusing on violence: *Journal of Interpersonal Violence (JIV)* and *Violence and Victims (VV)*.

We considered and rejected a variety of other academic journals.[2] Many were on specific aspects of criminology and criminal justice, such as *Journal of Police Science and Administration*, *Police Journal*, *Police Studies*, *Policing*, *The Prison Journal*, *Criminal Justice History*, *Victimology*, and *Juvenile and Family Court Journal*. Others were primarily concerned with other disciplines that bordered on criminology and criminal justice, such as the sociology of deviance (e.g., *Social Problems*, *Deviant Behavior*), socio-legal studies (e.g., *Law and Society Review*), legal psychology (e.g., *Law and Human Behavior*), and child and adolescent psychopathology (e.g., *Journal of Abnormal Child Psychology*, *Developmental Psychopathology*). In addition, we did not consider more mainstream journals in cognate disciplines such as sociology, psychology, psychiatry, economics, statistics, or drug and alcohol studies.[3] Overall, we believe that the 20 journals we have chosen would be widely viewed as mainstream criminology and criminal justice journals.

CITATIONS IN EACH OF THE 20 JOURNALS

Table 4.1 summarizes key statistics for the 20 journals included in this analysis, including the number of eligible articles published in 1990, the number of authors of these articles, the percentage of the authors who were American, and the total number of eligible citations in the journal. As stated in Chapter 2, we excluded editorial introductions, book review articles, letters to the editor, and obituaries. Eligible citations did not include self-citations (citations to the author of the article) or institutional authors (e.g., National Institute of Justice, Home Office). The number of citations does not necessarily imply that all the authors cited are different individuals. An author was counted each time he or she was cited and thus could be counted two or more times in 1990.

The reference lists for each article in each journal were entered into the computer using an optical scanner. After editing to correct scanner-induced errors, eliminate self-citations and institutional authors, and create multiple listings for multiple-author references, the lists were alphabetized (using the computer) and the number of references to each author were counted.

In the five American criminology journals, there were 127 articles, with 236 authors (82 percent of whom were American) and a total of 7,123 citations. In the five American criminal justice journals, there were 140 articles, with 245 authors (91 percent American), and a total of 6,661 citations. In the five international criminology journals, there were 124 articles, with 190 authors (only 7 percent American), and a total of 4,101 citations. In the five international criminal justice journals, there were 112 articles, with 186 authors (75 percent American), and a total of 5,812 citations. It is clear that the majority of authors in the international criminal justice journals were American; however, in all cases the American criminal justice journals had a higher percentage of American authors. In total, we studied 503 articles in these 20 journals (an average of 25 articles per journal), with 857 authors (66 percent American) and 23,697 citations (an average of 1,185 citations per journal).

Table 4.2 shows the most-cited five scholars (or more in the case of ties) in each of the 20 journals. For example, in *JQ*, the most-cited scholar was Alfred Blumstein, with 15 citations, followed by Travis Hirschi (14), Wesley G. Skogan (14), and Michael R. Gottfredson (12), with Denise B. Kandel and Eric D. Poole tied at 11 citations.

MOST-CITED SCHOLARS IN CATEGORIES OF JOURNALS

In order to compare each journal, the most-cited 25 scholars in each journal were given a score from 25 to 1, depending on their ranking. To be precise, each scholar was given a score of 26 minus the ranking, so that it was possible for more than 25 scholars to score, depending on ties. For example, in *JQ*, the most-cited scholar (ranked 1), Alfred Blumstein, was given a score of 25. The next-most-cited scholars, Travis Hirschi and Wesley G. Skogan (each ranked 2.5 because they were tied), were each given a score of 23.5. The ranking continued up to the seven scholars who were each ranked 25 and scored 1. A total of 28 scholars were given

Table 4.1
Journals Included in the Analysis

American Criminology Journals
Criminology (CRIM): 28 articles, 63 authors (71% U.S.), 2,493 citations.
Journal of Quantitative Criminology (JQC): 19 articles, 34 authors (62% U.S.), 823 citations.
Journal of Research in Crime and Delinquency (JRCD): 15 articles, 23 authors (91% U.S.), 1,014 citations.
Journal of Interpersonal Violence (JIV): 43 articles, 74 authors (96% U.S.), 1,672 citations.
Violence and Victims (VV): 22 articles, 42 authors (83% U.S.), 1,121 citations.
  TOTAL: 127 articles, 236 authors (82% U.S.), 7,123 citations.

American Criminal Justice Journals
Justice Quarterly (JQ): 29 articles, 58 authors (86% U.S.), 2,141 citations.
Journal of Criminal Justice (JCJ): 36 articles, 69 authors (93% U.S.), 1,777 citations.
Crime and Delinquency (CD): 29 articles, 54 authors (94% U.S.), 1,121 citations.
Criminal Justice Review (CJR): 10 articles, 12 authors (92% U.S.), 656 citations.
Federal Probation (FP): 36 articles, 52 authors (92% U.S.), 966 citations.
  TOTAL: 140 articles, 245 authors (91% U.S.), 6,661 citations.

International Criminology Journals
British Journal of Criminology (BJC): 25 articles, 38 authors (0% U.S.), 1,107 citations.
Australian and New Zealand Journal of Criminology (ANZ): 21 articles, 36 authors (0% U.S.), 688 citations.
Canadian Journal of Criminology (CJC): 46 articles, 70 authors (4% U.S.), 1,312 citations.
Criminologie (CRGE): 11 articles, 14 authors (0% U.S.), 378 citations.
Contemporary Crises (CC): 21 articles, 32 authors (31% U.S.), 616 citations.
  TOTAL: 124 articles, 190 authors (7% U.S.), 4,101 citations.

International Criminal Justice Journals
Crime and Justice (CJ): 7 articles, 9 authors (56% U.S.), 1,743 citations.
Criminal Justice and Behavior (CJB): 27 articles, 56 authors (79% U.S.), 1,462 citations.
International Journal of Comparative and Applied Criminal Justice (IJCA): 26 articles, 34 authors (76% U.S.), 725 citations.
International Journal of Offender Therapy and Comparative Criminology (IJOT): 22 articles, 46 authors (80% U.S.), 792 citations.
Social Justice (SJ): 30 articles, 41 authors (66% U.S.), 1,090 citations.
  TOTAL: 112 articles, 186 authors (75% U.S.), 5,812 citations.

Total American Journals: 267 articles, 481 authors (87% U.S.), 13,784 citations.

Total International Journals: 236 articles, 376 authors (40% U.S.), 9,913 citations.

Total Criminology Journals: 251 articles, 426 authors (48% U.S.), 11,224 citations.

Total Criminal Justice Journals: 252 articles, 431 authors (84% U.S.), 12,473 citations.

TOTAL FOR ALL JOURNALS: 503 articles, 857 authors (66% U.S.), 23,697 citations.

Table 4.2
Most-Cited Scholars in Each Journal in 1990

American Criminology Journals

CRIM: D.P. Farrington (20); T. Hirschi (19); A. Blumstein (18); S.A. Mednick (16); D.A. Smith (16)

JQC: D.P. Farrington (11); A. Blumstein (10); J. Cohen (10); L.E. Cohen (9); M.R. Gottfredson (9); C.G. Janson (9); M.G. Sirken (9)

JRCD: T. Hirschi (20); M.R. Gottfredson (16); L.E. Cohen (11); M.J. Hindelang (10); R. Quinney (9); R.J. Sampson (9)

JIV: M.A. Straus (21); D.G. Kilpatrick (14); J.V. Becker (12); R.J. Gelles (12); G.G. Abel (11); L.J. Veronen (11)

VV: M.A. Straus (30); R.J. Gelles (19); K. Yllo (10); D.G. Saunders (9); M.E. Wolfgang (9)

American Criminal Justice Journals

JQ: A. Blumstein (15); T. Hirschi (14); W.G. Skogan (14); M.R. Gottfredson (12); D.B. Kandel (11); E.D. Poole (11)

JCJ: E.D. Poole (19); L.W. Sherman (19); R.M. Regoli (18); M.A. Straus (11); R.G. Culbertson (10)

CD: J. Petersilia (16); B.S. Erwin (13); T.R. Clear (10); H. Edelhertz (10); G.A. Geis (10); B. Krisberg (10); R.M. Martinson (10); M.H. Tonry (10)

CJR: E.T. Glueck (9); S.E. Glueck (9); W.C. Bailey (8); M.E. Wolfgang (8); D.P. Farrington (7)

FP: T.R. Clear (11); R.M. Carter (8); H.E. Allen (6); E.J. Latessa (6); J.R. Lilly (6); L.E. Ohlin (6); J. Petersilia (6); L.T. Wilkins (6)

International Criminology Journals

BJC: S. Cohen (14); A.E. Bottoms (11); K. Pease (8); W.G. Carson (7); D. Downes (7)

ANZ: D. Brown (6); A.M. Morris (6); J. Braithwaite (5); H. Hiller (5); R. Quinney (5); P.R. Wilson (5)

CJC: R.V. Clarke (13); R.R. Ross (12); P. Gendreau (11); F.T. Cullen (10); T. Gabor (10); D.P. Rosenbaum (10)

CRGE: M. Baril (8); M. Cusson (5); R.V. Ericson (5); M. Frechette (4); S.K. Steinmetz (4)

CC: U. Rosenthal (7); M.B. Clinard (5); F.T. Cullen (5); D.P. Farrington (5); J.Q. Wilson (5)

International Criminal Justice Journals

CJ: D.P. Farrington (29); M.W. Klein (13); L.N. Robins (11); D.S. Elliott (10); S.A. Mednick (10)

CJB: P. Gendreau (22); R.D. Hare (14); R.R. Ross (14); J.S. Carroll (11); F.T. Cullen (9); R.M. Martinson (9)

IJCA: T. Hirschi (6); W. Clifford (5); M.J. Hindelang (5); J.J Doharia (5); J.G. Weis (5)

IJOT: J.V. Becker (14); D. Finkelhor (8); G.G. Abel (7); M. Kaplan (7); R. Deisher (6); H.J. Eysenck (6); P. Fehrenbach (6); N. Groth (6); H. Toch (6)

SJ: C. Smart (11); J. Young (11); C. MacKinnon (10); M. Cain (8); M. Chesney-Lind (8)

Note: Number of citations in parentheses

a score greater than zero, and all other scholars were scored zero. This procedure was adopted as a method of giving all journals equal weight. If we had simply added the number of citations, journals with a large number of citations (e.g., *CRIM*) would have contributed disproportionately to the total score.

Table 4.3 shows the scholars with the highest total scores in the five American criminology journals. For example, Marvin E. Wolfgang was ranked in the top 25 scholars in four of the five journals, scoring 19 in *CRIM*, 14 in *JQC*, 19 in *JRCD*, 0 in *JIV*, and 21.5 in *VV*, for a total score of 73.5. The next most-cited scholars in American criminology journals were Michael R. Gottfredson, Alfred Blumstein, and Travis Hirschi. Our aim was to show the top 20 scholars in each category of journals; because of ties, 21 scholars are shown in Table 4.3.

Table 4.3
Scores in Five American Criminology Journals

| Rank | Author | SCORE | | | | | TOTAL |
		CRIM	*JQC*	*JRCD*	*JIV*	*VV*	SCORE
1	Marvin E. Wolfgang	19	14	19	0	21.5	73.5
2	Michael R. Gottfredson	10.5	20.5	24	0	16	71
3	Alfred Blumstein	23	23.5	17.5	0	0	64
4	Travis Hirschi	24	14	25	0	0	63
5	Jacqueline Cohen	20	23.5	13	0	0	56.5
6.5	David P. Farrington	25	25	0	0	0	50
6.5	Murray A. Straus	0	0	0	25	25	50
8	Richard J. Gelles	0	0	0	22.5	24	46.5
9	Lawrence E. Cohen	0	20.5	23	0	0	43.5
10.5	Michael J. Hindelang	0	4.5	22	0	4.5	31
10.5	Robert J. Sampson	10.5	0	20.5	0	0	31
12	Susan K. Steinmetz	0	0	0	13.5	16	29.5
13	Dean G. Saunders	0	0	0	7.5	21.5	29
14	John L. Hagan	10.5	14	2	0	0	26.5
15	Dean G. Kilpatrick	0	0	0	24	0	24
16.5	David Finkelhor	0	0	0	18.5	4.5	23
16.5	K. Yllo	0	0	0	0	23	23
18.5	Judith V. Becker	0	0	0	22.5	0	22.5
18.5	Marcus Felson	0	9.5	13	0	0	22.5
20.5	Sarnoff A. Mednick	21.5	0	0	0	0	21.5
20.5	Douglas A. Smith	21.5	0	0	0	0	21.5

Note: Score=26 minus rank in each journal
   CRIM = *Criminology; JQC = Journal of Quantitative Criminology; JRCD = Journal of Research in Crime and Delinquency; JIV = Journal of Interpersonal Violence; VV = Violence and Victims*

Table 4.4 shows that the most-cited scholars in five American criminal justice journals were Joan Petersilia, Alfred Blumstein, Marvin E. Wolfgang, and Todd R. Clear. Table 4.5 shows that the most-cited scholars in five international criminol-

Table 4.4
Scores in Five American Criminal Justice Journals

Rank	Author	JQ	JCJ	SCORE CD	CJR	FP	TOTAL SCORE
1	Joan Petersilia	0	0	25	11.5	20.5	57
2	Alfred Blumstein	25	13	0	17.5	0	55.5
3	Marvin E. Wolfgang	18	13	0	22.5	0	53.5
4	Todd R. Clear	0	0	20.5	0	25	45.5
5.5	Travis Hirschi	23.5	0	7	0	14.5	45
5.5	Eric D. Poole	20.5	24.5	0	0	0	45
7	David P. Farrington	18	0	0	21	0	39
8	Robert M. Martinson	0	0	20.5	0	14.5	35
9	Ronald V.G. Clarke	0	19	0	11.5	0	30.5
11	Eleanor T. Glueck	0	0	0	24.5	0	24.5
11	Sheldon E. Glueck	0	0	0	24.5	0	24.5
11	Lawrence W. Sherman	0	24.5	0	0	0	24.5
14	Robert M. Carter	0	0	0	0	24	24
14	Francis T. Cullen	16	0	0	0	8	24
14	Billie S. Erwin	0	0	24	0	0	24
16	Wesley G. Skogan	23.5	0	0	0	0	23.5
17	Robert M. Regoli	0	23	0	0	0	23
18	William C. Bailey	0	0	0	22.5	0	22.5
20	Michael R. Gottfredson	22	0	0	0	0	22
20	John L. Hagan	9	13	0	0	0	22
20	Murray A. Straus	0	22	0	0	0	22

Note: Score=26 minus rank in each journal
JQ = Justice Quarterly; JCJ = Journal of Criminal Justice; CD = Crime and Delinquency;
CJR = Criminal Justice Review; FP = Federal Probation

ogy journals were John Braithwaite, Francis T. Cullen, Maurice Cusson, and James Q. Wilson. Table 4.6 shows that the most-cited scholars in five international criminal justice journals were Travis Hirschi, Delbert S. Elliott, Marvin E. Wolfgang, and David Finkelhor.

Table 4.7 shows the total scores of the top 30 scholars in all ten criminology journals. For example, Marvin E. Wolfgang scored 73.5 in American journals and 17.5 in international journals, for a total score of 91. The next most-cited scholars in these ten journals were Michael R. Gottfredson, David P. Farrington, Alfred Blumstein, and Travis Hirschi. While the score in any one journal may be based on a relatively small number of citations, at greater levels of aggregation (e.g., ten journals), the top scholars have to be among the most-cited scholars in several journals. Table 4.8 shows that the most-cited scholars in ten criminal justice journals were Travis Hirschi, Marvin E. Wolfgang, Alfred Blumstein, David P. Farrington, and Joan Petersilia. The similarities between the most-cited scholars in the two sets of journals is worth noting: Marvin E. Wolfgang, Alfred Blumstein, Travis Hirschi, and David P. Farrington are among the top five scholars cited in each of the two tables.

Table 4.5
Scores in Five International Criminology Journals

Rank	Author	SCORE BJC	ANZ	CJC	CRGE	CC	TOTAL SCORE
1	John Braithwaite	16.5	21.5	0	0	18	56
2	Francis T. Cullen	0	0	21	0	22.5	43.5
3	Maurice Cusson	0	0	14	23.5	0	37.5
4	James Q. Wilson	0	0	14	0	22.5	36.5
5	Patricia M. Mayhew	16.5	0	17.5	0	0	34
6	Anthony N. Doob	0	0	17.5	15.5	0	33
7.5	Richard V. Ericson	8	0	0	23.5	0	31.5
7.5	Richard Quinney	0	21.5	0	0	10	31.5
9	Micheline Baril	0	0	5	25	0	30
10	Stanley Cohen	25	4	0	0	0	29
11	Anthony E. Bottoms	4	24	0	0	0	28
12	Marcel Frechette	0	0	5	21	0	26
13.5	Ronald V.G. Clarke	0	0	25	0	0	25
13.5	Uriel Rosenthal	0	0	0	0	25	25
15.5	David Brown	0	24.5	0	0	0	24.5
15.5	Allison M. Morris	0	24.5	0	0	0	24.5
17	Robert R. Ross	0	0	24	0	0	24
18.5	Paul Gendreau	0	0	23	0	0	23
18.5	Kenneth Pease	23	0	0	0	0	23
20.5	Marshall B. Clinard	0	0	0	0	22.5	22.5
20.5	David P. Farrington	0	0	0	0	22.5	22.5

Note: Score=26 minus rank in each journal
BJC = *British Journal of Criminology*; *ANZ* = Australian and New Zealand Journal of Criminology; *CJC* = *Canadian Journal of Criminology*; *CRGE* = *Criminologie*; *CC* = *Contemporary Crises*

Table 4.9 aggregates the categories of journals differently, to show total scores in all ten American journals. The most-cited scholars were Marvin E. Wolfgang, Alfred Blumstein, Travis Hirschi, and Michael R. Gottfredson. Similarly, Table 4.10 shows that the most-cited scholars in all ten international journals were Francis T. Cullen, John Braithwaite, Marvin E. Wolfgang, and Travis Hirschi.

Table 4.11 aggregates all 20 journals to show the most-cited 40 scholars. Overall, the most-cited scholars were Marvin E. Wolfgang, Travis Hirschi, David P. Farrington, and Alfred Blumstein.

Table 4.12 shows the most-cited works of the eleven most-cited scholars (two scholars were tied for tenth place). For example, the most-cited work of Marvin E. Wolfgang was *Delinquency in a Birth Cohort* (Wolfgang, Figlio, and Sellin 1972), with 24 citations, and his second most-cited work was *Patterns in Criminal Homicide* (Wolfgang 1958), with 19 citations. Overall, 27 of Wolfgang's works were cited in these 20 criminology and criminal justice journals in 1990. David P. Farrington had 46 different works cited, while James Q. Wilson's citations were to only 10 different works. It was interesting that most of the works listed in Table 4.12 were books rather than journal articles.

Table 4.6
Scores in Five International Criminal Justice Journals

Rank	Author	CJ	SCORE CJB	IJCA	IJOT	SJ	TOTAL SCORE
1	Travis Hirschi	17	10.5	25	0	0	52.5
2	Delbert S. Elliott	21.5	0	17.5	0	0	39
3	Marvin E. Wolfgang	17	0	7	13.5	0	37.5
4	David Finkelhor	0	10.5	0	24	0	34.5
5	Paul Gendreau	0	22	7	0	0	29
6	Robert D. Hare	3.5	23.5	0	0	0	27
7.5	Judith V. Becker	0	0	0	25	0	25
7.5	David P. Farrington	25	0	0	0	0	25
9.5	Carol Smart	0	0	0	0	24.5	24.5
9.5	Jock Young	0	0	0	0	24.5	24.5
11.5	Jacqueline Cohen	12.5	0	0	0	11.5	24
11.5	Malcolm W. Klein	24	0	0	0	0	24
13	Robert R. Ross	0	23.5	0	0	0	23.5
14.5	Catherine MacKinnon	0	0	0	0	23	23
14.5	Lee N. Robins	23	0	0	0	0	23
18.5	Gene G. Abel	0	0	0	22.5	0	22.5
18.5	William Clifford	0	0	22.5	0	0	22.5
18.5	J.J. Doharia	0	0	22.5	0	0	22.5
18.5	Michael J. Hindelang	0	0	22.5	0	0	22.5
18.5	M. Kaplan	0	0	0	22.5	0	22.5
18.5	Joseph G. Weis	0	0	22.5	0	0	22.5

Note: Score=26 minus rank in each journal

CJ = Crime and Justice; CJB = Criminal Justice and Behavior; IJCA = International Journal of Comparative and Applied Criminal Justice; IJOT = International Journal of Offender Therapy and Comparative Criminology; SJ= Social Justice

CONCLUSION

Our analysis of citations in 20 journals in 1990 confirms and amplifies Cohn and Farrington's (1994a, 1994b, 1996) previous conclusions based on analyses of a smaller number of journals in 1986-90. Marvin E. Wolfgang, Alfred Blumstein, and James Q. Wilson were still among the most-cited authors. Generally, the most-cited works of the most-cited authors were concerned with criminal career research, confirming that this was the most influential issue of the late 1980s.

However, other authors and other issues are relatively more important in the present analysis than in our previous ones. In particular, Francis T. Cullen's work on rehabilitation and Ronald V.G. Clarke's work on situational crime prevention were found to be highly influential. Hence, it would be useful to expand our analyses to study more criminology and criminal justice journals.

Table 4.7
Scores in All Ten Criminology Journals

Rank	Author	US SCORE	INT SCORE	TOTAL SCORE
1	Marvin E. Wolfgang	73.5	17.5	91
2	Michael R. Gottfredson	71	4	75
3	David P. Farrington	50	22.5	72.5
4	Alfred Blumstein	64	0	64
5	Travis Hirschi	63	0	63
6	Jacqueline Cohen	56.5	0	56.5
7	John Braithwaite	0	56	56
8	Richard Quinney	20.5	31.5	52
9	Susan K. Steinmetz	29.5	21.5	51
10	Murray A. Straus	50	0	50
11	James Q. Wilson	13	36.5	49.5
12	Lawrence E. Cohen	43.5	5	48.5
13	Richard J. Gelles	46.5	0	46.5
14	Francis T. Cullen	0	43.5	43.5
15	Ronald V.G. Clarke	13	25	38
16	Maurice Cusson	0	37.5	37.5
17	John L. Hagan	26.5	10.5	37
18	Patricia M. Mayhew	2	34	36
19	James Garofalo	17.5	16.5	34
20	Rolf Loeber	18	15.5	33.5
21	Anthony N. Doob	0	33	33
22.5	Richard V. Ericson	0	31.5	31.5
22.5	Sarnoff A. Mednick	21.5	10	31.5
24.5	Michael J. Hindelang	31	0	31
24.5	Robert J. Sampson	31	0	31
26	Robert R. Ross	6.5	24	30.5
27	Micheline Baril	0	30	30
28.5	Stanley Cohen	0	29	29
28.5	Dean G. Saunders	29	0	29
30	Anthony E. Bottoms	0	28	28

Table 4.8
Scores in All Ten Criminal Justice Journals

Rank	Author	US SCORE	INT SCORE	TOTAL SCORE
1	Travis Hirschi	45	52.5	97.5
2	Marvin E. Wolfgang	53.5	37.5	91
3	Alfred Blumstein	55.5	12.5	68
4	David P. Farrington	39	25	64
5	Joan Petersilia	57	0	57
6	Robert M. Martinson	35	20.5	55.5
7	Delbert S. Elliott	9	39	48
8	Ronald V.G. Clarke	30.5	17	47.5
9	Todd R. Clear	45.5	0	45.5
10	Eric D. Poole	45	0	45
11	Francis T. Cullen	24	20.5	44.5
12	Jacqueline Cohen	14.5	24	38.5
13	Denise B. Kandel	20.5	17	37.5
14	David Finkelhor	0	34.5	34.5
16	Michael R. Gottfredson	22	9.5	31.5
16	Michael J. Hindelang	9	22.5	31.5
16	Joseph G. Weis	9	22.5	31.5
18	Lloyd E. Ohlin	20.5	10.5	31
19	Paul Gendreau	0	29	29
20	Donald J. West	11.5	17	28.5
21.5	Robert D. Hare	0	27	27
21.5	James Q. Wilson	17.5	9.5	27
23.5	Judith V. Becker	0	25	25
23.5	Franklin E. Zimring	14.5	10.5	25
27	Eleanor T. Glueck	24.5	0	24.5
27	Sheldon E. Glueck	24.5	0	24.5
27	Lawrence W. Sherman	24.5	0	24.5
27	Carol Smart	0	24.5	24.5
27	Jock Young	0	24.5	24.5
31	Robert M. Carter	24	0	24
31	Billie S. Erwin	24	0	24
31	Malcolm W. Klein	0	24	24

Table 4.9
Scores in All Ten American Journals

Rank	Author	CRIM SCORE	CJ SCORE	TOTAL SCORE
1	Marvin E. Wolfgang	73.5	53.5	127
2	Alfred Blumstein	64	55.5	119.5
3	Travis Hirschi	63	45	108
4	Michael R. Gottfredson	71	22	93
5	David P. Farrington	50	39	89
6	Murray A. Straus	50	22	72
7	Jacqueline Cohen	56.5	14.5	71
8	Richard J. Gelles	46.5	19	65.5
9	Joan Petersilia	0	57	57
10	John L. Hagan	26.5	22	48.5
11	Todd R. Clear	0	45.5	45.5
12	Eric D. Poole	0	45	45
13.5	Ronald V.G. Clarke	13	30.5	43.5
13.5	Lawrence E. Cohen	43.5	0	43.5
15	Lawrence W. Sherman	16.5	24.5	41
16	Michael J. Hindelang	31	9	40
17	Robert M. Martinson	0	35	35
18	Robert J. Sampson	31	1	32
19	Robert M. Figlio	20	11.5	31.5
20	James Q. Wilson	13	17.5	30.5
21	Susan K. Steinmetz	29.5	0	29.5
22	Dean G. Saunders	29	0	29
23.5	Eleanor T. Glueck	0	24.5	24.5
23.5	Sheldon E. Glueck	0	24.5	24.5
26.5	Robert M. Carter	0	24	24
26.5	Frances T. Cullen	0	24	24
26.5	Billie S. Erwin	0	24	24
26.5	Dean G. Kilpatrick	24	0	24
29	Wesley G. Skogan	0	23.5	23.5
31.5	Richard A. Berk	8	15	23
31.5	David Finkelhor	23	0	23
31.5	Robert M. Regoli	0	23	23
31.5	K. Yllo	23	0	23

Note: CRIM = Criminology journals; CJ = Criminal justice journals

Table 4.10
Scores in All Ten International Journals

Rank	Author	CRIM SCORE	CJ SCORE	TOTAL SCORE
1	Francis T. Cullen	43.5	20.5	64
2	John Braithwaite	56	0	56
3	Marvin E. Wolfgang	17.5	37.5	55
4	Travis Hirschi	0	52.5	52.5
5	Paul Gendreau	23	29	52
6.5	David P. Farrington	22.5	25	47.5
6.5	Robert R. Ross	24	23.5	47.5
8	Delbert S. Elliott	8	39	47
9	James Q. Wilson	36.5	9.5	46
10	Ronald V.G. Clarke	25	17	42
11	David Finkelhor	0	34.5	34.5
12	Patricia Mayhew	34	0	34
13	Anthony N. Doob	33	0	33
15	Richard V. Ericson	31.5	0	31.5
15	Sarnoff A. Mednick	10	21.5	31.5
15	Richard Quinney	31.5	0	31.5
17	Micheline Baril	30	0	30
18	Marshall B. Clinard	22.5	7	29.5
19	Stanley Cohen	29	0	29
20	Anthony E. Bottoms	28	0	28
21	Robert D. Hare	0	27	27
22	Marcel Frechette	26.5	0	26.5
24	Judith V. Becker	0	25	25
24	Michel Foucault	8	17	25
24	Uriel Rosenthal	25	0	25
28	David Brown	24.5	0	24.5
28	Robert M. Martinson	4	20.5	24.5
28	Allison M. Morris	24.5	0	24.5
28	Carol Smart	0	24.5	24.5
28	Jock Young	0	24.5	24.5

Note: CRIM = Criminology journals; CJ = Criminal Justice journals

Table 4.11
Scores in All Twenty Journals

Rank	Author	US	SCORE INT	CRIM	CJ	TOTAL[a]
1	Marvin E. Wolfgang	127	55	91	91	182
2	Travis Hirschi	108	52.5	63	97.5	160.5
3	David P. Farrington	89	47.5	72.5	64	136.5
4	Alfred Blumstein	119.5	12.5	64	68	132
5	Michael R. Gottfredson	93	13.5	75	31.5	106.5
6	Jacqueline Cohen	71	24	56.5	38.5	95
7	Francis T. Cullen	24	64	43.5	44.5	88
8	Ronald V.G. Clarke	43.5	42	38	47.5	85.5
9	James Q. Wilson	30.5	46	49.5	27	76.5
10.5	John Braithwaite	16	56	56	16	72
10.5	Murray A. Straus	72	0	50	22	72
12	Richard J. Gelles	65.5	0	46.5	19	65.5
13	Michael J. Hindelang	40	22.5	31	31.5	62.5
14.5	Delbert S. Elliott	12.5	47	11.5	48	59.5
14.5	Robert M. Martinson	35	24.5	4	55.5	59.5
16	John L. Hagan	48.5	10.5	37	22	59
17	David Finkelhor	23	34.5	23	34.5	57.5
18	Joan Petersilia	57	0	0	57	57
19	Robert R. Ross	6.5	47.5	30.5	23.5	54
20	Sarnoff A. Mednick	21.5	31.5	31.5	21.5	53
21.5	Paul Gendreau	0	52	23	29	52
21.5	Richard Quinney	20.5	31.5	52	0	52
23	Susan K. Steinmetz	29.5	21.5	51	0	51
24	Lawrence E. Cohen	43.5	5	48.5	0	48.5
25	Judith V. Becker	22.5	25	22.5	25	47.5
26	Todd R. Clear	45.5	0	0	45.5	45.5
27	Eric D. Poole	45	0	0	45	45
28	Gene Abel	20.5	22.5	20.5	22.5	43
29.5	Robert M. Figlio	31.5	9.5	20	21	41
29.5	Lawrence W. Sherman	41	0	16.5	24.5	41
31.5	Maurice Cusson	0	37.5	37.5	0	37.5
31.5	Denise B. Kandel	20.5	17	0	37.5	37.5
33	Patricia M. Mayhew	2	34	36	0	36
34	James Garofalo	17.5	16.5	34	0	34
35	Rolf Loeber	18	15.5	33.5	0	33.5
36.5	Anthony N. Doob	0	33	33	0	33
36.5	Lloyd E. Ohlin	22.5	10.5	2	31	33
38	Robert J. Sampson	32	0	31	1	32
39	Richard V. Ericson	0	31.5	31.5	0	31.5
40	Micheline Baril	0	30	30	0	30

[a]This column provides the total citations **either** in U.S. and international journals **or** in criminology and criminal justice journals.

Note: CRIM = Criminology journals;   CJ = Criminal Justice journals;   US = American journals;
         INT = International journals

Table 4.12
The Most-Cited Works of the Most-Cited Scholars

Rank	Author/Work	Number of Citations
1	**Marvin E. Wolfgang** (27)[a]	
	Delinquency in a Birth Cohort (Wolfgang et al. 1972)	24
	Patterns in Criminal Homicide (Wolfgang 1958)	19
2	**Travis Hirschi** (27)	
	Causes of Delinquency (Hirschi 1969)	26
	Measuring Delinquency (Hindelang et al. 1981)	12
	"The True Value of Lambda" (Gottfredson and Hirschi 1986)	12
3	**David P. Farrington** (46)	
	"Criminal Career Research" (Blumstein et al. 1988a)	9
	Understanding and Controlling Crime (Farrington et al.,1986)	8
4	**Alfred Blumstein** (28)	
	Criminal Careers and "Career Criminals" (Blumstein et al. 1986)[b]	17
	"Criminal Career Research" (Blumstein et al. 1988a)	9
5	**Michael R. Gottfredson** (28)	
	"The True Value of Lambda" (Gottfredson and Hirschi 1986)	12
	Decision-Making in Criminal Justice (Gottfredson and Gottfredson 1980/1988)	11
6	**Jacqueline Cohen** (22)	
	Criminal Careers and "Career Criminals" (Blumstein et al. 1986)[b]	19
	"Criminal Career Research" (Blumstein et al. 1988a)	9
7	**Francis T. Cullen** (21)	
	Reaffirming Rehabilitation (Cullen and Gilbert 1982)	9
	"Does Correctional Treatment Work?" (Andrews et al. 1990)	7
8	**Ronald V.G. Clarke** (18)	
	The Reasoning Criminal (Cornish and Clarke 1986)	9
	"Understanding Crime Displacement" (Cornish and Clarke 1987)	7
9	**James Q. Wilson** (10)	
	Crime and Human Nature (Wilson and Herrnstein 1985)	18
	Thinking about Crime (Wilson 1975/1983)	12
10.5	**John Braithwaite** (19)	
	To Punish or Persuade (Braithwaite 1985)[c]	4
10.5	**Murray A. Straus** (37)	
	Behind Closed Doors (Straus et al. 1980)	12
	"Societal Change and Change in Family Violence" (Straus and Gelles 1986)	8

[a]The total number of different works cited for each author is listed in parentheses.
[b]The difference in citation counts for Blumstein et al. 1986 is due to the fact that the work was cited twice in an article by Blumstein. These two citations were not credited to Blumstein because self-citations were not counted.
[c]The second-most-cited work by John Braithwaite is not shown here as there were four works (with three citations each) tied for this position.

NOTES

1. We did consider using the *Journal of Crime and Justice* and the *Howard Journal of Criminal Justice* but these journals contained too few citations. The most cited scholar in the *Journal of Crime and Justice* in 1990 had only four citations and only three scholars had four or more citations in the *Howard Journal of Criminal Justice* in 1990.

2. We did not consider non-academic journals such as *The Police Chief*.

3. For comprehensive lists of major journals in criminology and criminal justice, see Vaughn and del Carmen (1992) and Wright and Rogers (1996).

5

The Most-Cited Scholars in Criminology and Criminal Justice Since 1945: A Longitudinal Analysis of Four Data Sets

By comparing citation analyses over the last 50 years, it is possible to assess some of the continuities and the changes in the scholars who have influenced criminology and criminal justice since World War II. This chapter presents a longitudinal comparison of the most-cited scholars in four data sets. The first is from Wolfgang, Figlio, and Thornberry's (1978) analysis of known scholarly journal articles and research books dealing with crime-related topics published from 1945–1972, the second from our study (outlined in Chapter 2) of nine leading American and international criminology and criminal justice journals appearing from 1991–1995, the third from Wright and Soma's (1996) examination of all known introductory criminology textbooks published from 1963–1968, and the fourth from Wright's (1995a) and Wright and Cohn's (1996) analyses of all known introductory criminology and criminal justice textbooks appearing from 1989–1993. This analysis demonstrates the changing influence of scholars in criminology and criminal justice over time; we found that only one fourth of the most-cited scholars in the earlier data sets reappeared in the recent studies.

THE FOUR DATA SETS

We examined a large number of previous studies of the most-cited scholars in criminology and criminal justice before selecting the four primary data sets for our analyses of citation patterns over time. We intentionally chose data sets taken from both academic publications such as journals and research monographs and textbooks to enable the comparison of citation trends in different types of publications. Two of the data sets were selected because they listed the most-cited scholars in early publications: Wolfgang, Figlio, and Thornberry (1978) for academic journal publications and Wright and Soma (1996) for textbooks. The other two data sets were chosen as representative of current citation analysis: the data from Chapter 2 for academic journal publications, and Wright (1995a) and Wright and Cohn (1996) for textbooks.

As mentioned above, Wolfgang, Figlio, and Thornberry (1978) examined the most-cited authors and works in all known scholarly publications (excluding textbooks) dealing with criminological topics from 1945–1972. Altogether, this study analyzed the citations to 3,690 works, including 556 research-oriented books and monographs and 3,134 journal articles. The result was a list of the authors and titles of the 82 most-cited works in criminology, although reanalyses have converted these data into inventories of the most-cited scholars (see Geis and Meier 1978; Wright 1998). We have used Wright's (1998) conversion, listing the 47 most-cited scholars from the 82 most-cited works reported in Wolfgang, Figlio, and Thornberry (1978).[1] We refer to this as data set A.

Wright and Soma (1996) produced the first longitudinal study of the most-cited scholars in introductory criminology textbooks, examining all known books published during three periods: 1963–1968, 1976–1980, and 1989–1993.[2] The data for the earliest period reported in this study (1963–1968) listed the 31 most-cited scholars in ten textbooks; we included these in our analysis because they were taken from a period that partially overlaps the years examined by Wolfgang, Figlio, and Thornberry (1978). We refer to this as data set B.

Chapter 2 reports the 49 most-cited scholars in nine leading American and international criminology and criminal justice journals published from 1991–1995 (see Table 2.13). We selected this data set for our analysis because it offers the most current list of prominent scholars in academic publications. We refer to this as data set C.

Finally, for a comparable recent survey of the most-cited scholars in textbooks, we combined two data sets from 1989–1993: Wright's (1995a) report of the 47 most-cited authors in 23 introductory criminology textbooks, and Wright and Cohn's (1996) summary of the 22 most-cited figures in 16 introductory criminal justice textbooks. This combination (after the deletion of duplicate names) resulted in a list of 58 most-cited scholars in introductory criminology and criminal justice textbooks appearing between 1989 and 1993. We refer to this as data set D.

Table 5.1 describes the data sets and lists the most-cited scholars featured in our analysis. Altogether, 135 different names appeared on the most-cited scholar lists in the four data sets.

THE ANALYSIS

It is clear from the list in Table 5.1 that there are a variety of ways the four data sets may be examined. The most obvious is to consider each data set individually and compare it with the other three. There are also various combinations of the four data sets that provide intriguing prospects. The first possibility is to compare data sets A and B with data sets C and D, thus relating the two earlier data sets to the two more recent ones. This enables us to evaluate the levels of continuity and change in the most-cited scholars in all criminology and criminal justice publications (both academic publications and textbooks). We also compared the most-cited scholars in academic publications (data sets A and C) with those in textbooks (data sets B and D).

Table 5.1
The Most-Cited Scholars in Criminology and Criminal Justice Publications, 1945–1995

Data Set A

Description: Wolfgang, Figlio, and Thornberry (1978), Academic Publications (journals, research books, and monographs) from 1945–1972 (N = 47)

Scholars (in alphabetical order): David Abrahamsen, Harry J. Anslinger, David P. Ausubel, Milton L. Barron, Howard S. Becker, Albert D. Biderman, Herbert A. Bloch, Isidor Chein, Richard A. Cloward, Albert K. Cohen, Donald R. Cressey, Simon Dinitz, Franco Ferracuti, Donald R. Gerard, Eleanor T. Glueck, Sheldon E. Glueck, Emil T. Hartl, Louise A. Johnson, Solomon Kobrin, William C. Kvaraceus, Bernard Lander, Robert S. Lee, Alfred R. Lindesmith, David Matza, Joan McCord, William McCord, Eugene McDermott, Jennie McIntyre, Robert K. Merton, Walter B. Miller, Arthur Niederhoffer, Lloyd E. Ohlin, Austin L. Porterfield, Walter C. Reckless, Albert J. Reiss, Jr., Eva Rosenfield, Thorsten J. Sellin, William H. Sheldon, James F. Short, Jr., Fred L. Strodtbeck, Edwin H. Sutherland, Gresham M. Sykes, William F. Tompkins, George B. Vold, Adrianne Weir, Marvin E. Wolfgang, and Irving K. Zola

Data Set B

Description: Wright and Soma (1996), Textbooks from 1963–1968 (N = 31)

Scholars (in alphabetical order): Harry Elmer Barnes, Ruth Shonle Cavan, Marshall B. Clinard, Richard A. Cloward, Albert K. Cohen, Donald R. Cressey, Ralph W. England, Jr., Daniel Glaser, Eleanor T. Glueck, Sheldon E. Glueck, Jerome Hall, Frank E. Hartung, William Healy, Richard R. Korn, Orlando F. Lewis, David W. Maurer, Lloyd W. McCorkle, Robert K. Merton, Walter B. Miller, Lloyd E. Ohlin, Leon Radzinowicz, Walter C. Reckless, Thorsten J. Sellin, Clifford R. Shaw, James F. Short, Jr., Edwin H. Sutherland, Gresham M. Sykes, Paul W. Tappan, Negley K. Teeters, George B. Vold, and Marvin E. Wolfgang

Data Set C

Description: Chapter 2, Academic Publications (leading journals) from 1991–1995 (N = 49)

Scholars (in alphabetical order): Gene G. Abel, Suzanne S. Ageton, Ronald L. Akers, Don A. Andrews, Howard E. Barbaree, Judith V. Becker, Alfred Blumstein, James L. Bonta, John Braithwaite, Dante V. Cicchetti, Jacqueline Cohen, Lawrence E. Cohen, Francis T. Cullen, Delbert S. Elliott, Jeffrey A. Fagan, David P. Farrington, Marcus Felson, Timothy J. Flanagan, Paul Gendreau, Michael R. Gottfredson, John L. Hagan, Michael J. Hindelang, Travis Hirschi, David Huizinga, Marvin D. Krohn, George L. Kelling, Rolf Loeber, William L. Marshall, Martha A. Myers, Daniel S. Nagin, Lloyd E. Ohlin, Raymond Paternoster, Joan Petersilia, Vernon L. Quinsey, Robert M. Regoli, Albert J. Reiss, Jr., Robert J. Sampson, Lawrence W. Sherman, Wesley G. Skogan, Douglas A. Smith, Murray A. Straus, Terence P. Thornberry, Hans Toch, Michael H. Tonry, Christy A. Visher, Kirk R. Williams, James Q. Wilson, Marvin E. Wolfgang, and Jock Young

Data Set D

Description: Wright (1995a) and Wright and Cohn (1996), Textbooks from 1989–1993 (N = 58)

Scholars (in alphabetical order): Ronald L. Akers, Harry E. Allen, David H. Bayley, Thomas J. Bernard, Barbara Boland, John Braithwaite, William J. Chambliss, Todd R. Clear, Marshall B. Clinard, Richard A. Cloward, Albert K. Cohen, Donald R. Cressey, Francis T. Cullen, Emile Durkheim, Delbert S. Elliott, David P. Farrington, Timothy J. Flanagan, Gilbert Geis, Richard J. Gelles, Don C. Gibbons, Jack P. Gibbs, Eleanor T. Glueck, Sheldon E. Glueck, Herman Goldstein, Michael R. Gottfredson, Peter Greenwood, John L. Hagan, Richard J. Herrnstein, Michael J. Hindelang, Travis Hirschi, James A. Inciardi, George L. Kelling, Wayne R. LaFave, Edwin M. Lemert, David Matza, Sarnoff A. Mednick, Lloyd E. Ohlin, Joan Petersilia, Richard Quinney, Walter C. Reckless, Albert J. Reiss, Jr., Thorsten J. Sellin, Lawrence W. Sherman, James F. Short, Jr., Jerome H. Skolnick, Darrell J. Steffensmeier, Murray A. Straus, Edwin H. Sutherland, Gresham M. Sykes, Charles R. Tittle, Austin T. Turk, George B. Vold, Samuel Walker, Joseph G. Weis, Paul B. Wice, James Q. Wilson, Marvin E. Wolfgang, and Jock Young

---

FINDINGS

We first compared the two earlier data sets (A and B) to the two recent data sets (C and D). Sixteen scholars who appeared among the most-cited figures in earlier criminology and criminal justice publications reappeared on the recent most-cited lists. Of these 16 scholars, two appeared on two of the four most-cited lists (Marshall B. Clinard and David Matza), twelve appeared on three lists (Richard A. Cloward, Albert K. Cohen, Donald R. Cressey, Eleanor T. Glueck, Sheldon E. Glueck, Walter C. Reckless, Albert J. Reiss, Jr., Thorsten J. Sellin, James F. Short, Jr., Edwin H. Sutherland, Gresham M. Sykes, and George B. Vold), and only two (Lloyd E. Ohlin and Marvin E. Wolfgang) appeared on all four of the most-cited lists.

We then aggregated the data sets for academic publications and textbooks and obtained correlations between the resulting clusters. We found a weak relationship among the most-cited scholars in criminology and criminal justice over time (r = .27).[3] However, considering that 63 authors appeared on the combined lists of most-cited scholars from the earlier period, enduring prominence in criminology and criminal justice seems to be the exception rather than the rule: only 25.4 percent of the names from the earlier lists rated among the most-cited scholars in the recent data sets.

We also obtained correlation coefficients for each pair of data sets. The resulting correlation matrix, which permits an evaluation of the continuity over time in the most-cited scholars in different types of publications,[4] is shown in Table 5.2. It is clear that, while there was some stability between the most-cited scholars in earlier academic publications and recent textbooks (r = .29) and between the most-cited scholars in earlier and recent textbooks (r = .31), there was little similarity between the most-cited scholars in earlier and recent academic publications (r = .06) or between the most-cited scholars in earlier textbooks and recent academic publications (r = .05).

When the most-cited scholars from earlier academic publications (data set A) and recent textbooks (data set D) were compared, 15 names appeared on both lists.[5]

When the earlier and later textbooks were compared (data sets B and D), 14 authors rated among the most-cited scholars in both data sets.[6] In contrast, only Lloyd E. Ohlin, Albert J. Reiss, Jr., and Marvin E. Wolfgang appeared as most-cited scholars in earlier and in recent academic publications, and only Lloyd E. Ohlin and Marvin E. Wolfgang appeared as most-cited scholars in earlier textbooks and recent academic publications.

An even better indicator of continuity and change among the most-cited scholars may be the percentages of authors from the earlier lists who subsequently appeared on the more recent lists. An examination of the four data sets shows that 45.2 percent of the most-cited scholars in the earlier textbooks were also among the most-cited scholars in the later textbooks, 31.9 percent of the most-cited scholars in the earlier academic publications also appeared on the recent textbook list, 6.5 percent of the most-cited scholars on the earlier textbook list were among the most-cited scholars in recent academic publications, and 6.4 percent of the most-cited scholars in the earlier academic publications were also among the most-cited scholars in later academic publications. It is clear from this comparison that whatever continuity appeared among the most-cited scholars in the four data sets was largely a product of the two data sets taken from the textbooks, suggesting that prominence in criminology and criminal justice is particularly ephemeral in academic publications.

Table 5.2
Correlations among the Most-Cited Scholars in Four Data Sets[a]

	(A) Academic Publications, 1945–1972[b]	(B) Textbooks, 1963–1968[c]	(C) Academic Publications, 1991–1995[d]	(D) Textbooks, 1989–1993[e]
(A)	1.00	——	——	——
(B)	.38	1.00	——	——
(C)	.06	.05	1.00	——
(D)	.29	.31	.36	1.00

[a] See note 3.
[b] Taken from Wolfgang, Figlio, and Thornberry (1978).
[c] Taken from Wright and Soma (1996).
[d] Taken from Chapter 2, Table 2.13.
[e] Taken from Wright (1995a) and Wright and Cohn (1996).

The data also permit us to analyze citation patterns in academic publications compared to textbooks within each of the two time periods. Table 5.1 shows that 31.9 percent (15) of the 47 most-cited scholars in the earlier academic publications also appeared among the most-cited scholars in the earlier textbooks.[7] Similarly, 38.8 percent (19) of the 49 most-cited scholars in recent academic publications ranked among the most-cited figures in recent textbooks.[8] This suggests that a core level of agreement exists between the most-cited scholars in academic publications and in textbooks during any particular time period.

The correlation coefficients calculated on the data sets show reasonable relationships between the most-cited scholars in academic publications and textbooks in both time periods; it is also clear that the correlations remain stable across time. The correlation between the most-cited scholars in recent academic publications and recent textbooks ($r = .36$) is only slightly lower than the correlation between the most-cited scholars in earlier academic publications and textbooks ($r = .38$). In other studies, Wright (1995a, 1996a, 1997) has noted that only modest associations exist between the most-cited scholars in recent academic publications and recent textbooks in criminology and criminal justice. Apparently, the degree of disparity in citation patterns between academic publications and textbooks is not new.

Finally, when comparing the correlations among the most-cited scholars within the time periods to the correlations between time periods, higher levels of agreement were found among the former. Notably, the two highest correlation coefficients in Table 5.2 appeared between the most-cited scholars in academic publications and in textbooks *within* the time periods; the four lowest correlations were in associations *between* time periods. This suggests that time contributes more than different types of publications to the differences in the citation patterns observed in our analysis.

CONCLUSION AND DISCUSSION

Using four data sets taken from earlier and recent academic publications and textbooks, we conducted a longitudinal analysis of the most-cited scholars in criminology and criminal justice from 1945–1995. Although some similarity was found between the most-cited scholars in earlier and recent textbooks, almost no agreement existed between the most-cited scholars in earlier and recent academic publications. In general, we found more change than continuity over time when considering the most-cited scholars in criminology and criminal justice; most of the consistency that was observed in our analysis was attributed to some stability in the citation patterns between the earlier and recent textbooks.

We found greater levels of agreement between the most-cited scholars in the academic publications and the textbooks within each time period. However, the correlation coefficients calculated on these associations were only moderate, indicating more differences than similarities in the citation patterns between academic publications and textbooks. Overall, our analysis suggests that citation patterns in criminology and criminal justice differ markedly in different types of publications and over different time periods.

Comparisons of the most-cited scholars in criminology and criminal justice academic publications and textbooks over time do produce some rather interesting patterns (see Wright 1995a, 1996a, 1997, 1998). First, textbook authors clearly venerate the past more than do authors of academic publications. Many of the most-cited scholars in recent textbooks (including Donald R. Cressey, Emile Durkheim, Eleanor T. Glueck, Sheldon E. Glueck, Walter C. Reckless, Edwin H. Sutherland, and George B. Vold) made their major intellectual contributions decades ago and are now deceased. In contrast, virtually all the major works of the most-cited scholars in recent academic publications have appeared within the last 15 years. This is supported by our findings of modest correlations between the most-cited scholars in recent textbooks with earlier academic publications and earlier textbooks, but negligible associations between recent academic publications with earlier academic publications and earlier textbooks. As Wright (1997: 87) remarks, "[while leading] journals reflect the latest styles and fads in theories and research methods, textbook authors may be pressured by the conventional thinking of publishers, reviewers, and instructors to stick with 'tried and true' arguments and citations."

Second, a comparison of the most-cited scholars in academic publications and textbooks seems to support Wright's (1995a: 309) observation that "[recent] textbook authors shy away from reporting the quantitative research that dominates the journals" (see also Wright 1993, 1996a, 1997). The majority of the most-cited scholars in recent academic publications are known for their quantitative research. In contrast, many scholars who are extensively cited in recent textbooks (but not academic publications) are prominent criminological theorists and/or qualitative researchers.[9] In general, our analysis of citation patterns seems to support Wright's (1993) claim that a comparison of the content of academic publications and textbooks reveals "two criminologies." Furthermore, the moderate correlations between the most-cited scholars in academic publications and textbooks during both of the time periods we examined suggest that this bifurcation in crime-related scholarship is nothing new.

It appears that prominence in criminology and criminal justice is fleeting for the majority of scholars and enduring for only a few (see Wright and Soma 1996). Some qualitative and quantitative evaluations of this phenomenon may be appropriate, to determine what is distinctive about the professional careers of the 16 elite scholars who appeared on at least one earlier and one recent list of most-cited scholars.[10]

First, longevity and perseverance seem to be prerequisites for enduring prominence in criminology and criminal justice (Wright and Soma 1996). The publications of most of the 16 elite scholars who appeared on two or more most-cited lists over time span decades rather than years. For example, Thorsten J. Sellin's most influential works extended over 34 years, from *Culture Conflict and Crime* (Sellin 1938) to *Delinquency in a Birth Cohort* (Wolfgang, Figlio, and Sellin 1972). Gresham M. Sykes's important works currently span 35 years, from the publication of his article "Techniques of Neutralization" (Sykes and Matza 1957) to the second edition of his textbook *Criminology* (Sykes and Cullen 1992).

In addition, lasting prominence appears to be given primarily to those demonstrating considerable breadth in their work (Wright and Soma 1996). Many of the 16 most-cited scholars over time have made important theoretical and empirical contributions to criminology and criminal justice while conducting research in a number of different areas. Edwin H. Sutherland, for example, not only developed the differential association and differential social organization theories in the editions of his textbook *Principles of Criminology* (Sutherland 1934, 1939, 1947), but also wrote path-breaking empirical studies of professional crime (Sutherland 1937) and white-collar crime (Sutherland 1949). Besides offering outstanding commentary and interpretation of the differential association perspective in revisions of *Principles of Criminology* (see Sutherland and Cressey 1955, 1960, 1966) after Sutherland's death in 1950, Donald R. Cressey's original contributions included landmark theoretical and empirical analyses of embezzlement (Cressey 1953), organized crime (Cressey 1969), court processing (Rosett and Cressey 1976), and prison organizations and prisoner subcultures (Cressey 1960, 1961, 1965, Irwin and Cressey 1962).

Finally, most of those who achieve enduring fame have demonstrated repeated excellence in their professional work; it is clear that one or even two influential and well-received publications are not sufficient (Wright and Soma 1996). Consider, for example, the long catalog of Marvin E. Wolfgang's work which spans over 30 years and includes such monumental and seminal contributions as *Patterns in Criminal Homicide* (Wolfgang 1958), *The Measurement of Delinquency* (Sellin and Wolfgang 1964), *The Subculture of Violence* (Wolfgang and Ferracuti 1967), *Delinquency in a Birth Cohort* (Wolfgang, Figlio, and Sellin 1972), *Evaluating Criminology* (Wolfgang, Figlio, and Thornberry 1978), *The National Survey of Crime Severity* (Wolfgang et al. 1985), *From Boy to Man, From Delinquency to Crime* (Wolfgang, Thornberry, and Figlio 1987), and *Delinquency Careers in Two Birth Cohorts* (Tracy, Wolfgang, and Figlio 1990).

In summary, a qualitative evaluation of the scholars who have had an enduring impact on criminology and criminal justice suggests that they possess a rare combination of intellectual stamina, range, and brilliance. They seem to share a gift that academics seldom acknowledge in the work of their colleagues: that of genius (Wright and Soma 1996).

Our study yielded one interesting quantitative predictor of lasting prominence in criminology and criminal justice: whether a scholar appeared on both of the earlier most-cited lists. Of the 15 authors who were among the most-cited scholars in both earlier academic publications and textbooks, 13 (86.7 percent) reappeared among the most-cited scholars in recent criminology and criminal justice publications (the two exceptions were Robert K. Merton and Walter B. Miller). In contrast, of the 48 authors who appeared on only one earlier most-cited list, only three (6.3 percent) reappeared (Marshall B. Clinard, David Matza, and Albert J. Reiss, Jr.). This difference was found to be statistically significant ($\chi^2 = 39.01$; df = 1; $p < .001$).

Interestingly, this quantitative predictor can be used to forecast the scholars who are likely to turn up on most-cited lists 25 years from now. Among current criminologists and criminal justice scholars, those who seem destined for continued prominence include Ronald L. Akers, John Braithwaite, Francis T. Cullen, Delbert

S. Elliott, David P. Farrington, Timothy J. Flanagan, Michael R. Gottfredson, John L. Hagan, Michael J. Hindelang, Travis Hirschi, George L. Kelling, Lloyd E. Ohlin, Joan Petersilia, Albert J. Reiss, Jr., Lawrence W. Sherman, Murray A. Straus, James Q. Wilson, Marvin E. Wolfgang, and Jock Young. However, given the volatility of citation patterns in academic publications, this prediction probably only applies to the most-cited scholars in future criminology and criminal justice textbooks.

Until recently, citation analysis was used primarily to examine current patterns among the most-cited scholars and works (for exceptions, see Cole 1975; Wright and Soma 1996). We believe there is much to be learned through longitudinal citation studies similar to the one presented here. By comparing past and present citation patterns, trends can be discerned for predicting which scholars and works may be influential in the future.

NOTES

1. Geis and Meier (1978) converted the 82 most-cited works in Wolfgang, Figlio, and Thornberry (1978) into a list of 71 influential scholars. This inventory was not used in our study because it contained too many names to be comparable to data sets B and C (see Table 5.1). Because Wright's (1998) conversion, like Geis and Meier's (1978), reports the most-cited scholars in the most-cited works listed by Wolfgang, Figlio, and Thornberry (1978), and not the most-cited scholars per se, some caution must be exercised when comparing this list to the other data sets in Table 5.1.

2. For the 1976–1980 data, Wright and Soma (1996) relied on an earlier citation study of textbooks by Shichor (1982); for the 1989–1993 data, Wright and Soma reanalyzed the data reported by Wright (1995a). The list of textbooks examined by Wright and Soma was taken from a comprehensive bibliography of all introductory criminology textbooks published since 1918, prepared by Wright (1994a).

3. Throughout this chapter, we used a special formula devised by North et al. (1963) to calculate correlations in content analysis. Here,

$$r = \frac{2\,(M_{1,2})}{N_1 + N_2}$$

where "$M_{1,2}$" is the number of matches (or agreements) in two lists of data, while "$N_1 + N_2$" refers to the total population of the lists. The range of possible correlation coefficients produced by this formula is 0 to +1.00. Because this formula violates some of the conventional assumptions associated with correlation (e.g., interval-level data and linearity), we chose a cautious interpretation of these coefficients, foregoing the usual F tests of statistical significance used in correlation (see Blalock 1972).

4. The matrix in Table 5.2 reports bivariate correlations because we could find no theoretical justification for calculating partial correlations to control for the influences of different data sets. Without theoretical justification, interpretations of partial correlations calculated on our data sets would be conjectural at best and impossible at worst.

5. These are Richard A. Cloward, Albert K. Cohen, Donald R. Cressey, Eleanor T. Glueck, Sheldon E. Glueck, David Matza, Lloyd E. Ohlin, Walter C. Reckless, Albert J. Reiss, Jr., Thorsten J. Sellin, James F. Short, Jr., Edwin H. Sutherland, Gresham M. Sykes, George B. Vold, and Marvin E. Wolfgang.

6. These are Marshall B. Clinard, Richard A. Cloward, Albert K. Cohen, Donald R. Cressey, Eleanor T. Glueck, Sheldon E. Glueck, Lloyd E. Ohlin, Walter C. Reckless, Thorsten J. Sellin, James F. Short, Jr., Edwin H. Sutherland, Gresham M. Sykes, George B. Vold, and Marvin E. Wolfgang

7. These are Richard A. Cloward, Albert K. Cohen, Donald R. Cressey, Eleanor T. Glueck, Sheldon E. Glueck, Robert K. Merton, Walter B. Miller, Lloyd E. Ohlin, Walter C. Reckless, Thorsten J. Sellin, James F. Short, Jr., Edwin H. Sutherland, Gresham M. Sykes, George B. Vold, and Marvin E. Wolfgang.

8. These are Ronald L. Akers, John Braithwaite, Francis T. Cullen, Delbert S. Elliott, David P. Farrington, Timothy J. Flanagan, Michael R. Gottfredson, John L. Hagan, Michael J. Hindelang, Travis Hirschi, George L. Kelling, Lloyd E. Ohlin, Joan Petersilia, Albert J. Reiss, Jr., Lawrence W. Sherman, Murray A. Straus, James Q. Wilson, Marvin E. Wolfgang, and Jock Young.

9. For example, William J. Chambliss, Marshall B. Clinard, Richard A. Cloward, Albert K. Cohen, Donald R. Cressey, Emile Durkheim, Edwin M. Lemert, David Matza, Richard Quinney, Jerome H. Skolnick, Edwin H. Sutherland, Austin T. Turk, and George B. Vold.

10. These are Marshall B. Clinard, Richard A. Cloward, Albert K. Cohen, Donald R. Cressey, Eleanor T. Glueck, Sheldon E. Glueck, David Matza, Lloyd E. Ohlin, Walter C. Reckless, Albert J. Reiss, Jr., Thorsten J. Sellin, James F. Short, Jr., Edwin H. Sutherland, Gresham M. Sykes, George B. Vold, and Marvin E. Wolfgang.

6

Who Lands the Luminaries? Rating the Prestige of Criminology and Criminal Justice Journals Through an Analysis of Where Scholars Publish

Rating the prestige of academic journals is one of the favorite pastimes of scholars who research professional issues in criminology and criminal justice. It is an exercise with considerable practical significance: several studies have used the number of articles published in leading journals to measure the productivity of faculty in criminology and criminal justice graduate programs (see Chapter 1 for a review of this research). It is often assumed that these productivity rankings can be used to estimate the relative prestige of graduate departments. Even more pertinent to the careers of individual faculty, tenure and promotion decisions often are based in part on the number of articles published in the most prestigious journals. Because the professional judgment of one's work is clearly affected by where it is published, the ranking of academic journals is an important priority in an evaluation of criminology and criminal justice.

The two procedures currently available to rate the prestige of journals are *reputational* (or *subjective*) and *citation* (or *objective*) techniques (see Poole and Regoli 1981; Shichor, O'Brien, and Decker 1981; Stack 1987a; Weisheit and Regoli 1984). Both have been widely criticized. After reviewing these procedures and their limitations, we propose an alternative method, the *luminaries* technique, for rating the prestige of journals. This procedure avoids some of the pitfalls of previous approaches by ranking journals by the number of articles that they publish that are written by influential authors (or luminaries).

In this chapter, we have rated the prestige of 85 journals according to the percentage of articles and research notes published from 1990–1994 that were written by 76 scholars who rank among the most-cited in the criminology and criminal justice literature. By comparing our findings to three recent, methodologically sophisticated, studies that use rival ranking procedures we are able to assess the validity of the luminaries technique.

REPUTATIONAL AND CITATION STUDIES

Eleven previous studies have rated the prestige of journals in criminology and criminal justice. Eight of these studies have assessed journal prestige through the use of a reputational technique (DeZee 1980; Fabianic 1980; Greene, Bynum, and Webb 1985; McElrath 1990; Parker and Goldfeder 1979; Regoli, Poole, and Miracle 1982; Shichor, O'Brien, and Decker 1981; Williams, McShane, and Wagoner 1995), two have ranked journals through a citation technique (Poole and Regoli 1981; Stack 1987a), and one study combined these approaches by reanalyzing existing research (Sorensen, Patterson, and Widmayer 1992).

The reputational studies rely on peer evaluations from samples of criminologists and criminal justice scholars to rank the prestige of journals. Some of these studies use a technique originally developed by Glenn (1971) to rank journals in sociology in which an arbitrary baseline score (usually "10") is assigned to an "average" article appearing in a designated well-established journal. For example, DeZee (1980) and Regoli, Poole, and Miracle (1982) used the *Journal of Criminal Law and Criminology*. Similarly, McElrath (1990) used *Criminology*. Respondents are then asked to weigh and to compare the importance of average articles appearing in a list of other journals against those appearing in the selected baseline journal. Other reputational studies (e.g., Shichor, O'Brien, and Decker 1981; Williams, McShane, and Wagoner 1995) omitted baseline comparisons and simply asked respondents to rate the importance or prestige of average articles appearing in a list of journals on a scale, usually from "1" (least important or prestigious) to "10" (most important or prestigious).

In addition to the usual problems that plague survey research (e.g., low response rates and possible selection biases among respondents), reputational studies have some special difficulties. First, these studies assume that respondents are familiar with the journals they are ranking (Poole and Regoli 1981). It is hard to believe that all the raters in these surveys possess detailed knowledge about the quality of the average article appearing in so many different journals. To avoid this issue, reputational studies typically ask respondents to rate only those journals with which they are acquainted. This means that, in some reputational studies, only a handful of respondents (possibly as few as 10 percent) rate certain journals (see Shichor, O'Brien, and Decker 1981; Williams, McShane, and Wagoner 1995). As a result, highly specialized journals with a core group of loyal readers may be overrated in these studies.

In interdisciplinary fields such as criminology and criminal justice, respondents may overrate the importance of journals that cater to their discipline, while simultaneously underrating journals in rival areas (Williams, McShane, and Wagoner 1995). This creates the possibility that the discipline with the most respondents (typically sociology in reputational studies of criminology and criminal justice journals) will automatically garner the most favorable journal ratings.

Finally, there appears to be a cumulative inertia effect in reputational research, so that once a journal's reputation is "fixed" by one of these studies, it seldom changes. This suggests that, over the years, journals that improve in quality would be underrated in these surveys, while once-prestigious journals in decline could be overrated.

Citation studies of journal rankings developed in response to these problems (e.g., Poole and Regoli 1981). In criminology and criminal justice, these studies have ranked journals by the number of citations that articles receive in periodicals (e.g., Poole and Regoli 1981; Stack, 1987a), although citation studies in other fields have ranked journals by citations in textbooks (Christenson and Sigelman 1985).

Although citation studies avoid the problem of respondents' lack of familiarity with particular journals, they nevertheless have other drawbacks (Williams, McShane, and Wagoner 1995). For example, the source journal(s) used to collect citations appear to have a distinct advantage in the rankings, in part because contributors probably are careful to cite earlier relevant articles that appeared in the journals where they submit their papers. Although Stack's (1987a) study (which ranked all 26 criminology and criminal justice journals indexed in *SSCI* by the number of citations they received for articles published in 1983 and 1984) partially compensated for this problem by using a large number of source journals, any citation study that relies on *SSCI* is limited to an analysis of indexed journals. *SSCI* is slow to add new periodicals, a significant problem in a rapidly changing and growing field like criminal justice, which has produced many new journals during a relatively short period of time.

Poole and Regoli's (1981) citation study, which ranked 43 journals by the number of citations received in *Criminology* between 1975 and 1979, did not control for either the number of articles published in the journals or the age of the journals. Logically, older periodicals that published many articles had a significant advantage over newer periodicals with fewer articles available for citation. Although Stack (1987a) devised procedures to control for these difficulties, his analysis still does not address another serious problem in citation studies: the inability to distinguish the frequency of citations to particular articles from the prevalence of citations to all articles appearing in journals. A journal that published one or two important and widely cited articles would rank high in citation studies even if the average article that appeared in that periodical was rarely or never cited.

One possible solution to the weaknesses of reputational and citation studies is to combine their findings to create composite rankings of periodicals. Sorensen, Patterson, and Widmayer (1992) calculated z-scores for 37 criminology and criminal justice journals rated in nine previous studies and ranked the journals by their average z-scores. The composite ranking of journals is an important step forward in this type of research as the averaging of journal ratings at least partially corrects for the problematic findings of particular studies. However, Sorensen, Patterson, and Widmayer's (1992) approach has one significant drawback: to be included in such a composite analysis, a journal must have been rated in a previous study. Thus, relatively new journals are missing from their rankings. Two conspicuous omissions are *Justice Quarterly* (established in 1984) and the *Journal of Quantitative Criminology* (established in 1985). Certainly one of the chief limitations of reputational, citation, and composite studies is that they rank too few journals, and routinely exclude new publications.

THE LUMINARIES TECHNIQUE

Our new technique for rating the prestige of journals involves determining where the most-cited scholars, or luminaries, in criminology and criminal justice publish their works. Many of these scholars largely built their professional reputations by publishing important articles in the leading journals; in order to maintain their status as prominent scholars they have every incentive to continue contributing to these periodicals. Furthermore, editors of leading journals are often more likely to solicit papers from prominent scholars than from others, and to accept their unsolicited manuscripts through the peer review process. Together, these factors imply the existence of a direct relationship between the prestige of journals and the number of articles written by luminaries that are published in these journals. This suggests that the percentage of articles and research notes that are written by prominent scholars can be used to rank the prestige of different journals.

The basic resources required to rank journals through the luminaries technique are a core group of luminaries (identified through previous analyses of the most-cited scholars in journals and/or textbooks in criminology and criminal justice) and a recent bibliography providing a comprehensive, up-to-date list of scholarly periodicals in criminology and criminal justice. These are easily available to the criminal justice bibliographer.

The luminaries approach appears to have some advantages over reputational, citation, and composite procedures as a mechanism for ranking the prestige of journals. First, as an objective measure, the luminaries technique does not depend on respondents' familiarity with the average importance of articles appearing in many different journals. Even the most specialized and obscure journals, invisible and unknown to the majority of criminologists and criminal justice scholars, can be rated by the luminaries approach. This is the key strength of our technique over conventional reputational studies.

The comprehensive analysis of citations in journals (e.g., Stack 1987a) requires the use of *SSCI* to rank the prestige of periodicals. Unfortunately, this severely limits the number of periodicals that can be rated through this approach as only those journals indexed in *SSCI* may be examined. Theoretically, the only restriction on the number of journals that can be rated through the luminaries technique is the skill of the bibliographic scholar conducting the analysis.

Finally, because it involves averaging the ratings from previous studies, the composite approach cannot rank newer journals that have not been included in any prior research. However, to be included in a luminaries study, a new journal needs only a few years of sustained publication.

RESEARCH DESIGN

We used three recent studies of the most-cited scholars in criminology and criminal justice (Cohn and Farrington 1994b; Wright 1995a; Wright and Cohn 1996) to compile a master list of luminaries. Cohn and Farrington (1994b) identified the 47 most-cited scholars in six criminology and criminal justice journals (*Criminal Justice and Behavior*, *Criminology*, *Journal of Criminal Justice*, *Journal of Quantitative Criminology*, *Journal of Research in Crime and Delinquency*, and *Justice Quarterly*) published from 1986–1990. In an examination of textbooks published between 1989 and 1993, Wright (1995a) discovered the 47 most-cited scholars in 23 criminology textbooks and Wright and Cohn (1996) found the 22 most-cited scholars in 16 criminal justice textbooks. Merging the three lists and deleting duplications produced a master list of 76 luminaries.[1]

Two recent bibliographies of journals (Vaughn and del Carmen 1992; Wright and Rogers 1996), were used to compile a list of periodicals. Vaughn and del Carmen (1992) provide an annotated bibliography of 133 multidisciplinary journals that they say often publish articles written by criminologists and criminal justice scholars. Wright and Rogers (1996) list 98 scholarly periodicals that they claim predominantly publish articles dealing with crime and justice topics.

Several requirements were used when selecting journals from these bibliographies for our analysis. First, we examined only journals[2] that primarily publish articles and research notes[3] relating to criminology and/or criminal justice. Periodicals from other disciplines (e.g., sociology and psychology) were deleted from our list, unless they primarily featured articles on crime and/or justice.[4] Second, only scholarly journals, which appear to be aimed at an academic audience, were included in our study. Periodicals that cater entirely to practitioners or laypersons were omitted.[5] Finally, because journals require some track record for scrutiny through the luminaries technique, we analyzed only scholarly periodicals with at least a five-year publication history. Thus, only journals with a continuous publication record from 1990–1994 were included in our study.

We were able to identify a total of 85 journals that met all three requirements. This is the largest number of journals ever included in a study rating periodicals, examining 22 more journals than the study with the second largest number (Williams, McShane, and Wagoner 1995). By traveling to a number of different libraries, we were able to determine the authors of all the articles and research notes that appeared in all 85 journals during the years of our study.

We ranked the prestige of these 85 journals by determining the number and percent of articles and research notes that were authored or coauthored by luminaries from 1990–1994. Two ranking systems were used in the analysis. The first was an unweighted system that disregarded the number of authors listed on articles and research notes. Thus, if at least one luminary appeared as an author of the article, regardless of the number of non-luminary coauthors listed, the article was counted as being written by a luminary. In addition, we employed a weighted system that considered the fraction of authorship that could be attributed to a luminary for each article and research note.[6] In order to standardize the journals by the number of articles and research notes published, both the unweighted and the weighted rankings were based on percentages of articles and research notes authored or coauthored by luminaries.

FINDINGS

Table 6.1 shows both the unweighted and the weighted scores of the journals examined in our study. Forty-nine of the 85 journals (57.7 percent) published at least one article or research note authored or coauthored by a luminary from 1990–1994. These journals are ranked in the top part of the table, while the 36 periodicals that published no articles or research notes written by luminaries are listed in alphabetical order at the bottom of the table.

It is interesting to compare the unweighted and the weighted ratings in Table 6.1. The positions of a small number of journals change markedly when their ranks are weighted. For example, *Journal of Quantitative Criminology* falls from third to seventh place, *Journal of Criminal Justice* falls from 10.5th to 18th, and *Criminal Justice Policy Review* falls from 15th to 21st. In these journals, the majority of articles and research notes written by luminaries were coauthored with non-luminaries. Among the journals that benefit from the weighting of the ranks are *Current Issues in Criminal Justice* (rising from 22nd to 15th place), *International Review of Victimology* (rising from 28th to 19th), *and American Journal of Criminal Justice* (rising from 29.5th to 20th).

However, the positions of many of the journals remain largely the same when the unweighted and weighted scores are compared: 24 of the 49 periodicals (49.0 percent) change by three ranks or less. This is confirmed by a rank-order correlation calculated between the unweighted and weighted scores ($r = .92$; $p < .001$).[7] Because of this similarity, the remainder of this chapter will examine the unweighted ranks, as these data are simpler to analyze and to interpret.[8]

An examination of the unweighted ranks in Table 6.1 suggests that most of the journals that generally rate high in reputational, citation, and composite studies continue to do well in a luminaries analysis. *Criminology, Journal of Research in Crime and Delinquency, Crime and Delinquency*, and *Journal of Criminal Law and Criminology* all rank among the top seven journals in the table.[9] However, there are some surprises in the table. *Criminal Justice Ethics* (fourth place) and *The Prison Journal* (eighth) rank higher than one would anticipate from previous studies, while *Law and Society Review* (14th) ranks much lower. Several relatively new periodicals rank high in this analysis: *Journal of Quantitative Criminology* (third place), *Justice Quarterly* (sixth), and *Journal of Criminal Justice Education* (ninth)[10] all finished among the top ten periodicals.

Tables 6.2 and 6.3 assess the validity of the luminaries technique by comparing our journal rankings to the most recent reputational (Williams, McShane, and Wagoner 1995), citation (Stack 1987a), and composite (Sorensen, Patterson, and Widmayer 1992) studies. So that valid rank-order correlations may be calculated, these comparisons are limited to the 14 journals that are ranked in all four studies. Table 6.2 presents the rankings of these 14 journals in the four studies. Table 6.3 provides a correlation matrix, which shows the strong relationship between the rankings: all the rank-order correlations in Table 6.3 are statistically significant. This is particularly impressive when compared to Sorenson, Patterson, and

Widmayer's (1992) comparison of nine reputational and citation studies, in which 13 of the 36 correlations (36 percent) were *not* statistically significant.

Table 6.1
Ranking of Journals in Criminology and Criminal Justice, 1990–1994, by the Percentage of Articles/Research Notes Written by Luminaries (Most-Cited Scholars)

Journal	Unweighted Scores[a]			Weighted Scores[b]		
	Rank	%[c]	N[d]	Rank	%	N
Criminology	1	18.46	24	3	8.68	11.28
Journal of Research in Crime and Delinquency	2	17.20	16	1	10.57	9.83
Journal of Quantitative Criminology	3	13.25	11	7	5.92	4.91
Criminal Justice Ethics	4	12.24	6	2	9.18	4.50
Crime and Delinquency	5	10.76	17	5	6.82	10.77
Justice Quarterly	6	10.22	14	8	4.77	6.53
Journal of Criminal Law and Criminology	7	9.38	6	4	7.55	4.83
The Prison Journal	8	9.09	5	6	6.42	3.53
Journal of Criminal Justice Education	9	5.80	4	9	4.34	3.00
British Journal of Criminology	10.5	5.38	7	11	3.46	4.50
Journal of Criminal Justice	10.5	5.38	10	18	2.19	4.08
American Journal of Police	12	4.80	6	12	2.86	3.58
Australian and New Zealand Journal of Criminology	13	4.17	4	10	4.17	4.00
Law and Society Review	14	4.08	6	14	2.44	3.58
Criminal Justice Policy Review	15	4.04	4	21	1.85	1.83
Federal Probation	16	4.00	8	13	2.58	5.16
Journal of Drug Issues	17	3.72	9	17	2.20	5.33
Journal of Crime and Justice	18	3.57	3	16	2.38	2.00
Deviant Behavior	19	3.19	3	28	1.41	1.33
International Journal of Sociology of Law	20	3.13	3	31	1.13	1.08
Police Forum	21	2.94	1	26	1.47	0.50
Current Issues in Criminal Justice	22	2.91	3	15	2.43	2.50
Policing and Society	23	2.78	2	23	1.63	1.17
Crime, Law and Social Change	24	2.42	3	30	1.21	1.50
Law and Policy	25	2.25	2	37.5	0.84	1.00
Journal of Contemporary Criminal Justice	26	2.17	2	23	1.63	1.50
Law and Social Inquiry	27	2.04	1	32	1.02	0.50
International Review of Victimology	28	1.96	1	19	1.96	1.00
American Journal of Criminal Justice	29.5	1.89	1	20	1.89	1.00
Police Studies	29.5	1.89	2	41	0.66	0.70
Criminal Law Forum	31	1.79	1	35	0.89	0.50
Criminal Law Bulletin	32	1.77	2	29	0.33	1.50
Forum on Corrections Research	33	1.63	2	23	1.63	2.00
Social Justice	34	1.62	3	25	1.62	3.00

Journal						
Criminal Justice and Behavior	35	1.56	2	33	0.98	1.25
Journal of Psychiatry and Law	36	1.45	1	27	1.45	1.00
Justice System Journal	37	1.28	1	42	0.64	0.50
Journal of Interpersonal Violence	38	1.12	2	37.5	0.84	1.50
Howard Journal of Criminal Justice	39	1.10	1	43	0.55	0.50
International Journal of Comparative and Applied Criminal Justice	40	0.90	1	34	0.90	1.00
Youth and Society	41	0.86	1	44	0.43	0.50
Canadian Journal of Criminology	43	0.85	1	36	0.85	1.00
Journal of Family Violence	43	0.85	1	47	0.28	0.33
Violence and Victims	43	0.85	1	45	0.42	0.50
Contemporary Drug Problems	45.5	0.68	1	39	0.68	1.00
International Journal of Offender Therapy and Comparative Criminology	45.5	0.68	1	46	0.34	0.50
Journal of Offender Rehabilitation	47	0.67	1	40	0.67	1.00
Criminal Law Review	48	0.47	1	48	0.24	0.50
FBI Law Enforcement Bulletin	49	0.33	1	49	0.17	0.50

Journals with No Articles/Research Notes Written by Luminaries:

American Criminal Law Review, American Journal of Criminal Law, American Journal of Legal History, Behavioral Sciences and the Law, Corrections Today, Criminal Justice Review, Criminal Law Quarterly, The Criminologist (England), Drugs and Society: A Journal of Contemporary Issues, Family Violence and Sexual Assault Bulletin, International Criminal Police Review, International Journal of Law and Psychiatry, Journal of Addictive Diseases, Journal of Correctional Education, Journal of Criminal Law, Journal of Drug Education, Journal of Forensic Sciences, Journal of Human Justice, Journal of Law and Society, Journal of Legal Studies, Journal of Offender Monitoring, Journal of Police and Criminal Psychology, Journal of Prison and Jail Health, Judicature, Jurimetrics: Journal of Law, Science and Technology, Justice Professional, Juvenile and Family Court Journal, Law and Human Behavior, Law and Philosophy: An International Journal for Jurisprudence and Legal Philosophy, Legal Studies Forum, Police Chief, Police Journal, Police Liability Review, Policing, Terrorism and Political Violence, and *Women and Criminal Justice.*

[a] Unweighted scores disregard the number of authors on articles written by luminaries.
[b] Weighted scores, for articles with multiple authors, take into account the fraction of authorship that can be attributed to luminaries (see note 6).
[c] The percentage of articles written by luminaries.
[d] The number of articles written by luminaries.

It is important to note that two of the three highest correlation coefficients in Table 6.3 involve the luminaries ranking: $r = .80$ with Sorensen, Patterson, and Widmayer's (1992) methodologically sophisticated composite ranking, and $r = .78$ with Williams, McShane, and Wagoner's (1995) recent reputational ranking.[11] These high correlations strongly support the validity of the luminaries technique as a measure of journal prestige.

Table 6.2
A Comparison of Journal Rankings in Four Studies

Journal	(A) Luminaries Rank	(B) Reputational Rank[a]	(C) Citation Rank[b]	(D) Composite Rank[c]
Criminology	1	1	2	2
Journal of Research in Crime and Delinquency	2	4	3	4
Crime and Delinquency	3	5	6	5
Journal of Criminal Law and Criminology	4	3	7	1
British Journal of Criminology	5.5	7	5	7
Journal of Criminal Justice	5.5	6	11	6
Law and Society Review	7	2	1	3
Federal Probation	8	14	13	10
Crime, Law and Social Change	9	10	12	12.5
Criminal Justice and Behavior	10	8	10	9
Justice System Journal	11	13	8	11
Canadian Journal of Criminology	12	9	9	12.5
International Journal of Offender Therapy and Comparative Criminology	13	11	14	14
Judicature	14	12	4	8

[a] From Williams, McShane, and Wagoner (1995).
[b] From Stack (1987a).
[c] From Sorensen, Patterson, and Widmayer (1992).

CONCLUSION

The luminaries procedure, which ranks the prestige of journals by examining where the most-cited scholars publish their articles and research notes, appears to be a promising new way to evaluate periodicals. This technique does not depend on respondent familiarity with the quality of an average article in a large number of periodicals (as does the reputational approach), nor is it restricted to the analysis of criminology and criminal justice journals included in *SSCI* (as is the citation approach). When compared to the best and most recent previous studies that rank criminology and criminal justice journals, the luminaries procedure produces similar results. Thus, our technique appears to be a simple, quick, and valid way to evaluate the prestige of a large number of periodicals.

The luminaries procedure has certain limitations. First, it is no more accurate than the studies of the most-cited scholars on which it is based. To date, recent citation studies of criminology and criminal justice journals and textbooks (see Cohn and Farrington 1994a, 1994b; Wright 1995a; Wright and Cohn 1996) have paid little attention to the sociology of law, specifically ignoring the *Journal of Criminal Law and Criminology* and *Law and Society Review* because they use

Table 6.3
Correlations of Journal Rankings in Four Studies

	(A) Luminaries Study	(B) Reputational Study[a]	(C) Citation Study[b]	(D) Composite Study[c]
(A)	1.00	——	——	——
(B)	.78**	1.00	——	——
(C)	.47*	.66**	1.00	——
(D)	.80**	.85**	.74**	1.00

Note: $* p < .05$; $** p < .01$.
[a] Williams, McShane, and Wagoner (1995).
[b] Stack (1987a).
[c] Sorensen, Patterson, and Widmayer (1992).

complex legal styles of footnoting, with no comprehensive lists of references at the ends of articles. As a result, few luminaries from this area appear on existing lists of the most-cited scholars in criminology and criminal justice; this is probably why law journals in general, and *Law and Society Review* in particular, scored so poorly in our study.

Another problem is the confusion of the terms "prestige" and "importance" in existing studies that rank criminology and criminal justice journals. Researchers typically use these concepts interchangeably when, in fact, there are clear and significant differences between the two terms. Prestige refers to status, or in Max Weber's (1922/1978: 932) classic definition, the "social estimation of honor," while importance probably is closer to Weber's concept of power, defined in part as the ability "to realize [one's] own will" (1922/1978: 926). Thus, while prestigious journals are respected, important journals have a significant impact, changing entire disciplines. It is likely that a few prestigious journals publish mostly unimportant articles, while articles with great impact do occasionally appear in journals with little status.

The prestige of journals is perhaps better measured through reputational studies, while citation studies are probably better indicators of a journal's importance. Ironically, the luminaries approach is an objective technique that appears to measure prestige more than importance. This may be one reason why, in the rank-order correlations reported in Table 6.3, the luminaries ranking is much more highly associated with Williams, McShane, and Wagoner's (1995) reputational findings than Stack's (1987a) citation study.

A more serious drawback to our study, and perhaps the luminaries approach in general, is that some journals may publish few or no articles by luminaries. We found 18 journals that published only one article or research note written by a luminary. In these cases, our technique ranks journals more by the number of articles that they publish than by their prestige. We are particularly suspicious of the validity of the luminaries approach in differentiating among the journals ranked from 36th to 49th place in Table 6.1; in reality, there may be few meaningful differences among the prestige of most of these journals.

Despite these limitations and concerns, the luminaries procedure for ranking journals demonstrates once more the usefulness of attempts to identify the most-cited scholars and works in criminology and criminal justice. Advances in citation analysis should result in even more valid applications of the luminaries approach in the future.

NOTES

1. In alphabetical order, these 76 luminaries are Suzanne S. Ageton, Ronald L. Akers, Harry E. Allen, David H. Bayley, Richard A. Berk, Thomas J. Bernard, Alfred Blumstein, Barbara Boland, John Braithwaite, William J. Chambliss, Todd R. Clear, Marshall B. Clinard, Richard A. Cloward, Albert K. Cohen, Jacqueline Cohen, Lawrence E. Cohen, Donald R. Cressey, Francis T. Cullen, Emile Durkheim, Delbert S. Elliott, David P. Farrington, Marcus Felson, Robert M. Figlio, Timothy J. Flanagan, Gilbert Geis, Richard J. Gelles, Don C. Gibbons, Jack P. Gibbs, Eleanor T. Glueck, Sheldon E. Glueck, Herman Goldstein, Don M. Gottfredson, Michael R. Gottfredson, David F. Greenberg, Peter W. Greenwood, John L. Hagan, Richard J. Herrnstein, Michael J. Hindelang, Travis Hirschi, James A. Inciardi, James B. Jacobs, George L. Kelling, Marvin D. Krohn, Wayne R. LaFave, Edwin M. Lemert, Robert M. Martinson, David Matza, Sarnoff A. Mednick, Lloyd E. Ohlin, Joan Petersilia, Eric D. Poole, Richard Quinney, Walter C. Reckless, Robert M. Regoli, Albert J. Reiss, Jr., Robert J. Sampson, Thorsten J. Sellin, Lawrence W. Sherman, James F. Short, Jr., Wesley G. Skogan, Jerome H. Skolnick, Darrell J. Steffensmeier, Murray A. Straus, Edwin H. Sutherland, Gresham M. Sykes, Charles R. Tittle, Hans Toch, Austin T. Turk, George B. Vold, Andrew Von Hirsch, Samuel Walker, Joseph G. Weis, Paul B. Wice, James Q. Wilson, Marvin E. Wolfgang, and Jock Young (see Cohn and Farrington 1994b; Wright 1995a; Wright and Cohn 1996).

2. We also gathered data from three criminology and criminal justice annuals: *Advances in Criminological Theory*, *Crime and Justice: An Annual Review of Research*, and *Criminal Justice History: An International Annual*. Because these annuals are technically not journals and are usually cataloged by librarians as reference works, discussions of their rankings are provided in notes in this chapter (see especially note 9).

3. Comments, replies, book review essays, book reviews, and other miscellaneous items (e.g., obituaries and notices) were omitted from the analysis.

4. Because several previous studies include a few prestigious general interest sociology journals (especially *American Journal of Sociology* and *American Sociological Review*) in their rankings (see Regoli, Poole, and Miracle 1982; Sorensen, Patterson, and Widmayer 1992), we gathered data from four of these periodicals: *American Journal of Sociology*, *American Sociological Review*, *Social Forces*, and *Social Problems*. In these journals, only articles and research notes dealing with crime and/or justice topics were included in our analysis. Discussions of the rankings of these journals are included in notes to this chapter (see especially note 9).

5. Because it is often extremely difficult to distinguish between scholarly and non-scholarly publications when examining individual journals, we chose to err on the side of inclusion. Consequently, such borderline periodicals as *Corrections Today* and *the FBI Law Enforcement Bulletin* were examined in our analysis.

6. In the weighted journal rankings, articles and research notes were scored "1.00" if authored or coauthored only by luminaries, ".50" if half of the listed authors on coauthored articles and research notes were luminaries (i.e., one luminary and one non-luminary on articles with two authors, two luminaries and two non-luminaries on articles with four authors, etc.), ".33" if one-third of the listed authors on coauthored articles and research notes were luminaries (i.e., one luminary and two non-luminaries on articles with three authors), and so on.

7. Spearman's *r* was used to calculate all the rank-order correlations. Standard *z*-scores were computed to determine levels of statistical significance (see Blalock 1972).

8. There is reason to believe that the unweighted ranks are actually more valid than the weighted ranks. Although luminaries may share the work responsibilities in papers co-authored with non-luminaries, they probably exert a decisive influence in determining where these articles are published. The unweighted ranks may better reflect this form of influence.

9. With annuals added to the unweighted findings (see note 2), *Advances in Criminological Theory* ranks first (with 20.0 percent, or 11 articles written by luminaries), *Crime and Justice: An Annual Review of Research* is third (17.2 percent, or 10 articles by luminaries), and *Criminal Justice History: An International Annual* is unranked (no luminaries). Several general interest sociology journals also score high when included in the unweighted rankings (see note 4). Excluding the annuals, *American Sociological Review* finishes first (38.5 percent, or five articles by luminaries), *American Journal of Sociology* is second (36.5 percent, or four articles by luminaries), *Social Forces* is third (21.1 percent, or four articles by luminaries), and *Social Problems* is twelfth (8.1 percent, or three articles by luminaries). It is worth noting that these four general interest sociology journals rank high whenever they are included in prestige studies; in Sorensen, Patterson, and Widmayer's (1992) composite analysis of 36 periodicals, *American Sociological Review* ranks first, *American Journal of Sociology* is sixth, *Social Problems* is eighth, and *Social Forces* is eleventh.

10. *Journal of Criminal Justice Education* began publication in 1990.

11. Stack's (1987a) citation study is responsible for the three lowest coefficients in Table 6.3, including the relatively disappointing correlation (*r* = .47) between his rankings and the luminaries rankings. The inclusion of Stack's (1987a) findings in Sorensen, Patterson, and Widmayer's (1992) composite scores partially explains the much higher correlation (*r* = .74) between these rankings.

7

A Page-Coverage Analysis of the Most Influential Scholars in Criminology Textbooks

The last chapter proposed a new method for rating the prestige of journals by considering the number of articles in those journals that were authored by "luminaries" in the field. The most common way of determining who are the luminaries is through the use of citation counts. However, here we suggest an alternative method of measuring the influence of scholars and works, by using procedures developed in the content analysis of themes and topics in the print media. In this chapter we will rank scholars in introductory criminology textbooks and compare the results using this procedure to those obtained from a citation analysis of the same textbooks. Our procedure employs content analysis techniques to examine the amount of coverage (in pages) devoted to scholars in introductory criminology textbooks, and then uses page-coverage as the unit of analysis to rank the 100 most influential scholars in the textbooks. An earlier citation analysis study (Wright 1995a) ranked the 47 most-cited scholars in the same textbooks, enabling us to compare page-coverage rankings and citation rankings. We conclude with some comments about the relative merits of measuring the influence of scholars and works through the page-coverage procedures used here and traditional citation analysis.

UNITS OF ANALYSIS IN CONTENT ANALYSIS

Despite the large number of citation analysis studies to appear in criminology and criminal justice journals in recent years, some criminologists and criminal justice scholars do not consider citation analysis to be a valid measure of the influence of scholars and works. Critics have argued that citation patterns may reflect attempts of authors to curry favor with journal editors and reviewers, may ignore the content of the discussion of the scholar and/or work (i.e., the scholar and/or work may be viewed favorably, unfavorably, or seen in a neutral context), and may reflect past rather than current contributions to a field (see Cohn and Farrington 1994a, 1994b; Cole and Cole 1973).

The defenders of citation analysis have countered that high citation counts are strongly correlated with other indicators of influence in a discipline, such as the receipt of prestigious awards and elections to offices in professional associations (Cohn and Farrington 1994a, 1994b). Cohn and Farrington (1994b: 531) conclude that "large numbers of citations . . . provide an imperfect but nevertheless reasonably valid measure of influence on a field."

However, as a type of manifest, or quantitative, content analysis of print media (see Berelson 1952; Budd, Thorp, and Donahew 1967; Carney 1979; Wright 1988),[1] citation analysis procedures rely on somewhat unusual units of analysis to measure and to tabulate influence. The key elements are names (in the analysis of the influence of particular scholars) and titles (in the analysis of the influence of particular works) that are accompanied by references. One possible problem with these units of analysis is that they measure influence by how often scholars and works are cited (the frequency of citation), rather than by the amount of space that is devoted to the discussion of these scholars and works. Traditionally in the manifest content analysis of print media, length of coverage, which is usually measured by inches-of-print or in pages, is considered to be a superior unit of analysis when measuring the importance of themes or topics (Berelson 1952; Budd, Thorp, and Donahew 1967; Carney 1979; Wright 1988). In this chapter we consider whether the two measures of influence, length of coverage and citation analysis, identify different scholars as influential in criminology and criminal justice.

To offer a hypothetical example of the potential differences between length of coverage and citations as measurements of influence, let us consider an article that cites two scholars. In this article, scholar A has one study cited in a five-inch discussion of his/her research, while scholar B has five studies cited in a one-inch review of his/her work. Using citations as a unit of analysis, B would be ranked as much more influential in this article than A; using inches-of-print as a unit of analysis, A would be rated as much more influential than B. In this circumstance, length of coverage may offer a more realistic measure of the relative influence of these scholars in the article.

Manifest content analysis researchers in deviance and criminology and criminal justice have made extensive use of length of coverage measurements (see e.g., Phillips 1979, 1980; Bollen and Phillips 1981; Stack 1987b; Wright 1987, 1988, 1992, 1994b, 1995c, 1995d, 1995e, 1996b; Wright and Friedrichs 1991). For example, studies of major newspapers that have tried to link suicide stories to subsequent motor vehicle accidents (Phillips 1979; Bollen and Phillips 1981), or publicized executions to subsequent homicides (Phillips 1980; Stack 1987b), have typically used inches-of-print in newspaper columns as the unit of analysis for measuring the amount of publicity devoted to news stories.

In a series of articles critical of introductory criminology textbooks, Wright used both inches-of-print and page-coverage to argue that textbooks devote insufficient attention to criminal career studies (Wright 1994b), deterrence research (Wright 1996b), the free will/determinism controversy (Wright 1995d), white-collar crime (Wright and Friedrichs 1991), and women and crime topics (Wright 1987, 1988,

1992, 1995e). In these studies, Wright follows the standard convention in the manifest content analysis of print by assuming that the length of coverage devoted to a topic like deterrence is a more valid indicator of the influence of this research than the number of times that authors mention key words like deterrence. The same reasoning can be used to argue that length of coverage might be a more valid indicator than simple citations when measuring the influence of particular scholars and works.

This chapter measures the influence of 2,076 scholars in 23 introductory criminology textbooks published from 1989–1993, using length of coverage (in inches-of-print and pages) as the unit of analysis. The total amount of page-coverage devoted to each scholar in the textbooks is calculated to rank the 100 most influential scholars; these rankings are then compared to a recent citation analysis (Wright 1995a) of the 47 most influential scholars in the same 23 textbooks. Notable differences emerge when the results from these two studies are compared.

RESEARCH DESIGN

A total of 23 introductory criminology textbooks published from 1989–1993 were included in this study; the same time frame and textbooks used in Wright's (1995a) study of the most-cited scholars in recent criminology textbooks.[2] However, unlike citation analysis research, we examined inches of print and page coverage.[3] When the name of a scholar[4] was mentioned in a textbook (either in the text, in citations within the text, or in a footnote), the number of inches of print coverage devoted to the scholar was recorded.[5] All scholars receiving at least one inch of print coverage in at least one of the textbooks were included in the study; scholars receiving peripheral attention (less than one inch of print coverage in at least one textbook) were excluded. Because of inaccuracies in the textbook indexes, all 23 books were read in their entirety during the analysis.

We also determined the number of inches of print included in each textbook on a typical page. Once information was collected on the amount of coverage for every scholar in all textbooks, the data were reconfigured so that the reported unit of analysis for ranking the most influential scholars was page length (see e.g., Wright 1994b, 1995c, 1995d, 1996b for additional examples of the use of this procedure in manifest content analysis).

FINDINGS

Altogether, 2,076 different scholars were covered in at least one inch of print in at least one of the criminology textbooks examined. However, the majority of these scholars received minimal attention; when the total inches-of-print measures were reconfigured into coverage in total pages, only 196 scholars (9.4 percent) were discussed in 1.33 or more pages (in all 23 textbooks combined).[6]

Table 7.1 lists the 100 most influential scholars in these textbooks, as ranked by the amount of page-coverage received. The two scholars who received the most page-coverage in these textbooks were Edwin H. Sutherland and Travis Hirschi.

An examination of the table shows that Sutherland impressively outdistanced Hirschi by 36.47 pages for first place. Although 14.06 pages of coverage separate Hirschi in second place from Marvin E. Wolfgang in third place, Wolfgang's coverage only slightly exceeded the page-coverage for Lloyd E. Ohlin, Donald R. Cressey, and Robert K. Merton, the next three scholars listed in the table.

Table 7.1
The 100 Most Influential Scholars in 23 Criminology Textbooks, 1989–1993, Measured in Page-Coverage

Rank	Scholar	Pages Devoted to the Scholar
1	Edwin H. Sutherland	102.85
2	Travis Hirschi	66.38
3	Marvin E. Wolfgang	52.32
4	Lloyd E. Ohlin	51.93
5	Donald R. Cressey	51.25
6	Robert K. Merton	50.02
7	Karl Marx	47.67
8	Emile Durkheim	46.65
9	David Matza	43.72
10	Cesare Lombroso	41.49
11	James Q. Wilson	41.23
12	Richard A. Cloward	40.80
13	Clifford R. Shaw	36.49
14	Gresham M. Sykes	36.01
15	Albert K. Cohen	35.87
16	Sigmund Freud	33.02
17	Henry D. McKay	32.42
18	Richard Quinney	32.25
19	Cesare Beccaria	31.24
20	William J. Chambliss	30.67
21	Thorsten J. Sellin	30.44
22	Walter B. Miller	28.36
23	Richard J. Herrnstein	24.07
24	Robert M. Figlio	22.56
25	Marshall B. Clinard	20.47
26	Jeremy Bentham	20.31
27	Hans J. Eysenck	19.88
28	Walter C. Reckless	18.54
29	Edwin M. Lemert	17.97
30	Austin T. Turk	16.98
31	Darrell J. Steffensmeier	16.51
32	Michael R. Gottfredson	16.50
33	Friedrich Engels	16.29
34	Stanton E. Samenow	15.98
35	Jerome H. Skolnick	15.97
36	Samuel Yochelson	15.41
37	William H. Sheldon	14.82

38	Ronald L. Akers	14.09
39	James F. Short, Jr.	13.12
40	Howard S. Becker	12.83
41	Gabriel Tarde	12.61
42	Delbert S. Elliott	12.60
43	Sarnoff A. Mednick	12.28
44	Charles Goring	11.99
45	Adolphe Quetelet	11.70
46	John Irwin	11.36
47	Carl B. Klockars	11.28
48	Paul E. Tracy	11.12
49	John Braithwaite	10.79
50	Simon I. Singer	10.36
51	Jack P. Gibbs	10.25
52	Suzanne S. Ageton	10.11
53	Hervey M. Cleckley	9.99
54	Timothy J. Flanagan	9.76
55	Willem A. Bonger	9.70
56	Eleanor T. Glueck	9.61
57	Peter W. Greenwood	9.58
58	Freda Adler	9.50
59	Jack Katz	9.38
60	Franco Ferracuti	9.26
61.5	Herman Schwendinger	9.24
61.5	Julia Schwendinger	9.24
63	Joan Petersilia	9.20
64	Sheldon E. Glueck	9.14
65	Richard J. Gelles	9.01
66	Ernest A. Hooton	8.93
67	Jerome Hall	8.90
68	George B. Vold	8.73
69	Charles R. Tittle	8.71
70	Michael J. Hindelang	8.62
71	Lawrence W. Sherman	8.51
72	Gilbert Geis	8.25
73	Elliott Currie	8.03
74	Nicholas A. Groth	7.91
75	Daniel Glaser	7.89
76	David Huizinga	7.72
77	Murray A. Straus	7.61
78	Jock Young	7.58
79	Peter C. Yeager	7.48
80.5	David P. Farrington	7.46
80.5	Francis A.J. Ianni	7.46
82.5	Lawrence E. Cohen	7.43
82.5	Kathleen F. Maguire	7.43
84	Albert J. Reiss, Jr.	7.41
85	James A. Inciardi	7.27
86.5	Thomas J. Bernard	7.26
86.5	Neal Shover	7.26

88	Enrico Ferri	7.01
89	Mary Owen Cameron	6.93
90	John E. Conklin	6.91
91	Robert M. Martinson	6.58
92	Marcus Felson	6.42
93	Marcia R. Chaiken	6.40
94	Menachem Amir	6.24
95	Don C. Gibbons	6.22
96	Alan A. Block	6.19
97	Charles H. McCaghy	6.18
98	Edwin M. Schur	6.17
99	Paul W. Tappan	6.13
100	C. Ray Jeffery	6.12

There is a noticeable diversity of names in Table 7.1. Included among the page-coverage influentials are scholars representing many different generations (starting from the eighteenth century, with Cesare Beccaria in 19th place), disciplines (from physician William H. Sheldon in 37th place to cartographer Adolphe Quetelet in 45th place), and perspectives (from radical philosopher Karl Marx in 7th place to conservative political scientist James Q. Wilson in 11th place and biocriminologist C. Ray Jeffery in 100th place).

Table 7.2 compares the page-coverage data with the 47 most-cited scholars in the 23 criminology textbooks (see Wright 1995a). It is clear that there is some agreement between the two lists: 26 of the 47 most-cited scholars in the textbooks also are among the 47 most-covered scholars ($r = .55$).[7] This suggests that the two units of analysis produce roughly equivalent results.

A closer inspection reveals some important differences between the two lists of influential scholars. First, it is clear that page-coverage analysis is much more likely to favor important historical figures in criminology than is citation analysis. Karl Marx, Cesare Lombroso, Clifford R. Shaw, Sigmund Freud, Henry D. McKay, Cesare Beccaria, Jeremy Bentham, Friedrich Engels, William H. Sheldon, Gabriel Tarde, Charles Goring, and Adolphe Quetelet all rank among the 47 most-covered scholars in the textbooks, but not among the 47 most-cited scholars. Altogether, 14 of the 47 most-covered scholars in the textbooks (29.8 percent) published all of their major works before 1950[8] while only four of the 47 most-cited scholars (8.5 percent) share this distinction[9] ($\chi^2 = 6.86$; df $= 1$; $p < .01$). It appears that textbooks provide extensive discussion of early criminological scholars but do not adequately cite their works.

Furthermore, scholars known primarily for one renowned work in criminology, including Cesare Beccaria (1764/1963), Howard S. Becker (1963), Charles Goring (1913), Robert K. Merton (1938), and Stanton E. Samenow and Samuel Yochelson (Yochelson and Samenow 1976, 1977), are disadvantaged by citation analysis. For example, Merton (1938) parsimoniously outlined anomie theory in one famous early article; he seldom returned to the analysis of crime in his subsequent illustrious career as a sociologist. Although most criminology textbooks include

Table 7.2

A Comparison of the 47 Most Influential Scholars in Criminology Textbooks, 1989–1993, as Measured Through Citation Analysis and Page-Coverage Analysis

Citation Analysis Rank[a]	Page-Coverage Analysis Rank	Scholar
1	2	Travis Hirschi
2	11	James Q. Wilson
3	3	Marvin E. Wolfgang
4	1	Edwin H. Sutherland
5	5	Donald R. Cressey
6	20	William J. Chambliss
7	25	Marshall B. Clinard
8	21	Thorsten J. Sellin
9	32	Michael R. Gottfredson
10	42	Delbert S. Elliott
11	—(70[b])	Michael J. Hindelang
12	18	Richard Quinney
13.5	23	Richard J. Herrnstein
13.5	—(68[b])	George B. Vold
15	—(72[b])	Gilbert Geis
16	8	Emile Durkheim
17	4	Lloyd E. Ohlin
18.5	—(85[b])	James A. Inciardi
18.5	29	Edwin M. Lemert
20	—(102[c])	Francis T. Cullen
21	—(86.5[b])	Thomas J. Bernard
22	15	Albert K. Cohen
23	—(69[b])	Charles R. Tittle
24	9	David Matza
25.5	—(49[b])	John Braithwaite
25.5	14	Gresham M. Sykes
27	43	Sarnoff A. Mednick
28.5	—(84[b])	Albert J. Reiss, Jr.
28.5	35	Jerome H. Skolnick
30	38	Ronald L. Akers
31	39	James F. Short, Jr.
32	—(51[b])	Jack P. Gibbs
33	31	Darrell J. Steffensmeier
34	—(80.5[b])	David P. Farrington
35	12	Richard A. Cloward
36	—(95[b])	Don C. Gibbons
37.5	—(71[b])	Lawrence W. Sherman
37.5	—(78[b])	Jock Young
39.5	28	Walter C. Reckless
39.5	30	Austin T. Turk
42	—(64[b])	Sheldon E. Glueck
42	—(142[c])	John L. Hagan
42	—(63[b])	Joan Petersilia
44	—(77[b])	Murray A. Straus

45	—(56[b])	Eleanor T. Glueck
46	—(65[b])	Richard J. Gelles
47	—(158[c])	Joseph G. Weis
—	6	Robert K. Merton
—	7	Karl Marx
—	10	Cesare Lombroso
—	13	Clifford R. Shaw
—	16	Sigmund Freud
—	17	Henry D. McKay
—	19	Cesare Beccaria
—	22	Walter B. Miller
—	24	Robert M. Figlio
—	26	Jeremy Bentham
—	27	Hans J. Eysenck
—	33	Friedrich Engels
—	34	Stanton E. Samenow
—	36	Samuel Yochelson
—	37	William H. Sheldon
—	40	Howard S. Becker
—	41	Gabriel Tarde
—	44	Charles Goring
—	45	Adolphe Quetelet
—	46	John Irwin
—	47	Carl B. Klockars

[a] With self-citations deleted; taken from Wright (1995a).
[b] Rank in Table 7.1.
[c] Rank in an extended list of 196 scholars receiving the most page-coverage.

an extensive discussion of anomie theory and generally cite this article, these citations are insufficient to rank Merton as one of the 47 most-cited scholars in Table 7.2.

While citation analysis may underestimate the influence of historical figures and scholars known mostly for one celebrated work, it simultaneously appears to overestimate the influence of modern scholars who are exceptionally prolific. Some contemporary scholars who rank high in citations but lower in page coverage are very widely published, but have produced no single highly significant or seminal work.

In general, these findings seem to suggest that citation analysis as a measure of the influence of scholars has certain disadvantages which may not be shared by page-coverage analysis. Specifically, while a citation analysis of criminology textbooks appeared to underestimate the influence of historical figures and scholars mostly known for one famous work, and exaggerate the influence of prolific contemporary scholars, page-coverage analysis compensates for these shortcomings, arguably offering a more balanced assessment of influence. The data reported here suggest that page-coverage analysis may be a promising supplement to citation analysis for measuring the influence of scholars.

SUMMARY AND DISCUSSION

Citation analysis research has recently emerged as an important way to measure the influence of scholars in criminology and criminal justice, despite some persistent doubts about its validity. This chapter has offered an alternative way to measure the influence of scholars by considering the use of inches-of-print and page-coverage as units of analysis. A comparison of the findings from a citation analysis of influential scholars in 23 criminology textbooks published from 1989–1993 (Wright 1995a) to a page-coverage analysis of scholars in the same books indicates that, while citation analysis underestimates the influence of certain scholars in the textbooks, page-coverage analysis compensates for these distortions.

In particular, page-coverage analysis appears to correct for certain citation analysis shortcomings relating to the measurement of the influence of important historical figures in criminology and criminal justice, scholars known mostly for one renowned work, and prodigious contemporary scholars. However, our extensive experience as content analysts conducting both citation analysis and page-coverage research convinces us that the latter does not offer an immediate remedy. The major problem is the immense amount of time and effort required to conduct this type of page-coverage analysis. The current study demanded the tedious and painstaking tracking of the coverage of over 2,000 scholars in about 10,000 pages of text; merely coding the accumulated data took almost three months. Our estimate is that the analysis reported here required approximately 600 hours of research time; the earlier citation analysis of the same 23 textbooks involved about 200 hours. Any researcher who considers pursuing a similar study is warned of the arduous nature of the task.

One possible way to reduce the demands of this research is to choose random or representative samples of passages for page-coverage analysis. In future studies, it may be more practical to select a random sample of perhaps 10 percent of the pages of books or periodicals for analysis. This could actually make page-coverage research less burdensome than traditional citation analysis. Before conducting random sample studies of the page-coverage devoted to influential scholars, the validity of this approach should be tested against an analysis of an entire population of books and/or periodicals.

The next step in evaluating the potential of page-coverage analysis as a technique for studying the influence of scholars is to extend this research to criminology and criminal justice journals. In particular, page coverage studies could be conducted which consider the same journals and time intervals studied in works such as Cohn and Farrington's (1994a, 1994b, 1996) citation analyses of influential scholars and in Chapters 2 and 4. A comparison between the citation analyses and concomitant page-coverage studies could help to establish whether the differences between page-coverage and citation analysis findings reported here are idiosyncratic to textbooks or also affect journals. In addition, this research could shed more insight into the strengths and limitations of both citation analysis and page-coverage analysis.

NOTES

1. The other general type of content analysis is latent, or qualitative. Latent content analysis "requires the researcher to draw inferences regarding deeper, contextual meanings" (Wright 1988: 41), while manifest content analysis simply counts "surface meanings" such as names, words, sentences, paragraphs, and/or pages (see also Berelson 1952; Budd, Thorp, and Donahew 1967; Carney 1979).

2. Only introductory criminology textbooks published in the United States were included in the study. When more than one edition of a textbook appeared from 1989–1993, only the most recent edition was used. The list of the textbooks examined in the study can be found in Wright (1994a).

3. It is possible that, if different font sizes were used in the printing of the various textbooks, the number of words per inch of print could vary between the textbooks. Similarly, we could have expressed the number of inches devoted to a scholar in each book as a fraction of the total number of inches in the book, to correct for the different size of each book. However, previous page-coverage analyses have not raised this issue and we believe that our results would be substantially unchanged if we were able to correct for unequal fonts.

4. Names of nonacademics (e.g., novelists, politicians, criminals) were excluded.

5. All discussions of scholars, including critical assessments and biographical treatments, were included in the data analysis, as it was assumed that these were also prima facie important indicators of their influence.

6. The complete list of all 196 scholars is available from the authors on request.

7. A rank-order correlation was not calculated here because different names appeared on the two lists of influential scholars. See Chapter 5, note 3.

8. These were Cesare Beccaria, Jeremy Bentham, Emile Durkheim, Friedrich Engels, Sigmund Freud, Charles Goring, Cesare Lombroso, Karl Marx, Henry D. McKay, Adolphe Quetelet, Clifford R. Shaw, William H. Sheldon, Edwin H. Sutherland, and Gabriel Tarde.

9. These were Emile Durkheim, Eleanor T. Glueck, Sheldon E. Glueck, and Edwin H. Sutherland.

8

Finis for the Convergence Controversy? A Citation Analysis of the Complementarity Between Criminology and Criminal Justice

One of the most heated debates in the fields of criminology and criminal justice has centered around the degree of divergence or convergence between the two areas as academic disciplines (cf., Conrad and Myren 1979; Holmes and Taggart 1990; Langworthy and Latessa 1989; Morn 1980; Pearson et al. 1980; Sherman 1978; Sorensen, Widmayer, and Scarpitti 1994; Ward and Webb 1984; Zalman 1981). Those who see a divergence between the two fields generally argue that, while criminology is primarily concerned with the theoretical and empirical study of the etiology of crime, criminal justice is a more practitioner-oriented discipline focused around the study of the criminal justice system and its institutions and agencies (Ward and Webb 1984; Zalman 1981). Convergence proponents usually counter that, while criminology and criminal justice may have developed as separate fields with different purposes, they recently have come back together so that few meaningful boundaries today remain to distinguish the two disciplines (Langworthy and Latessa 1989).

Various scholars have attempted to clarify this issue. One approach has been to focus on the different rankings assigned to various professional criminology and criminal justice journals by those who identify themselves primarily as criminologists or criminal justice scholars (Regoli, Poole, and Miracle 1982; Williams, McShane, and Wagoner 1995). Another technique has been to consider the methodological and thematic differences between articles appearing in criminology and criminal justice periodicals (Holmes and Taggart 1990). Finally, some researchers have conducted surveys that examine the differences between faculty in criminology and criminal justice programs (Greene, Bynum, and Webb 1984; Ward and Webb 1984) or the members of criminology and criminal justice associations (Sorensen, Widmayer, and Scarpitti 1994).

We propose an alternative approach for assessing the degree of convergence or divergence between the two fields: a comparison of the most-cited scholars in criminology and criminal justice publications. Although we have found fairly weak associations between those scholars who are extensively cited in criminology publications and those who are heavily cited in criminal justice publications (results that appear to support the divergence perspective), we instead suggest that this may in fact demonstrate an emerging complementarity between criminology and criminal justice.

THE CONVERGENCE CONTROVERSY

In a review of the differences between criminology and criminal justice as fields of inquiry, Sorensen, Widmayer, and Scarpitti (1994) note that there has historically been a "dual paradigm" in crime-related education and research. Since the International Association of Police Professors (later renamed the Academy of Criminal Justice Sciences) split off from the American Society of Criminology in 1963, there have been two separate disciplines, with different orientations, interests, professional associations, and publications, devoted to the study of crime and justice in the United States.

"Criminology" historically has been considered a specialization within the larger discipline of sociology; most of those who identify themselves as criminologists obtained their graduate training in sociology (Sorensen, Widmayer, and Scarpitti 1994). The subject matter of criminology is primarily etiological: criminologists are interested in the theoretical and empirical study of the correlates of crime (Zalman 1981). The national professional association of criminologists is the American Society of Criminology, while some of the major journals in the discipline include *Criminology*, *Journal of Quantitative Criminology*, and *Journal of Research in Crime and Delinquency*. However, criminologists traditionally have also given high ratings to articles published in leading sociology journals, especially *American Journal of Sociology*, *American Sociological Review*, and *Social Forces* (Greene, Bynum, and Webb 1984; Regoli, Poole, and Miracle 1982).

"Criminal justice" originally emerged as a practitioner-oriented, interdisciplinary field that drew on research from sociology, psychology, political science, and the law. Today, however, it has evolved into a distinct academic discipline with its own programs and graduate degrees. Criminal justice scholars specialize in studying the institutional (or agency) components of criminal justice, usually from a systems perspective that recognizes the interdependence of law enforcement, courts, and corrections (Zalman 1981). The national professional association of criminal justice scholars is the Academy of Criminal Justice Sciences, while some of the leading journals in the discipline include *Justice Quarterly*, *Journal of Criminal Justice*, and *Criminal Justice and Behavior*. Criminal justice scholars today regularly give high ratings to articles published in the leading criminology journals, especially *Criminology*, *Journal of Quantitative Criminology*, and *Journal of Research in Crime and Delinquency* (Williams, McShane, and Wagoner 1995). In general, criminologists have focused on basic research on the social causes of crime while criminal justice scholars have been more interested in applied research on institutional responses to crime and criminals.

In the early 1980s, the Joint Commission on Criminology and Criminal Justice

Standards and Goals, a cooperative venture by the American Society of Criminology and the Academy of Criminal Justice Sciences to assess the future of criminal justice education, documented the divergence between the disciplines of criminology and criminal justice (Ward and Webb 1984; see also DeZee 1980; Felkenes 1980; Greene, Bynum, and Webb 1984; Regoli, Poole, and Miracle 1982). For example, one Commission study found that, when asked to rate the most prestigious places to publish articles, members of the American Society of Criminology tended to list leading sociology journals while members of the Academy of Criminal Justice Sciences rated only criminology and criminal justice journals as the most prestigious places to publish (Regoli, Poole, and Miracle 1982). Another Commission study of the doctoral graduates of criminology and criminal justice programs found that the former mostly claimed expertise in basic research and theory while the latter generally reported expertise primarily in institutional criminal justice, particularly corrections (Felkenes 1980). The Commission's final report (Ward and Webb 1984; see also Greene, Bynum, and Webb 1984) noted that a paradigmatic split existed between those faculty with doctorates (primarily criminologists), who taught in graduate programs, had little or no practical experience in criminal justice agencies, and highly valued basic research, and faculty without doctorates (mostly criminal justice scholars), who taught in undergraduate programs, had extensive criminal justice agency experience, and highly valued teaching and agency consultation. The former group tended to embrace a theoretical or "analytical" approach to scholarship, while the latter favored a "pragmatic, agency-based" approach (Ward and Webb 1984; Greene, Bynum, and Webb 1984).

Several recent studies, however, have found signs of convergence between criminology and criminal justice (Holmes and Taggart 1990; Sorensen, Widmayer, and Scarpitti 1994; Williams, McShane, and Wagoner 1995). In an analysis of the differences between articles appearing in *Criminology, Journal of Criminal Justice* and *Justice Quarterly* from 1976–1989, Holmes and Taggart (1990) noted that criminal justice scholars increasingly were using the same sophisticated, multivariate statistics that earlier had been employed almost solely by criminologists. However, throughout the period of the research, the criminal justice journals were more likely to publish articles focusing on criminal justice institutions and agencies, while *Criminology* published more articles that analyzed the correlates of crime.[1] Another study (Williams, McShane, and Wagoner 1995) found that among 253 members of the Academy of Criminal Justice Sciences, those who identified themselves as criminologists rated the prestige of criminology and criminal justice journals in almost exactly the same way as those who identified themselves as criminal justice scholars.[2]

Another study that suggests some convergence between the disciplines of criminology and criminal justice is Sorensen, Widmayer, and Scarpitti's (1994) survey of the backgrounds, characteristics, and interests of 305 members of the American Society of Criminology and/or the Academy of Criminal Justice Sciences. While important differences distinguished respondents who belonged only to the American Society of Criminology from respondents who belonged only to the Academy of Criminal Justice Sciences (the former had little agency experience and were committed to research and publication, while the latter had considerable agency experience and were committed to teaching and agency consultation), the authors noted an emerging area of convergence among "dual members" (respondents who belonged to both associations). Specifically, dual members often had backgrounds involving agency experience, but also reported a strong commitment to research and publication. Sorensen, Widmayer, and Scarpitti (1994: 164-165) conclude that a "third paradigm may be coming into existence" that acknowledges that the "study of criminal justice agencies and the etiology of crime should be considered two sides of the same coin."

One method that has not previously been used to examine the convergence controversy is citation analysis. In a reanalysis of the data appearing in studies of the most-cited scholars in criminology and criminal justice textbooks (Wright 1995a; Wright and Cohn 1996) and journals (Cohn and Farrington 1994b; Chapter 2), we found fairly weak associations between scholars who are extensively cited in criminology publications and criminal justice publications. While at first glance this seems to support the divergence perspective, we instead argue that it is additional support for Sorensen, Widmayer, and Scarpitti's (1994) claim for a "third paradigm," which we call "complementarity."

RESEARCH DESIGN

A comparison of the lists of the most-cited scholars in criminology and criminal justice publications (textbooks and/or journals) provides a new approach for evaluating the degree of divergence, convergence, or complementarity that exists between criminology and criminal justice. A low correlation between the most-cited scholars in criminology and criminal justice publications would appear to indicate either divergence or complementarity between the fields, especially if a comparison of these two sets of scholars shows that they have different areas of specialization (i.e., etiological for the criminologists and institutional for the criminal justice scholars). A high correlation between the most-cited scholars in criminology and criminal justice publications would suggest support for the convergence argument, unless those who are extensively cited in both sets of publications are primarily generalists who publish on both etiological and institutional topics.

We reanalyzed data from four previous citation studies of criminology and criminal justice textbooks (Wright 1995a; Wright and Cohn 1996) and journals (Cohn and Farrington 1994b; Chapter 2) to examine the convergence controversy. In the textbook research, Wright (1995a) compiled a list of the 47 most-cited scholars in 23 criminology textbooks published from 1989–1993, while Wright and Cohn (1996) compiled a list of the 22 most-cited scholars in 16 criminal justice textbooks published during the same time period. Cohn and Farrington (1994b) compiled lists of the 25 most-cited scholars in three leading criminology journals (*Criminology, Journal of Quantitative Criminology*, and *Journal of Research in*

Crime and Delinquency) and the 20 most-cited scholars in three leading criminal justice journals (*Criminal Justice and Behavior*, *Journal of Criminal Justice*, and *Justice Quarterly*) published from 1986–1990. In Chapter 2 of this book, we examined these same six leading periodicals from 1991–1995 to offer lists of the 30 most-cited scholars in criminology journals (see Table 2.4) and the 30 most-cited scholars in criminal justice journals (see Table 2.8). Drawing on these studies, we prepared lists of the most-cited scholars in criminology *or* criminal justice publications (suggesting divergence or complementarity) and in criminology *and* criminal justice publications (suggesting convergence).

FINDINGS

Table 8.1 lists the most-cited scholars in criminology and criminal justice textbooks. Eleven of the 58 scholars in Table 8.1 (19.0 percent) ranked among the most-cited in both criminology and criminal justice textbooks; the other 47 (81.0 percent) ranked among the most-cited in either criminology or criminal justice textbooks, but not both. Only a weak association ($r = .32$) exists between the most-cited scholars in criminology and criminal justice textbooks, apparently contradicting the convergence perspective.[3]

An examination of the specific areas of expertise of the scholars listed in Table 8.1 further weakens the case for the convergence perspective and strengthens the arguments for either the divergence or complementarity approach. Virtually all of the scholars who are extensively cited in criminology but not criminal justice textbooks (see Table 8.1, section 1) are known mostly for important theoretical and/or empirical contributions to the study of the etiology of crime (e.g., Ronald L. Akers' development of social learning theory, Thomas J. Bernard's contributions to conflict theory, and Delbert S. Elliott's analysis of the National Youth Survey). Similarly, most of the scholars who are extensively cited in criminal justice but not criminology textbooks (see Table 8.1, section 2) are well known for studying particular criminal justice institutions or subsystems (David H. Bayley, Herman Goldstein, and George L. Kelling for law enforcement, Wayne R. LaFave and Paul B. Wice for the courts and criminal law, and Harry E. Allen, Todd R. Clear, and Peter W. Greenwood for corrections).

If anything, Table 8.1 may overstate the degree of convergence found in the textbooks, since numerous scholars who rank among the most-cited in both criminology and criminal justice textbooks (see Table 8.1, section three) are generalists who have made important contributions to both the study of the etiology of crime and the institutions of justice. For example, Gresham M. Sykes is well-known in criminology for proposing neutralization theory (Sykes and Matza 1957), and in criminal justice for his classic study of prisons, *The Society of Captives* (Sykes 1958). It is possible that criminology textbooks are mostly citing and discussing Sykes's etiological studies, while criminal justice textbooks are primarily citing and discussing his institutional studies. The same may be true for many of the other scholars appearing in Table 8.1, section 3.[4]

Table 8.1
The Most-Cited Scholars in Criminology and Criminal Justice Textbooks, 1989–1993[a]

Ranked Among the Most-Cited in Criminology Textbooks Only:

N = 36 (62.1%)

Scholars: Ronald L. Akers, Thomas J. Bernard, John Braithwaite, Marshall B. Clinard, Richard A. Cloward, Albert K. Cohen, Emile Durkheim, Delbert S. Elliott, David P. Farrington, Gilbert Geis, Richard J. Gelles, Don C. Gibbons, Jack P. Gibbs, Eleanor T. Glueck, Sheldon E. Glueck, Michael R. Gottfredson, John L. Hagan, Richard J. Herrnstein, Michael J. Hindelang, Travis Hirschi, James A. Inciardi, Edwin M. Lemert, David Matza, Sarnoff A. Mednick, Lloyd E. Ohlin, Richard Quinney, Walter C. Reckless, Thorsten J. Sellin, James F. Short, Jr., Darrell J. Steffensmeier, Murray A. Straus, Charles R. Tittle, Austin T. Turk, George B. Vold, Joseph G. Weis, Jock Young

Ranked Among the Most-Cited in Criminal Justice Textbooks Only:

N = 11 (19.0%)

Scholars: Harry E. Allen, David H. Bayley, Barbara Boland, Todd R. Clear, Timothy J. Flanagan, Herman Goldstein, Peter W. Greenwood, George L. Kelling, Wayne R. LaFave, Samuel L. Walker, Paul B. Wice

Ranked Among the Most-Cited in Criminology and Criminal Justice Textbooks:

N = 11 (19.0%)

Scholars: William J. Chambliss, Donald R. Cressey, Francis T. Cullen, Joan Petersilia, Albert J. Reiss, Jr., Lawrence W. Sherman, Jerome H. Skolnick, Edwin H. Sutherland, Gresham M. Sykes, James Q. Wilson, Marvin E. Wolfgang

---

[a]Adapted from Wright (1995a) and Wright and Cohn (1996).

Despite what appears to be fairly strong support for the divergence or complementarity arguments, a troublesome shortcoming hinders any attempt to draw straightforward conclusions about the convergence debate from a comparison of the most-cited scholars in criminology and in criminal justice textbooks. The amount of divergence or complementarity between these textbooks is obviously due, at least in part, to basic curriculum imperatives that have little to do with larger research agendas and disciplinary trends. Course descriptions and sequencing in criminology and criminal justice programs require criminology textbooks to cover mostly etiological issues, while criminal justice textbooks adopt a general systems approach. Even if convergence were a reality in criminological and criminal justice research, there still would be considerable pressures on the authors and publishers of textbooks to avoid overlapping subject matter and citations.

However, such pressures should not affect citation patterns in periodicals. Thus, an examination of the most-cited scholars in criminology and criminal justice journals, as shown in Tables 8.2 and 8.3, provides far more compelling arguments for those involved in the convergence debate. Only eight of the 37 scholars in Table

8.2 (21.6 percent) ranked among the most-cited scholars in both criminology and criminal justice journals in the 1986–1990 time period. As in textbooks, the majority of the scholars (78.4 percent) were among the most-cited in either criminology or criminal justice journals, but not in both. As with the data obtained from textbooks, the relationship between the most-cited scholars in the two sets of journals is fairly weak ($r = .36$).

Table 8.2
The Most-Cited Scholars in Criminology and Criminal Justice Journals, 1986–1990[a]

Ranked Among the Most-Cited in Criminology Journals Only

N = 17 (46.0%)

Scholars: Suzanne S. Ageton, Ronald L. Akers, Richard A. Berk, Richard A. Cloward, Lawrence E. Cohen, Delbert S. Elliott, David P. Farrington, Marcus Felson, Robert M. Figlio, Jack P. Gibbs, David F. Greenberg, Marvin D. Krohn, Robert J. Sampson, Thorsten J. Sellin, Edwin H. Sutherland, Charles R. Tittle, Joseph G. Weis

Ranked Among the Most-Cited in Criminal Justice Journals Only

N = 12 (32.4%)

Scholars: Donald R. Cressey, Francis T. Cullen, Timothy J. Flanagan, Don M. Gottfredson, James B. Jacobs, Robert M. Martinson, Eric D. Poole, Robert M. Regoli, Lawrence W. Sherman, Wesley G. Skogan, Hans Toch, Andrew Von Hirsch

Ranked Among the Most-Cited in Criminology and Criminal Justice Journals

N = 8 (21.6%)

Scholars: Alfred Blumstein, Jacqueline Cohen, Michael R. Gottfredson, John L. Hagan, Michael J. Hindelang, Travis Hirschi, James Q. Wilson, Marvin E. Wolfgang

[a]Adapted from Cohn and Farrington (1994b).

Table 8.3 shows somewhat more agreement between the most-cited scholars in criminology and criminal justice journals in the 1991–1995 data. Fifteen (32.6 percent) of the 46 scholars in Table 8.3 ranked among the most-cited in both criminology and criminal justice journals and 31 other scholars (67.4 percent) were among the most-cited in either criminology or criminal justice journals. A correlation calculated on these data ($r = .50$) was higher than those calculated on either the textbook data or the earlier journal data.[5] In general, however, the data from the journals show fairly weak associations between the most-cited scholars in criminology and criminal justice journals and appear to offer more persuasive support for the divergence or complementarity arguments than for the convergence approach.

Support for divergence and/or complementarity remains strong when the specializations of the scholars in Tables 8.2 and 8.3 are examined. Choosing some

Table 8.3
The Most-Cited Scholars in Criminology and Criminal Justice Journals, 1991–1995[a]

Ranked Among the Most-Cited in Criminology Journals Only

N = 15 (32.6%)

Scholars: Suzanne S. Ageton, Ronald L. Akers, Richard A. Berk, Robert J. Bursik, Harold G. Grasmick, David F. Greenberg, Marvin D. Krohn, John H. Laub, Kenneth C. Land, Rolf Loeber, Daniel S. Nagin, Raymond Paternoster, Edwin H. Sutherland, Charles R. Tittle, Christy A. Visher

Ranked Among the Most-Cited in Criminal Justice Journals Only

N = 16 (34.8%)

Scholars: Gene G. Abel, Don A. Andrews, Howard E. Barbaree, Judith V. Becker, Dante V. Cicchetti, Francis T. Cullen, Paul Gendreau, William L. Marshall, Martha A. Myers, Joan Petersilia, Vernon L. Quinsey, Lawrence W. Sherman, Wesley G. Skogan, Murray A. Straus, Hans Toch, Michael H. Tonry

Ranked Among the Most-Cited in Criminology and Criminal Justice Journals

N = 15 (32.6%)

Scholars: Alfred Blumstein, Jacqueline Cohen, Lawrence E. Cohen, Delbert S. Elliott, David P. Farrington, Marcus Felson, Michael R. Gottfredson, John L. Hagan, Michael J. Hindelang, Travis Hirschi, David Huizinga, Robert J. Sampson, Douglas A. Smith, James Q. Wilson, Marvin E. Wolfgang

---

[a]Adapted from Chapter 2, Tables 2.4 and 2.8.

examples from Table 8.2, it can be seen that most of the scholars who are extensively cited in criminology (but not criminal justice) journals have made important theoretical and/or empirical contributions to the study of crime causation (e.g., Suzanne S. Ageton, Ronald L. Akers, Richard A. Cloward; see Table 8.2, section 1). Despite a few notable exceptions such as Donald R. Cressey and Francis T. Cullen,[6] the scholars who are extensively cited in criminal justice (but not criminology) journals (see Table 8.2, section 2) are renowned primarily for studying particular criminal justice institutions and subsystems (e.g., Don M. Gottfredson, James B. Jacobs, Robert M. Martinson, and Hans Toch are prominent correctional researchers). Finally, the scholars who are extensively cited in both criminology and criminal justice journals are generalists who have made lasting contributions to the study of the causes of crime and the institutions of justice. For example, consider Alfred Blumstein's pivotal roles in the development of the criminal career paradigm in criminology and the systems approach to the study of criminal justice (see Blumstein 1994; Blumstein, Cohen, and Farrington 1988a, 1988b; Blumstein et al. 1986).

DIVERGENCE, CONVERGENCE, OR COMPLEMENTARITY?

Until recently, the divergence-convergence debate has been predominantly framed as an argument over whether criminology and criminal justice as two distinct disciplines have grown farther apart or are coming closer together. Stated in these terms, the data in this chapter favor the divergence perspective. Our analysis of the most-cited scholars in recent criminology and criminal justice textbooks and journals shows fairly weak associations between the two disciplines. It is clear that publications in criminology cite different prominent scholars than do publications in criminal justice. In addition, the specializations of these scholars correspond closely to the conventional definitional distinctions between criminology and criminal justice. Specifically, criminology publications (both textbooks and journals) extensively cite scholars who specialize primarily in theoretical and/or empirical studies of the etiology of crime while criminal justice publications extensively cite scholars who specialize in the study of the institutions of justice.

It is conceivable, however, that the entire convergence controversy has been based on a misunderstanding of the developing relationship between criminology and criminal justice. Perhaps the modern analysis of crime and justice should not be conceptualized from the perspective of criminology *or* criminal justice, however far apart or close together these disciplines may be, but rather from the perspective of criminology *and* criminal justice. Like Plato's belief that lovers originally were one person with two parts that, although separated and lost, desire to be rejoined once found, criminology and criminal justice now may be bound together in a truly complementary relationship. It may be that what the citation data really show is not so much the divergence between two disciplines, but instead the complementarity between two parts of one discipline.

Several recent commentators on the convergence debate have anticipated our argument for the emerging complementarity between criminology and criminal justice. As we mentioned, Holmes and Taggart (1990) concluded that few methodological differences now distinguish articles published in *Criminology* from those appearing in *Justice Quarterly*. However, they also argued that a thematic selection process has been gradually emerging, one in which *Criminology* mostly published papers that analyze the correlates of crime, while most of the articles appearing in *Justice Quarterly* have examined the criminal justice system and associated institutions.

As noted earlier, in their comparisons of the members of the American Society of Criminology and the Academy of Criminal Justice Sciences, Sorensen, Widmayer, and Scarpitti (1994: 165) went even further by concluding that criminology and criminal justice are "two sides of the same coin." They stated that, "in order to ensure the survival of *the* discipline, it is necessary to merge theory and practice to refrain from mutually exclusive identification with 'criminology' or 'criminal justice'" (italics added).

In short, we contend that current indicators of what appears to be divergence (e.g., the differences in citation patterns between publications) between criminology and criminal justice reflect a much more fundamental complementarity between the two. Criminology and criminal justice now may be very much like Tweedledum and Tweedledee, who, as Alice discovered in *Through the Looking-Glass*, perpetually quarreled, but still managed to finish each other's sentences.

NOTES

1. Holmes and Taggart (1990) examined these journals during the years that they were the official publications of the American Society of Criminology (1976–1989 for *Criminology*) and the Academy of Criminal Justice Sciences (1976–1983 for the *Journal of Criminal Justice* and 1984–1989 for *Justice Quarterly*).

2. Williams, McShane, and Wagoner (1995) found a correlation of $r = .92$ between the two sets of journal rankings. However, this study is limited by the fact that the survey only considered members of the Academy of Criminal Justice Sciences and not members of the American Society of Criminology.

3. See Chapter 5, note 3.

4. To test this assumption empirically, it would be necessary to examine the most-cited works of the most-cited scholars in criminology and criminal justice publications. However, most recent citation studies (with the exception of Cohn and Farrington 1996) have not examined the most-cited works of scholars.

5. The higher level of association between the most-cited scholars in criminology journals and criminal justice journals in the later time period (1991–1995) than in the earlier time period (1986–1990) could suggest a shift toward support for the convergence argument (although this change is not statistically significant; $\chi^2 = 1.38$, df $= 2, p > .10$).

6. Donald R. Cressey and Francis T. Cullen are generalists who are well known for both etiological and institutional research. Cressey, for example, assisted in the modification and qualification of Edwin H. Sutherland's differential association theory (Sutherland and Cressey 1960), developed a theory of embezzlement (Cressey 1953) and an organizational model of the Mafia (Cressey 1969), but also wrote extensively on the processing of offenders through the courts (Rosett and Cressey 1976) and corrections (Cressey 1958, 1959).

9

The Way Forward

We hope that this book has demonstrated how much citation analysis has taught us about a wide variety of topics. The most pressing need in the future is for funding to carry out citation analyses of larger numbers of journals and books in criminology and criminal justice. With funding, it would be possible to expand citation analyses to earlier periods of time, and to trace citation careers of scholars and works over long time periods. We believe that it would be useful to apply criminal career concepts such as onset, duration, termination, frequency, versatility, specificity, and escalation to the study of citation careers.

With funding, it would be possible to compare the results of citation analyses with a variety of alternative methods of measuring prestige and influence, such as surveys of criminologists and criminal justice scholars, numbers of publications, and receipt of honors and major offices in scholarly societies. With funding, more extensive analyses of topics addressed by articles and books could be carried out, to identify and aim to predict changes in key issues over time. It would be possible to carry out more extensive analyses of the most-cited works of the most-cited scholars, to document changes over time in the most influential scholars and works in more detail. Ideally, vitae of the most influential scholars should be collected, so that citations of all their works could be studied. It would also be important to relate the changing influence of scholars and works to changes in theoretical, empirical, methodological, and political concerns, and to the changing priorities of funding agencies. Crucial questions that should be addressed include why certain scholars become pre-eminent in certain time periods and how far it is possible to predict trajectories of influence of scholars and works.

Further advances in the methodology of citation analysis are needed. In particular, the prevalence of citations (the number of different articles or books in which a work is cited) seems a more valid measure of influence than the more usual measure of the frequency of citations. It would be desirable to develop a sensitive classification system for types of citations: whether they are favorable or unfavorable, how far they are perfunctory, how central to the argument they are, and so on. Measures of the number of column inches occupied by citations, or the number of pages on which a work is cited (as in Chapter 7), are also useful. In addition, the prestige of citing and cited journals could be taken into account in weighting citations.

In order to overcome problems of undesirable citation behavior (e.g., citing friends and departmental colleagues deliberately to boost their citations rather than because of their salience for the argument), research on citation behavior is needed. With funding, it would be possible to survey authors of books and journal articles to ask them why they cited certain scholars rather than others. This survey could include questions designed to investigate how far citation behavior is designed to curry favor with journal editors, likely reviewers, key staff members of funding agencies, and other individuals with power (e.g., heads of departments and presidents of scholarly societies). The effects of the specific interests of journal editors on the topics of articles published should be investigated. In addition to eliminating self-citations, coauthor citations could be excluded from analyses (see Chapter 1) and even citations of scholars in the same department or the same university.

Overall, we believe that citation analyses can be a very useful method of investigating changing scholarly influences over time. However, funding is needed to transform it from its Cinderella status to an accepted discipline, to overcome future threats to its validity, and to establish it as a valuable method of documenting changes in influential scholars and topics in criminology and criminal justice over time.

Bibliography

Abel, Gene G., M.S. Mittelman, Judith V. Becker, J. Rathner, and J.L. Rouleau. (1988). "Predicting Child Molesters' Response to Treatment." *Annals of the New York Academy of Sciences* 528:223–234.

Akers, Ronald L. (1985). *Deviant Behavior: A Social Learning Approach*, 3rd ed. Belmont, CA: Wadsworth.

Allen, Harry E. (1983). "Comment: A Reaction to 'An Analysis of Citations in Introductory Criminology Textbooks,' *Journal of Criminal Justice* 10(3)." *Journal of Criminal Justice* 11:177–178.

Andrews, Don A., Ivan Zinger, Robert D. Hoge, James Bonta, Paul Gendreau, and Francis T. Cullen. (1990). "Does Correctional Treatment Work? A Clinically Relevant and Psychologically Informed Meta-Analysis." *Criminology* 28:369–404.

Bagby, R. Michael, James D.A. Parker, and Alison S. Bury. (1990). "A Comparative Citation Analysis of Attribution Theory and the Theory of Cognitive Dissonance." *Personality and Social Psychology Bulletin* 16:274–283.

Bain, Reed. (1962). "The Most Important Sociologists?" *American Sociological Review* 27:746–748.

Barbaree, H.E., and W.L. Marshall. (1989). "Erectile Responses among Heterosexual Child Molesters, Father-Daughter Incest Offenders and Matched Nonoffenders: Five Distinct Age-Preference Profiles." *Canadian Journal of Behavioral Science* 21:70–82.

Beccaria, Cesare. (1764/1963). *On Crimes and Punishments*. Indianapolis, IN: Bobbs-Merrill.

Becker, Howard S. (1963). *Outsiders: Studies in the Sociology of Deviance*. New York: Free Press.

Berelson, Bernard. (1952). *Content Analysis in Communication Research*. Glencoe, IL: Free Press.

Blackburn, Richard S., and Michelle Mitchell. (1981). "Citation Analysis in the Organizational Sciences." *Journal of Applied Psychology* 66:337–342.

Blalock, Hubert M., Jr. (1972). *Social Statistics*. 2nd ed. New York: McGraw-Hill.

Blumstein, Alfred. (1994). "The Task Force on Science and Technology." In John A. Conley (ed.), *The 1967 President's Crime Commission Report: Its Impact 25 Years Later*, pp. 145–157. Cincinnati: ACJS/Anderson.

Blumstein, Alfred, Jacqueline Cohen, and David P. Farrington. (1988a). "Criminal Career Research: Its Value for Criminology." *Criminology* 26:1–35.

———. (1988b). "Longitudinal and Career Criminal Research: Further Clarifications." *Criminology* 26:57–74.

Blumstein, Alfred, Jacqueline Cohen, Susan E. Martin, and Michael H. Tonry, eds. (1983). *Research on Sentencing*. Washington, DC: National Academy Press.

Blumstein, Alfred, Jacqueline Cohen, Jeffrey A. Roth, and Christy A. Visher, eds. (1986). *Criminal Careers and "Career Criminals."* Washington, DC: National Academy Press.

Bollen, Kenneth A., and David P. Phillips. (1981). "Suicidal Motor Vehicle Fatalities in Detroit: A Replication." *American Journal of Sociology* 87:404–412.

Bott, David M., and Lowell L. Hargens. (1991). "Are Sociologists' Publications Uncited? Citation Rates of Journal Articles, Chapters, and Books." *The American Sociologist* 22:147–158.

Braithwaite, John. (1985). *To Punish or Persuade*. Albany, NY: State University of New York Press.

———. (1989). *Crime, Shame and Reintegration*. Cambridge: Cambridge University Press.

Budd, Richard W., Robert K. Thorp, and Lewis Donahew. (1967). *Content Analysis of Communications*. New York: Macmillan.

Buss, A.R. (1976). "Evaluation of Canadian Psychology Departments Based upon Citation and Publication Counts." *Canadian Psychological Review* 17:143–150.

Cano, V., and N.C. Lind. (1991). "Citation Life Cycles of Ten Citation Classics." *Scientometrics* 22:297–312.

Carney, Thomas F. (1979). *Content Analysis: A Technique for Systematic Inference from Communications*. Winnipeg, Canada: University of Manitoba Press.

Chapman, Antony J. (1989). "Assessing Research: Citation-Count Shortcomings." *The Psychologist* 8:336–344.

Christenson, James A., and Lee Sigelman. (1985). "Accrediting Knowledge: Journal Stature and Citation Impact in Social Science." *Social Science Quarterly* 66:964–975.

Cloward, Richard A., and Lloyd E. Ohlin. (1960). *Delinquency and Opportunity: A Theory of Delinquent Gangs*. New York: Free Press.

Cohen, Albert K. (1955). *Delinquent Boys: The Culture of the Gang*. New York: Free Press.

Cohen, Lawrence E., and Marcus Felson. (1979). "Social Change and Crime Rate Trends: A Routine Activity Approach." *American Sociological Review* 44: 588–607.

Cohen, Stanley. (1985). *Visions of Social Control: Crime, Punishment and Classification*. Cambridge: Polity.

Cohn, Ellen G., and David P. Farrington. (1990). "Differences Between British and American Criminology: An Analysis of Citations." *British Journal of Criminology* 30:467–482.

———. (1994a). "Who Are the Most Influential Criminologists in the English-Speaking World?" *British Journal of Criminology* 34:204–225.

———. (1994b). "Who Are the Most-Cited Scholars in Major American Criminology and Criminal Justice Journals?" *Journal of Criminal Justice* 22:517–534.

———. (1996). "*Crime and Justice* and the Criminology and Criminal Justice Literature." In Norval Morris and Michael Tonry (eds.), *Crime and Justice: A Review of Research*, vol. 20, pp. 265–300. Chicago: University of Chicago Press.

———. (1998a). "Changes in the Most-Cited Scholars in Major American Criminology and Criminal Justice Journals Between 1986–1990 and 1991–1995." *Journal of Criminal Justice* 26.

———. (1998b). "Changes in the Most-Cited Scholars in Major International Journals Between 1986–90 and 1991–95." *British Journal of Criminology* 38:156–170.

———. (1998c). "Assessing the Quality of American Doctoral Program Faculty in Criminology and Criminal Justice, 1991–95." *Journal of Criminal Justice Education* 9.

Cole, Jonathan R., and Stephen Cole. (1971). "Measuring the Quality of Sociological Research: Problems in the Use of the *Science Citation Index.*" *The American Sociologist* 6:23–29.

———. (1972). "The Ortega Hypothesis." *Science* 178 (27 Oct.):368–375.

———. (1973). *Social Stratification in Science.* Chicago: University of Chicago Press.

Cole, Stephen. (1975). "The Growth of Scientific Knowledge: Theories of Deviance as a Case Study." In Lewis A. Coser (ed.), *The Idea of Social Structure: Papers in Honor of Robert K. Merton*, pp. 175–220. New York: Harcourt Brace Jovanovich.

Conrad, John P., and Richard A. Myren. (1979). *Two Views of Criminology and Criminal Justice: Definitions, Trends, and the Future.* Chicago: Joint Commission on Criminology and Criminal Justice Standards and Goals.

Cornish, Derek, and Ronald V.G. Clarke, eds. (1986). *The Reasoning Criminal: Rational Choice Perspectives on Offending.* New York: Springer-Verlag.

———. (1987). "Understanding Crime Displacement: An Application of Rational Choice Theory." *Criminology* 25:933–947.

Courtney, John C., Karman B. Kawchuk, and Duff Spafford. (1987). "Life in Print: Citation of Articles Published in Volumes 1–10 of the *Canadian Journal of Political Science/Revue canadienne de science politique.*" *Canadian Journal of Political Science* 20:625–637.

Crawford, A., Trevor Jones, Tom Woodhouse, and Jock Young. (1990). *The Second Islington Crime Survey.* London: Middlesex Polytechnic, Centre for Criminology.

Cressey, Donald R. (1953). *Other People's Money.* New York: Free Press.

———. (1958). "The Nature and Effectiveness of Correctional Techniques." *Law and Contemporary Problems* 23:754–777.

———. (1959). "Contradictory Directives in Complex Organizations: The Case of the Prison." *Administrative Science Quarterly* 4:1–19.

———. (1960). "Limitations on Organization of Treatment in the Modern Prison." In Richard A. Cloward, Donald R. Cressey, George H. Grosser, Richard McCleary, Lloyd E. Ohlin, Gresham M. Sykes, and Sheldon L. Messinger (eds.) *Theoretical Studies in Social Organization of the Prison*, pp. 78–110. New York: Social Science Research Council.

———, ed. (1961). *The Prison.* New York: Holt, Rinehart, and Winston.

———. (1965). "Prison Organizations." In James G. March (ed.), *Handbook of Organizations*, pp. 1930–1932. Chicago: Rand McNally.

———. (1969). *Theft of the Nation.* New York: Harper and Row.

Cullen, Francis T., and Karen E. Gilbert. (1982). *Reaffirming Rehabilitation.* Cincinnati: Anderson.

Cullen, Francis T., Bruce G. Link, Nancy T. Wolf, and J. Frank. (1985). "The Social Dimensions of Correctional Officer Stress." *Justice Quarterly* 2:505–533.

DeLacey, Gerald, Carol Record, and Jenny Wade. (1985). "How Accurate are Quotations and References in Medical Journals?" *British Medical Journal* 291 (Sept. 28):884–886.

DeZee, Matthew R. (1980). *The Productivity of Criminology and Criminal Justice Faculty*. Chicago: Joint Commission on Criminology and Criminal Justice Education and Standards.

Diamond, Arthur M., Jr. (1986). "What is a Citation Worth?" *Journal of Human Resources* 21:200–215.

Doerner, William G., Matthew R. DeZee, and Steven P. Lab. (1982). "Responding to the 'Call for Papers.'" *Criminology* 19:650–658.

Doob, Anthony N. (1992). "Trends in the Use of Custodial Dispositions for Young Offenders." *Canadian Journal of Criminology* 34:75–84.

Doob, Anthony N., and Julian V. Roberts. (1983). *Sentencing: An Analysis of the Public's View*. Ottawa: Department of Justice.

Douglas, Robert J. (1992). "How to Write a Highly Cited Article Without Even Trying." *Psychological Bulletin* 112:405–408.

Elliott, Delbert S., David Huizinga, and Suzanne S. Ageton. (1985). *Explaining Delinquency and Drug Use*. Beverly Hills, CA: Sage.

Endler, Norman S. (1977). "Research Productivity and Scholarly Impact of Canadian Psychology Departments." *Canadian Psychological Review* 18:152–168.

Endler, Norman S., J. Phillipe Rushton, and H.L. Roediger, III. (1978). "Productivity and Scholarly Impact (Citations) of British, Canadian, and US Departments of Psychology (1975)." *American Psychologist* 33:1064–1083.

Fabianic, David A. (1979). "Relative Prestige of Criminal Justice Doctoral Programs." *Journal of Criminal Justice* 7:135–145.

———. (1980). "Perceived Scholarship and Readership of Criminal Justice Journals." *Journal of Police Science and Administration* 8:15–20.

Farrington, David P. (1986). "Age and Crime." In Michael Tonry and Norval Morris (eds.), *Crime and Justice: A Review of Research*, vol. 7, pp. 189–250. Chicago: University of Chicago Press.

Farrington, David P., Lloyd E. Ohlin, and James Q. Wilson. (1986). *Understanding and Controlling Crime: Toward a New Research Strategy*. New York: Springer-Verlag.

Felkenes, George T. (1980). *The Criminal Justice Doctorate: A Study of Doctoral Programs in the United States*. Chicago: Joint Commission on Criminology and Criminal Justice Education and Standards.

Ferber, Marianne A. (1986). "Citations: Are They an Objective Measure of Scholarly Merit?" *Journal of Women in Culture and Society* 11:381–389.

Foucault, Michel. (1977). *Discipline and Punish: The Birth of the Prison*. New York: Pantheon.

Fox, Richard G., and Arie Freiberg. (1985). *Sentencing: State and Federal Law in Victoria*. Melbourne: Oxford University Press.

Garfield, Eugene. (1977a). "The 250 Most-Cited Primary Authors, 1961–1975. Part I. How the Names Were Selected." *Current Contents* 77(49):5–15.

———. (1977b). "The 250 Most-Cited Primary Authors, 1961–1975. Part II. The Correlation Between Citedness, Nobel Prizes and Academy Memberships." *Current Contents* 77(50):5–15.

———. (1977c). "The 250 Most-Cited Primary Authors, 1961–1975. Part III. Each Author's Most-Cited Publication." *Current Contents* 77(51):5–20.

———. (1977d). "A List of 100 Most Cited (Chemical) Articles. *Current Contents* 10:5–12.

———. (1979). "Is Citation Analysis a Legitimate Evaluation Tool?" *Scientometrics* 1:359–375.

Garfield, Eugene, and Alfred Welljams-Dorof. (1990). "Language Use in International Research: A Citation Analysis." *Annals of the American Academy of Political and Social Science* 511:10–24.

Geis, Gilbert, and Robert F. Meier. (1978). "Looking Backward and Forward: Criminologists on Criminology as a Career." *Criminology* 16:273–288.

Gilbert, G. Nigel. (1977). "Referencing as Persuasion." *Social Studies of Science* 7:113–122.

Glenn, Norval. (1971). "American Sociologists' Evaluations of Sixty-Three Journals." *The American Sociologist* 6:298–303.

Goffman, Erving. (1961). *Asylums: Essays on the Social Situation of Mental Patients and Other Inmates*. Garden City, NY: Anchor.

Goodrich, June E., and Charles G. Roland. (1977). "Accuracy of Published Medical Reference Citations." *Journal of Technical Writing and Communication* 7:15–19.

Gordon, Randall A., and Pamela J. Vicari. (1992). "Eminence in Social Psychology: A Comparison of Textbook Citation, Social Sciences Citation Index, and Research Productivity Rankings." *Personality and Social Psychology Bulletin* 18:26–38.

Gorenflo, Daniel W., and James V. McConnell. (1991). "The Most Frequently Cited Journal Articles and Authors in Introductory Psychology Textbooks." *Teaching of Psychology* 18:8–12.

Goring, Charles. (1913). *The English Convict: A Statistical Study*. London: His Majesty's Stationery Office.

Gottfredson, Michael R., and Don R. Gottfredson. (1980/1988). *Decisionmaking in Criminal Justice: Toward the Rational Exercise of Discretion*. Cambridge, MA: Ballinger.

Gottfredson, Michael R., and Travis Hirschi. (1986). "The True Value of Lambda Would Appear to be Zero: An Essay on Career Criminals, Criminal Careers, Selective Incapacitation, Cohort Studies, and Related Topics." *Criminology* 24:213–234.

———. (1990). *A General Theory of Crime*. Stanford, CA: Stanford University Press.

Grabosky, Peter, and John Braithwaite. (1986). *Of Manners Gentle: Enforcement Strategies of Australian Business Regulatory Agencies*. Melbourne: Oxford University Press.

Greene, Jack R., Timothy S. Bynum, and Vincent J. Webb. (1984). "Patterns of Entry, Professional Identity, and Attitudes Toward Crime-Related Education: A Study of Criminal Justice and Criminology Faculty." *Journal of Criminal Justice* 12:39–59.

———. (1985). "Paradigm Development in Crime-Related Education: The Role of the Significant Others." *Criminal Justice Review* 10:7–17.

Hagan, John L. (1974). "Extra-Legal Attributes and Criminal Sentencing: An Assessment of a Sociological Viewpoint." *Law and Society Review* 8:357–381.

Hagan, John L., A.R. Gillis, and J. Simpson. (1987). "Class in the Household: A Power-Control Theory of Gender and Delinquency." *American Journal of Sociology* 92:788–816.

Hamermesh, Daniel S., George E. Johnson, and Burton A. Weisbrod. (1982). "Scholarship, Citations and Salaries: Economic Reward in Economics." *Southern Economics Journal* 49:472–481.

Hindelang, Michael J., Travis Hirschi, and Joseph G. Weis. (1981). *Measuring Delinquency*. Beverly Hills, CA: Sage.

Hirschi, Travis. (1969). *Causes of Delinquency*. Berkeley: University of California Press.

Hirschi, Travis, and Michael R. Gottfredson. (1983). "Age and the Explanation of Crime." *American Journal of Sociology* 89:552–584.

Holmes, Malcolm D., and William A. Taggart. (1990). "A Comparative Analysis of Research in Criminology and Criminal Justice Journals." *Justice Quarterly* 7:421–437.

Hough, J. Michael, and Patricia M. Mayhew. (1983). *The British Crime Survey: First Report*. London: Home Office.

———. (1985). *Taking Account of Crime: Key Findings from the 1984 British Crime Survey*. London: Her Majesty's Stationery Office.

Irwin, John, and Donald R. Cressey. (1962). "Thieves, Convicts and the Inmate Culture." *Social Problems* 10:142–155.

Jones, Trevor, Brian MacLean, and Jock Young. (1986). *The Islington Crime Survey: Crime, Victimization and Policing in Inner City London*. Aldershot: Gower.

Langworthy, Robert, and Edward Latessa. (1989). "Criminal Justice Education: A National Assessment." *The Justice Professional* 4:172–188.

Lenton, R.L. (1995). "Power Versus Feminist Theories of Wife Abuse." *Canadian Journal of Criminology* 38:305–330.

Lindsey, Duncan. (1980). "Production and Citation Measures in the Sociology of Science: The Problem of Multiple Authorship." *Social Studies of Science* 10:145–162.

Logan, Elisabeth L., and W.M. Shaw, Jr. (1991). "A Bibliometric Analysis of Collaboration in a Medical Speciality." *Scientometrics* 20:417–426.

Long, J. Scott, Robert McGinnis, and Paul D. Allison. (1980). "The Problem of Junior-Authored Papers in Constructing Citation Counts." *Social Studies of Science* 10:127–143.

Lotz, Roy, and Robert M. Regoli. (1977). "Police Cynicism and Professionalism." *Human Relations* 30:175–186.

Marenin, Otwin. (1993). "Faculty Productivity in Criminal Justice Ph.D. Programs: Another View." *Journal of Criminal Justice Education* 4:189–192.

Marshall, William L., and Howard E. Barbaree. (1988). "The Long-Term Evaluation of a Behavioral Treatment Program for Child Molesters." *Behaviour Research and Therapy* 26:499–511.

Mayhew, Patricia M., David Elliott, and Liz Anne Dowds. (1989). *The 1988 British Crime Survey*. London: Her Majesty's Stationery Office.

McElrath, Karen. (1990). "Standing in the Shadows: Academic Mentoring in Criminology." *Journal of Criminal Justice Education* 1:135–151.

Meadows, A.J. (1974). *Communication in Science*. London: Butterworths.

Megargee, Edwin I., and Martin J. Bohn. (1979). *Classifying Criminal Offenders: A New System Based on the MMPI*. Beverly Hills, CA: Sage.

Merton, Robert K. (1938). "Social Structure and Anomie." *American Sociological Review* 3:672–682.

Mijares, Tomas, and Robert Blackburn. (1990). "Evaluating Criminal Justice Programs: Establishing Criteria." *Journal of Criminal Justice* 18:33–41.

Morn, Frank T. (1980). *Academic Disciplines and Debates: An Essay on Criminal Justice and Criminology as Professions in Higher Education*. Chicago: Joint Commission on Criminology and Criminal Justice Education and Standards.

Mullens, Nicholas C., Lowell L. Hargens, Pamela K. Hecht, and Edward L. Kick. (1977). "The Group Structure of Co-Citation Clusters: A Comparative Study." *American Sociological Review* 42:552–562.

Myers, C.R. (1970). "Journal Citations and Scientific Eminence in Contemporary Psychology." *American Psychologist* 25:1041–1048.

Nagin, Daniel S., and Douglas A. Smith. (1990). "Participation in and Frequency of Delinquent Behavior: A Test For Structural Differences." *Journal of Quantitative Criminology* 6:335–356.

North, Robert C., Ole Holsti, M. George Zaninovich, and Dina A. Zinnes. (1963). *Content Analysis: A Handbook with Applications for the Study of International Crisis.* Evanston, IL: Northwestern University Press.

Oromaner, Mark J. (1968). "The Most-Cited Sociologists: An Analysis of Introductory Text Citations." *The American Sociologist* 3:124–126.

Pardeck, John T., Beverly J. Arndt, Dionna B. Light, Gladys F. Mosley, Stacy D. Thomas, Mary A. Werner, and Kathryn E. Wilson. (1991). "Distinction and Achievement Levels of Editorial Board Members of Psychology and Social Work Journals." *Psychological Reports* 68:523–527.

Parker, L. Craig, Jr., and Eileen Goldfeder. (1979). "Productivity Ratings of Graduate Programs in Criminal Justice Based on Publication in Ten Critical Journals." *Journal of Criminal Justice* 7:125–133.

Pearson, Richard, Theodore K. Moran, James C. Berger, Kenneth C. Landon, Janice R. McKenzie, and Thomas J. Bonita III. (1980). *Criminal Justice Education: The End of the Beginning.* New York: John Jay Press.

Peritz, B.C. (1983). "Are Methodological Papers More Cited than Theoretical or Empirical Ones? The Case of Sociology." *Scientometrics* 5:211–218.

Petersilia, Joan. (1980). "Criminal Career Research: A Review of Recent Evidence." In Norval Morris and Michael Tonry (eds.), *Crime and Justice: A Review of Research*, vol. 2, pp. 321–379. Chicago: University of Chicago Press.

Petersilia, Joan, Susan Turner, J. Kahan, and J. Peterson. (1985). *Granting Felons Probation: Public Risks and Alternatives.* Santa Monica, CA: Rand Corporation.

Phillips, David P. (1979). "Suicide, Motor Vehicle Fatalities, and the Mass Media: Evidence Toward a Theory of Suggestion." *American Journal of Sociology* 84:1150–1174.

———. (1980). "The Deterrent Effect of Capital Punishment: New Evidence on an Old Controversy." *American Journal of Sociology* 86:139–148.

Poole, Eric D., and Robert M. Regoli. (1981). "Periodical Prestige in Criminology and Criminal Justice: A Comment." *Criminology* 19:470–478.

Poyer, Robert K. (1979). "Inaccurate References in Significant Journals of Science." *Bulletin of the Medical Library Association* 67:396–398.

Regoli, Robert M., Eric D. Poole, and Andrew W. Miracle, Jr. (1982). "Assessing the Prestige of Journals in Criminal Justice: A Research Note." *Journal of Criminal Justice* 10:57–67.

Richards, J.M., Jr. (1991). "Years Cited: An Alternative Measure of Scientific Accomplishment." *Scientometrics* 20:427–438.

Roche, Thomas, and David Lewis Smith. (1978). "Frequency of Citations as Criterion for the Ranking of Departments, Journals, and Individuals." *Sociological Inquiry* 48:49–57.

Rosenberg, Milton J. (1979). "The Elusiveness of Eminence." *American Psychologist* 34:723–725.

Rosett, Arthur, and Donald R. Cressey. (1976). *Justice by Consent.* Philadelphia: Lippincott.

Rushton, J. Philippe. (1984). "Evaluating Research Eminence in Psychology: The Construct Validity of Citation Counts." *Bulletin of The British Psychological Society* 37:33–36.

Rushton, J. Philippe, and Norman S. Endler. (1977). "The Scholarly Impact and Research Productivity of Departments of Psychology in the United Kingdom." *Bulletin of the British Psychological Society* 30:369–373.

————. (1979). "More To-Do About Citation Counts in British Psychology." *Bulletin of the British Psychological Society* 32:107–109.

Rushton, J. Philippe, Christine H. Littlefield, Robin J.H. Russell, and Sari J. Meltzer. (1983). "Research Production and Scholarly Impact in British Universities and Departments of Psychology: An Update." *Bulletin of the British Psychological Society* 36:41–44.

Sampson, Robert J. (1987). "Urban Black Violence: The Effect of Male Joblessness and Family Disruption." *American Journal of Sociology* 93: 348–382.

Sampson, Robert J., and John H. Laub. (1993). *Crime in the Making: Pathways and Turning Points Through Life.* Cambridge, MA: Harvard University Press.

Sellin, Thorsten J. (1938). *Culture Conflict and Crime.* New York: Social Science Research Council.

Sellin, Thorsten J., and Marvin E. Wolfgang. (1964). *The Measurement of Delinquency.* New York: Wiley.

Sherman, Lawrence W. (1978). *The Quality of Police Education: A Critical Review with Recommendations for Improving Programs in Higher Education.* San Francisco: Jossey-Bass.

————. (1992). *Policing Domestic Violence: Experiments and Dilemmas.* New York: The Free Press.

Sherman, Lawrence W., and Richard A. Berk. (1984). "The Specific Deterrent Effects of Arrest For Domestic Assault." *American Sociological Review* 49: 261–272.

Sherman, Lawrence W., Patrick R. Gartin, and Michael E. Buerger. (1989). "Hot Spots of Predatory Crime: Routine Activities and the Criminology of Place." *Criminology* 27:27–55.

Shichor, David. (1982). "An Analysis of Citations in Introductory Criminology Textbooks: A Research Note." *Journal of Criminal Justice* 10:231–237.

————. (1983). "Citations in Introductory Criminology Textbooks: A Response to Allen's Comment." *Journal of Criminal Justice* 11:179.

Shichor, David, Robert M. O'Brien, and David L. Decker. (1981). "Prestige of Journals in Criminology and Criminal Justice." *Criminology* 19:461–469.

Smith, Adrian. (1989). "Citation Counting." *Association of University Teachers Bulletin* Jan.:5.

Smith, Douglas A., Christy A. Visher, and Roger Jarjoura. (1991). "Dimensions of Delinquency: Estimating the Correlates of Participation, Frequency, and Persistence of Delinquent Behavior." *Journal of Research in Crime and Delinquency* 28: 6–32.

Sorensen, Jonathan R., Amy L. Patterson, and Alan Widmayer. (1992). "Publication Productivity of Faculty Members in Criminology and Criminal Justice Doctoral Programs." *Journal of Criminal Justice Education* 3:1–33.

————. (1993). "Measuring Faculty Productivity in a Multidisciplinary Field: A Response to Professor Marenin." *Journal of Criminal Justice Education* 4:193–196.

Sorensen, Jonathan R., Alan G. Widmayer, and Frank R. Scarpitti. (1994). "Examining the Criminal Justice and Criminological Paradigms: An Analysis of ACJS and ASC Members." *Journal of Criminal Justice Education* 5:149–166.

Stack, Steven. (1987a). "Measuring the Relative Impacts of Criminology and Criminal Justice Journals: A Research Note." *Justice Quarterly* 4:475–484.

————. (1987b). "Publicized Executions and Homicide, 1950-1980." *American Sociological Review* 52: 532–540.

Straus, Murray A., and Richard J. Gelles. (1986). "Societal Change and Change in Family Violence from 1975 to 1985 as Revealed by Two National Surveys." *Journal of Marriage and the Family* 48:465–479.

Straus, Murray A., Richard J. Gelles, and Susan Steinmetz. (1980). *Behind Closed Doors: Violence in the American Family.* New York: Doubleday.

Sutherland, Edwin H. (1934). *Principles of Criminology.* 2nd ed. Philadelphia: Lippincott.

———. (1937). *The Professional Thief.* Chicago: University of Chicago Press.

———. (1939). *Principles of Criminology.* 3rd ed. Philadelphia: Lippincott.

———. (1947). *Principles of Criminology.* 4th ed. Philadelphia: Lippincott.

———. (1949). *White Collar Crime.* New York: Dryden.

Sutherland, Edwin H., and Donald R. Cressey. (1955). *Principles of Criminology.* 5th ed. Philadelphia: Lippincott.

———. (1960). *Principles of Criminology.* 6th ed. Philadelphia: Lippincott.

———. (1966). *Principles of Criminology.* 7th ed. Philadelphia: Lippincott.

Sweetland, James H. (1989). "Errors in Bibliographic Citations: A Continuing Problem." *The Library Quarterly* 59:291–304.

Sykes, Gresham M. (1958). *The Society of Captives: A Study of a Maximum Security Prison.* Princeton, NJ: Princeton University Press.

Sykes, Gresham M., and Francis T. Cullen. (1992). *Criminology.* 2nd ed. Fort Worth, TX: Harcourt Brace Jovanovich.

Sykes, Gresham M., and David Matza. (1957). "Techniques of Neutralization: A Theory of Delinquency." *American Sociological Review* 22:664–670.

Taylor, Ian, Paul Walton, and Jock Young. (1973). *The New Criminology: For a Social Theory of Deviance.* London: Routledge and Kegan Paul.

Thomas, Charles W. (1987). "The Utility of Citation-Based Quality Assessments." *Journal of Criminal Justice* 15:165–171.

Thomas, Charles W., and Matthew J. Bronick. (1984). "The Quality of Doctoral Programs in Deviance, Criminology, and Criminal Justice: An Empirical Assessment." *Journal of Criminal Justice* 12:21–37.

Tracy, Paul E., Marvin E. Wolfgang, and Robert M. Figlio. (1990). *Delinquency Careers in Two Birth Cohorts.* New York: Plenum.

Travis, Lawrence F., III. (1987). "Assessing the Quality of Doctoral Programs in Deviance, Criminology, and Criminal Justice: A Response to Thomas and Bronick." *Journal of Criminal Justice* 15:157–163.

Vaughn, Michael, and Rolando V. del Carmen. (1992). "An Annotated List of Journals in Criminal Justice and Criminology: A Guide for Authors." *Journal of Criminal Justice Education* 3:93–142.

Ward, Richard H., and Vincent J. Webb. (1984). *Quest for Quality.* New York: University Publications.

Weber, Max. (1922/1978). *Economy and Society: An Outline of Interpretive Sociology.* Berkeley: University of California Press.

Weisheit, Ralph A., and Robert M. Regoli. (1984). "Ranking Journals." *Scholarly Publishing* 15:313–325.

West, Donald J., and David P. Farrington. (1973). *Who Becomes Delinquent?* London: Heinemann.

Williams, Frank P., Marilyn D. McShane, and Carl P. Wagoner. (1992). "The Relative Prestige of Criminal Justice and Criminology Journals." Paper presented at the Annual Meeting of the American Society of Criminology, New Orleans, LA.

————. (1995). "Differences in Assessments of Relative Prestige and Utility of Criminal Justice and Criminology Journals." *American Journal of Criminal Justice* 19:301–324.

Wilson, James Q. (1968). *Varieties of Police Behavior*. Cambridge, MA: Harvard University Press.

————. (1975/1983). *Thinking About Crime*. New York: Vintage.

Wilson, James Q., and Richard J. Herrnstein. (1985). *Crime and Human Nature*. New York: Simon and Schuster.

Wolfgang, Marvin E. (1958). *Patterns in Criminal Homicide*. New York: Wiley.

Wolfgang, Marvin E., and Franco Ferracuti. (1967). *The Subculture of Violence*. New York: Barnes and Noble.

Wolfgang, Marvin E., Robert M. Figlio, and Thorsten Sellin. (1972). *Delinquency in a Birth Cohort*. Chicago: University of Chicago Press.

Wolfgang, Marvin E., Robert M. Figlio, and Terence P. Thornberry. (1978). *Evaluating Criminology*. New York: Elsevier.

Wolfgang, Marvin E., Robert M. Figlio, Paul E. Tracy, and Simon I. Singer. (1985). *The National Survey of Crime Severity*. Washington, DC: Bureau of Justice Statistics.

Wolfgang, Marvin E., Terence P. Thornberry, and Robert M. Figlio. (1987). *From Boy to Man, from Delinquency to Crime*. Chicago: University of Chicago Press.

Wright, Richard A. (1987). "Are 'Sisters in Crime' Finally Being Booked? The Coverage of Women and Crime in Journals and Textbooks." *Teaching Sociology* 15:418–422.

————. (1988). *"Victim" and "Resister" Conceptualizations of Oppression: An Assessment Through a Content Analysis of the Depiction of Women in Criminology Textbooks*. Ph.D. Dissertation, Department of Sociology, Kansas State University, Manhattan.

————. (1992). "From Vamps and Tramps to Teases and Flirts: Stereotypes of Women in Criminology Textbooks, 1956 to 1965 and 1981 to 1990." *Journal of Criminal Justice Education* 3:223–236.

————. (1993). "The Two Criminologies: The Divergent Worldviews of Textbooks and Journals." *The Criminologist* 18(3):1, 8, 10.

————. (1994a). "Criminology Textbooks, 1918 to 1993. A Comprehensive Bibliography." *Journal of Criminal Justice Education* 5:251–256.

————. (1994b). "Stopped for Questioning, But Not Booked: The Coverage of Career Criminals in Criminology Journals and Textbooks, 1983 to 1992." *Journal of Criminal Justice Education* 5:205–215.

————. (1995a). "The Most-Cited Scholars in Criminology: A Comparison of Textbooks and Journals." *Journal of Criminal Justice* 23:303–311.

————. (1995b). "Was There a 'Golden Past' for the Introductory Sociology Textbook? A Citation Analysis of Leading Journals." *The American Sociologist* 26:41–48.

————. (1995c). "Rehabilitation Affirmed, Rejected, and Reaffirmed: Assessments of the Effectiveness of Offender Treatment Programs in Criminology Textbooks, 1956 to 1965 and 1983 to 1992." *Journal of Criminal Justice Education* 6:21–39.

————. (1995d). "Where There's a Will, There's No Way: The Treatment of the Choice Debate in Criminology Textbooks, 1956 to 1965 and 1983 to 1992." *Teaching Sociology* 23:8–15.

————. (1995e). "Women as 'Victims' and as 'Resisters': Depictions of the Oppression of Women in Criminology Textbooks." *Teaching Sociology* 23:111–121.

———. (1996a). "Do Introductory Criminology Textbooks Cite the Most Influential Criminologists? Estimating the 'Match' Between What Journals Report and What Textbooks Discuss." *American Journal of Criminal Justice* 20:225–236.

———. (1996b) "The Missing or Misperceived Effects of Punishment: The Coverage of Deterrence in Criminology Textbooks, 1956 to 1965 and 1984 to 1993." *Journal of Criminal Justice Education* 7:1–22.

———. (1997). "Do Introductory Criminal Justice Textbooks Cite the Most Influential Criminal Justicians? Further Estimations of the 'Match' Between What Journals Report and What Textbooks Discuss." *Journal of Criminal Justice Education* 8:81–90.

———. (1998). "From Luminary to Lesser-Known: The Declining Influence of Criminology Textbook Authors on Scholarship." *Journal of Criminal Justice Education* 9:104–115

Wright, Richard A., and Kelly Carroll. (1994). "From Vanguard to Vanished: The Declining Influence of Criminology Textbooks on Scholarship." *Journal of Criminal Justice* 22:559–567.

Wright, Richard A., and Ellen G. Cohn. (1996). "The Most-Cited Scholars in Criminal Justice Textbooks, 1989 to 1993." *Journal of Criminal Justice* 24:459–467

Wright, Richard A., and David O. Friedrichs. (1991). "White-Collar Crime in the Criminal Justice Curriculum." *Journal of Criminal Justice Education* 2:95–121.

Wright, Richard A., and Joseph W. Rogers. (1996). "An Introduction to Teaching Criminology: Resources and Issues." In Richard A. Wright (ed.), *Teaching Criminology: Resources and Issues*, pp. 1–33. Washington, DC: American Sociological Association.

Wright, Richard A., and Colette Soma. (1995). "The Declining Influence of Dissertations on Sociological Research." *American Sociological Association Footnotes* 23(1):8.

———. (1996). "The Most-Cited Scholars in Criminology Textbooks, 1963 to 1968, 1976 to 1980, and 1989 to 1993." *Journal of Crime and Justice* 19:45–60.

Yochelson, Samuel, and Stanton E. Samenow. (1976). *The Criminal Personality*, Vol. 1. New York: Aronson.

———. (1977). *The Criminal Personality*, Vol. 2. New York: Aronson.

Yoels, William C. (1973). "The Fate of the Ph.D. Dissertation in Sociology: An Empirical Examination." *The American Sociologist* 8:87–89.

Zalman, Marvin. (1981). *A Heuristic Model of Criminology and Criminal Justice*. Chicago: Joint Commission on Criminology and Criminal Justice Education and Standards.

Index

Abel, Gene G., 39, 41, 50, 69, 73, 78, 83, 120

Abrahamsen, David, 83

Academy of Criminal Justice Sciences, 114-16, 121, 122 nn.1, 2

Adler, Freda, 107

"Age and Crime" (Farrington), 48

"Age and the Explanation of Crime" (Hirschi and Gottfredson), 29-30

Ageton, Suzanne S., 14, 28, 30, 32, 34, 35, 41, 42, 49, 52, 83, 101 n.1, 107, 119

AHCI (Arts and Humanities Citation Index), 2

Akers, Ronald L., 28, 31, 32, 34, 35, 41, 49, 52, 83, 84, 88, 90 n.8, 101 n.1, 107, 109, 117, 118, 119, 120

Alder, Christine, 47

Allen, Harry E., 14, 69, 84, 101 n.1, 117, 118

Allen, Judith, 47

Allison, Paul D., 5

Alpert, Geoffrey P., 37

American Journal of Criminal Justice, 96, 97

American Journal of Sociology, 12, 13, 101 n.4, 102 n.9, 114

American Psychological Association, 2, 10

American Society of Criminology, xii, 114-16, 121, 122 nn.1, 2

American Sociological Review, 12, 13, 101 n.4, 102 n.9, 114

American University, 19

Amir, Menachem, 108

Andrews, Don A., 38, 39, 41, 45, 50, 83, 120

Anslinger, Harry J., 83

Arizona State University, 19

Asylums (Goffman), 24

Australian and New Zealand Journal of Criminology (ANZ), 16-17, 23-24, 46, 48, 51, 57, 58, 62, 66, 68, 69, 72, 97

Ausubel, David P., 83

Bachman, Jerald G., 32

Bagby, R. Michael, 10

Bailey, William C., 69, 71

Bala, Nicholas, 45, 48

Baldwin, John, 44

Barbaree, Howard E., 39, 40, 41, 50, 83, 120

Baril, Micheline, 69, 72, 74, 77, 78

Barnes, Harry E., 83

Barron, Milton L., 83

Bayley, David H., 38, 45, 84, 101 n.1, 117, 118

Beaulieu, Lucien A., 45

Beccaria, Cesare, 106, 108, 110, 112 n.8

Becker, Howard S., 83, 107, 108, 110

Becker, Judith V., 38, 39, 40, 41, 50, 69,
    70, 73, 75, 77, 78, 83, 120
Bennett, Trevor H., 44
Bentham, Jeremy, 106, 108, 110, 112 n.8
Bentler, Peter M., 52
Berk, Richard A., 14, 30, 32, 34, 35, 37,
    51, 76, 101 n.1, 119, 120
Bernard, Thomas J., 84, 101 n.1, 107, 109,
    117, 118
Bersten, Michael, 47
Biderman, Albert D., 83
Biles, David, 46, 48
Bittner, Egon, 44
Black, Donald J., 29
Blackburn, Richard S., 9, 65
Blackburn, Robert, 3
Bloch, Herbert A., 83
Block, Alan A., 108
Blumstein, Alfred, 17, 23, 24, 28, 30, 32,
    34, 35, 37, 40, 41, 42, 43, 45, 48, 49,
    51, 61, 67, 69, 70, 71, 72, 73, 74, 75,
    76, 78, 79, 83, 101 n.1, 119, 120
Bohn, Martin J., 38
Boland, Barbara, 84, 101 n.1, 118
Bonger, Willem A., 107
Bonta, James L., 39, 50, 83
Bott, David M., 11
Bottoms, Anthony E., 43, 47, 48, 69, 72,
    74, 77
Bowling Green University, 19
Box, Steven, 43
Braithwaite, John, 29, 33, 43, 46, 47, 48,
    49, 51, 52, 69, 71, 72, 74, 77, 78, 79,
    83, 84, 88, 90 n.8, 101 n.1, 107, 109,
    118
Brissot, Jacques-Pierre, 38
British Crime Survey (Hough and May-
    hew), 43
British Journal of Criminology (BJC), 16,
    23-24, 42-43, 48, 51, 52 n.1, 53 n.13,
    55-56, 57, 58, 61, 62, 66, 68, 69, 72, 97,
    99
Broadhurst, Roderic G., 47
Brogden, Michael, 47
Bronick, Matthew J., 18-19
Brown, David, 47, 69, 72, 77
Bursik, Robert J., 28, 32, 34, 120
Bury, Alison S., 10
Bynum, Timothy S., 115

Cain, M., 69
Cameron, Mary Owen, 108
Canadian Journal of Criminology (CJC),
    16, 23-24, 44-45, 48, 51, 53 nn.13, 14,
    57, 58, 62, 66, 68, 69, 72, 97, 99
Canadian Journal of Political Sci-
    ence/Revue canadienne de science poli-
    tique (CJPS/Rcsp), 10
Cano, V., 11
Caplan, Aaron, 45
Carlen, Pat, 44
Carroll, J.S., 69
Carroll, Kelly, 15
Carson, W.G., 69
Carter, Robert M., 69, 71, 75, 76
Causes of Delinquency (Hirschi), 29, 30,
    31, 33, 40, 52
Cavan, Ruth Shonle, 83
Chaiken, Jan M., 31
Chaiken, Marcia R., 108
Chambliss, William J., 84, 90 n.9, 101 n.1,
    106, 109, 118
Chan, Janet, 47
Chaplin, Terry C., 39
Chapman, Antony J., 4, 6, 7, 8
Chappell, Duncan, 47
Chein, Isidor, 83
Chesney-Lind, Meda, 35, 69
Chiricos, Theodore G., 29, 31-32
Christenson, James A., 1
Cicchetti, Dante V., 39, 41, 50, 83, 120
Citation: careers, 17, 123; classics, 11, 12;
    frequency, 2, 9, 11, 24, 26, 29, 36, 44,
    104; prevalence, 24, 29, 30, 35, 36, 38,
    43, 44, 46, 50, 51; reliability, 3-4; sex
    discrimination in, 10; social factors
    influencing, 8; studies (see Journals,
    ranking of); validity, 3-4, 104
Citations in: biochemistry, 1, 5, 11; chem-
    istry, 7; economics, 1; medicine, 1, 5,
    11; organizational science, 1, 9, 63;
    physics, 1; population, 9, 10; psychol-
    ogy, 1, 3, 7, 9, 11-13; social psychology,
    9, 10, 12; social work, 11-12; sociology,
    1, 7, 9, 11, 12-13, 14, 15, 18-19
Clarke, Ronald V. G., 29, 32, 34, 45, 48,
    51, 69, 71, 72, 73, 74, 75, 76, 77, 78, 79
"Class in the Household: A Power-Control
    Theory of Gender and Delinquency"
    (Hagan, Gillis, and Simpson), 41

Classifying Criminal Offenders (Megargee and Bohn), 38

Clear, Todd R., 36, 57, 69, 70, 71, 75, 76, 78, 84, 101 n.1, 117, 118

Cleckley, Hervey M., 197

Clifford, William, 69, 73

Clinard, Marshall B., 14, 47, 69, 72, 77, 83, 84, 88, 90 nn.6, 9, 10, 101 n.1, 106, 109, 118

Cloward, Richard A., 7, 29, 32, 83, 84, 88, 89 n.5, 90 nn.6, 7, 9, 10, 101 n.1, 106, 109, 118, 119

Coauthor citation, 27, 124

Co-citation analysis, 1, 2

Cohen, Albert K., 7, 14, 32, 83, 84, 89 n.5, 90 nn.6, 7, 9, 10, 101 n.1, 106, 109, 118

Cohen, Jacob, 39

Cohen, Jacqueline, 14, 28, 30, 32, 34, 35, 37, 41, 42, 44, 49, 51, 61, 69, 70, 73, 74, 75, 76, 78, 79, 83, 101 n.1, 119, 120

Cohen, Lawrence E., 28, 30, 32, 34, 35, 37, 41, 49, 51, 69, 70, 74, 76, 78, 83, 101 n.1, 107, 119, 120

Cohen, Stanley, 43, 46, 47, 48, 51, 52, 69, 72, 74, 77

Cohn, Ellen G., 2, 4, 6, 7, 8, 14, 15, 16-18, 20, 23, 24, 26, 27, 55-56, 65-66, 73, 81, 82, 83-84, 85, 94-95, 104, 111, 116-117, 118, 119, 120

Cole, Jonathan R., 2, 4, 6-7

Cole, Stephen, 2, 4, 6-7

Complementarity. *See* Criminology and criminal justice, relations between

Composite. *See* Journals, ranking of

Conklin, John E., 108

Contemporary Crises (CC), 66, 68, 69, 72. *See also Crime, Law and Social Change*

Content analysis, 23, 103, 111. *See also* Latent content analysis; Manifest content analysis

Convergence. *See* Criminology and criminal justice, relations between

Cook, Philip J., 30

Corns, Chris, 47

Corrado, Raymond R., 45, 48

Courtney, John C., 6, 10

Cressey, Donald R., 14, 33, 38, 51, 83, 84, 87, 88, 89 n.5, 90 nn.6, 7, 9, 10, 101 n.1, 106, 109, 118, 119, 120, 122 n.6

Crime and Delinquency (CD), 25-27, 66, 67, 71, 96, 97, 99

Crime and Human Nature (Wilson and Herrnstein), 23, 42

Crime and Justice: A Review of Research (CJ), 17, 24, 66, 68, 69, 73, 101 n.2, 102 n.9

Crime in the Making (Sampson and Laub), 33, 41

Crime, Law and Social Change, 52 n.2, 66, 97, 99. *See also Contemporary Crises*

Crime, Shame and Reintegration (Braithwaite), 48

"Criminal Career Research: A Review of Recent Evidence" (Petersilia), 42

"Criminal Career Research: Its Value for Criminology" (Blumstein, Cohen, and Farrington), 30, 33, 42

Criminal Careers and "Career Criminals" (Blumstein et al.), 23, 24, 42

Criminal Justice and Behavior (CJB), 23-26, 38-39, 40, 41, 50-51, 56-61, 62, 66, 68, 69, 73, 95, 98, 99, 114, 117

Criminal Justice Ethics, 96, 97

Criminal Justice History, 66, 101 n.2

Criminal Justice Policy Review, 96, 97

Criminal Justice Review (CJR), 25-26, 66, 68, 69, 71, 98

Criminologie (CRGE), 66, 68, 69, 71

Criminology (CRIM), 15-16, 17, 23-26, 28-29, 33, 34, 50, 53 n.11, 55-56, 57-58, 61, 62, 65, 68, 69, 70, 92-93, 95, 96-97, 99, 114-16, 121, 122 n.1

Criminology (Sykes and Cullen), 87

Criminology and criminal justice, relations between: complementarity, 113-14, 116-19, 121; convergence, 23, 113, 115-19, 121, 122 n.5; divergence, 23, 113, 115-19, 121

Crittenden, Patricia M., 39

Cross-pollination index, 9

Culbertson, R.G., 69

Cullen, Francis T., 29, 32, 34-35, 36, 37, 39, 40, 41, 42, 45, 49, 50-51, 53 n.12, 61, 69, 70, 71, 72, 73, 74, 75, 76, 77, 78, 79, 83, 84, 88, 90 n.8, 101 n.1, 107, 109, 118, 119, 120, 122 n.6

Culture Conflict and Crime (Sellin), 87

Cunneen, Chris, 46

Current Issues in Criminal Justice, 96, 97

Currie, Elliott, 107
Cusson, Maurice, 69, 71, 72, 74, 78

Daly, Kathleen, 35
Daro, D., 39
Davies, Graham M., 39
Decker, David L., 16, 25-26
Deisher, R., 69
del Carmen, Rolando V., 37, 53 n.3, 80
  n.3, 95
Delinquency Careers in Two Birth Cohorts
  (Tracy, Wolfgang, and Figlio), 88
Delinquency in a Birth Cohort (Wolfgang,
  Figlio, and Sellin), 23-24, 31, 42, 72,
  87, 88
Developmental Psychopathology, 53 n.7,
  66
Deviant Behavior (Akers), 41
Deviant Behavior (journal), 53 n.4, 66, 97
DeZee, Matthew R., 18, 19, 92
Diamond, Arthur M., Jr., 2
"Dimensions of Delinquency: Estimating
  the Correlates of Participation, Fre-
  quency, and Persistence of Delinquent
  Behavior" (Smith, Visher, and Jarjoura),
  42
Dinitz, Simon, 83
Discipline and Punish (Foucault), 24
Divergence. *See* Criminology and criminal
  justice, relations between
Dobash, R. Emerson, 45
Dobash, Russell P., 45
Doctoral programs. *See* University depart-
  ments, citations and
"Does Correctional Treatment Work? A
  Clinically Relevant and Psychologically
  Informed Meta-Analysis" (Andrews et
  al.), 40, 42
Doharia, J.J., 69, 73
Doob, Anthony N., 44, 45, 48, 51, 72, 74,
  77, 78
Dorn, Nicholas, 44
Douglas, Robert J., 7
Downes, David M., 43, 53 n.13, 69
Durkheim, Emile, 14, 84, 87, 90 n.9, 101
  n.1, 106, 109, 112 nn.8, 9, 118
Dutton, Donald G., 45

Earles, C.M., 39
Edelhertz, H., 69

Egeland, Byron R., 39
Elliott, Delbert S., 28, 30, 31, 32, 33, 34,
  35, 38, 41, 42, 43, 45, 49, 50, 51, 61,
  69, 71, 73, 75, 77, 78, 83, 84, 88-89, 90
  n.8, 101 n.1, 107, 109, 117, 118, 119,
  120
Endler, Norman S., 2, 3, 4, 9
Engels, Friedrich, 106, 108, 110, 112, n.8
England, Ralph W., Jr., 83
"Erectile Responses among Heterosexual
  Child Molesters, Father-Daughter Incest
  Offenders and Matched Nonoffenders"
  (Barbaree and Marshall), 38
Erickson, Martha F., 39
Ericson, Richard V., 45, 47, 69, 72, 74, 77,
  78
Erwin, Billie S., 69, 71, 75, 76
Evaluating Criminology (Wolfgang, Fig-
  lio, and Thornberry), 88
Explaining Delinquency and Drug Use
  (Elliott, Huizinga, and Ageton), 33, 41
"Extra-Legal Attributes and Criminal Sen-
  tencing: An Assessment of a Sociologi-
  cal Viewpoint" (Hagan), 36, 40, 42
Eysenck, Hans J., 69, 106, 110

Fabianic, David A., 3, 25
Fagan, Jeffrey A., 29, 32, 35, 50, 83
Farrington, David P., 2, 4, 6, 7, 8, 14, 15,
  16-18, 20, 23-24, 26, 27, 28, 30, 31, 32,
  33, 34, 35, 37, 39, 40, 41, 42, 43, 45,
  47, 48-49, 50, 51, 55-56, 61, 65-66, 69,
  70, 71, 72, 73, 74, 75, 76, 77, 78, 79,
  81, 82, 83, 84, 85, 89, 90 n.8, 94-95,
  101 n.1, 104, 107, 109, 111, 116-17,
  118, 119, 120
Federal Probation, 25, 26, 67, 68, 97, 99
Fehrenbach, P., 69
Felson, Marcus, 29, 31, 32, 35, 37, 41, 50,
  70, 83, 101 n.1, 108, 119, 120
Ferber, Marianne A., 8, 9-10
Ferracuti, Franco, 83, 107
Ferri, Enrico, 108
Figlio, Robert M., 1, 4, 5, 13, 24, 29, 30,
  33, 38, 52, 76, 78, 81, 82, 83, 85, 89
  n.1, 101 n.1, 106, 110, 119
Finkelhor, David, 39, 69, 70, 71, 73, 75,
  76, 77, 78
Fisse, Brent, 46
Flanagan, Timothy J., 35, 40, 50, 52, 83,

84, 89, 90 n.8, 101 n.1, 107, 118, 119

Florida State University, 18

Folkman, S., 37

Foucault, Michel, 24, 43, 47, 48, 77

Fox, Richard G., 46, 47

Frechette, Marcel, 45, 69, 72, 77

Freiberg, Arie, 47

Freud, Sigmund, 8, 106, 108, 110, 112 n.8

Freund, Kurt, 39

From Boy to Man, From Delinquency to Crime (Wolfgang, Thornberry, and Figlio), 88

Fyfe, James J., 35, 38

Gabor, T., 69

Garfield, Eugene, 2, 4, 7, 8, 10

Garland, David, 44, 46, 48

Garofalo, James, 74, 78

Geis, Gilbert, 5, 46, 52, 69, 84, 89 n.1, 101 n.1, 107, 109, 118

Gelles, Richard J., 36, 45, 69, 70, 74, 76, 78, 84, 101 n.1, 107, 110, 118

Gendreau, Paul, 35, 38, 39, 41, 45, 50, 52, 69, 72, 73, 75, 77, 78, 83, 120

A General Theory of Crime (Gottfredson and Hirschi), 29-31, 33, 40-41, 48, 52

Gerard, Douglas R., 83

Gibbons, Don C., 84, 101 n.1, 109, 118

Gibbs, Jack P., 29, 52, 84, 101 n.1, 107, 109, 118, 119

Gilbert, G. Nigel, 8

Glaser, Daniel, 83, 107

Glenn, Norval, 92

Glueck, Eleanor T., 30, 69, 71, 75, 76, 83, 84, 87, 89 n.5, 90 nn.6, 7, 10, 101 n.1, 107, 110, 112 n.9, 118

Glueck, Sheldon E., 30, 69, 71, 75, 76, 83, 84, 87, 89 n.5, 90 nn.6, 7, 10, 101 n.1, 107, 109, 112 n.9, 118

Goffman, Erving, 24

Goldfeder, Eileen, 25

Goldstein, Herman, 35, 84, 101 n.1, 117, 118

Goodrich, June E., 5

Gordon, Randall A., 2, 12

Gorenflo, Daniel W., 12

Goring, Charles, 107, 108, 110, 112 n.8

Gottfredson, Don M., 37, 101 n.1, 119, 120

Gottfredson, Michael R., 28, 30, 32, 33, 34, 35, 37, 40-41, 43, 45, 48, 49, 50, 51, 61, 67, 69, 70, 71, 72, 74, 75, 76, 78, 79, 83, 84, 89, 90 n.8, 101 n.1, 106, 109, 118, 119, 120

Gove, Walter R., 31

Grabosky, Peter, 46, 48

Granting Felons Probation (Petersilia et al.), 42

Grasmick, Harold G., 28, 32, 34, 120

Greenberg, David F., 29, 30, 52, 101 n.1, 119, 120

Greene, Jack R., 115

Greenwood, Peter W., 84, 101 n.1, 107, 117, 118

Griffiths, Curt T., 46

Groth, Nicholas A., 69, 107

Habermas, Jurgen, 37

Hackler, James C., 45

Hagan, John L., 28, 31, 32, 33, 34, 35, 36, 37, 40, 41, 42, 49, 50, 51, 59, 70, 71, 74, 75, 78, 83, 84, 89, 90 n.8, 101 n.1, 109, 118, 119, 120

Hall, G.C.N., 39

Hall, Jerome, 83, 107

Hamermesh, Daniel S., 2

Hare, Robert D., 39, 69, 73, 75, 77

Harer, Miles D., 31

Hargens, Lowell L., 11

Harris, Grant T., 39

Hartl, Emil T., 83

Hartung, Frank E., 83

Hawkins, Gordon J., 46

Hawkins, Richard, 36

Healy, William, 83

Herrnstein, Richard J., 84, 101 n.1, 106, 109, 118

Hiller, H., 69

Hindelang, Michael J., 17, 23, 24, 28, 30, 32, 33, 34, 35, 37, 41, 42, 45, 49, 51, 69, 70, 73, 74, 75, 76, 79, 83, 84, 89, 90 n.8, 101 n.1, 107, 109, 118, 119, 120

Hirschi, Travis, 28, 29, 30, 32, 31, 33, 34, 35, 36, 37, 39, 40, 41, 42, 43, 45, 47, 48, 49, 50, 51, 52, 61, 67, 69, 70, 71, 72, 73, 74, 75, 76, 77, 78, 79, 83, 84, 89, 90 n.8, 101 n.1, 105-6, 109, 118, 119, 120

Hoge, Robert D., 45

Holmes, Malcolm D., 115, 121, 122 n.1

Home Office, 67
Hooton, Ernest A., 107
Hope, Timothy J., 44
"Hot Spots of Predatory Crime" (Sherman, Gartin, and Buerger), 34, 40, 42
Hough, J. Michael, 43, 48, 52
Huizinga, David, 28, 29, 30, 31, 32, 33, 34, 35, 37, 41, 42, 49, 50, 61, 83, 107, 120

Ianni, Francis A.J., 107
Importance of journals. *See* Journals, ranking of
Inches-of-print. *See* Length of coverage, as measure of influence
Inciardi, James A., 84, 101 n.1, 107, 109, 118
Inside-outside index, 9
International Journal of Comparative and Applied Criminal Justice (ICJA), 52, n.2, 66, 68, 69, 73, 98
International Journal of Offender Therapy and Comparative Criminology (IJOT), 52 n.2, 66, 68, 69, 73, 98, 99
International Review of Victimology, 96, 97
Irving, Barrie L., 44
Irwin, John, 107, 110
ISI (Institute for Scientific Information), 2, 5, 10
The Islington Crime Survey (Jones, MacLean, and Young), 47

Jackson, Mona, 47
Jacobs, James B., 52, 101 n.1, 119, 120
Jaffe, Peter G., 45, 48
Janson, C.G., 69
Jefferson, Tony, 43, 47
Jeffery, C. Ray, 108
Jensen, Gary F., 29, 32, 35
Jesness, Carl F., 40
John Jay College, 18
Johnson, George E., 2
Johnson, Louise A., 83
Jones, Trevor, 44
Journal of Abnormal Child Psychology, 53 n.7, 66
Journal of Crime and Justice, 26, 80 n.1, 97
Journal of Criminal Justice (JCJ), 23-26,

36-37, 38, 40-41, 50, 52 n.1, 57-59, 61, 62, 66, 68, 69, 71, 95, 96, 97, 99, 114-15, 117, 122 n.1
Journal of Criminal Justice Education, 96, 97, 102 n.10
Journal of Criminal Law and Criminology (JCLC), 25-26, 66, 92, 96, 97, 99
Journal of Economic Literature, 9
Journal of Fertility and Sterility, 11
Journal of Interpersonal Violence (JIV), 53 n.8, 66, 68, 69, 70, 98
Journal of Police Science and Administration, 53 n.8, 66
Journal of Quantitative Criminology (JQC), 23-26, 30-31, 33, 50, 53 n.10, 57, 58, 61, 62, 65, 67, 68, 70, 93, 95-97, 114, 116
Journal of Research in Crime and Delinquency (JRCD), 23-26, 31-32, 34, 50, 57, 58, 61, 62, 65, 67, 68, 69, 95-97, 99, 114, 116-17
Journals, ranking of: citation studies (objective), 91, 92-94, 96-97, 99-100; composite, 93, 94, 96, 98, 100, 102 n.11; importance of journals, 100; luminaries, 20-21, 91, 94-96, 98-101, 102 nn.6, 8, 9, 103; prestige of journals, 15, 21, 101; reputational (subjective), 91, 92-94, 96-98, 99-100
Jurik, Nancy C., 37
Justice Quarterly (JQ), 6, 23-26, 34-36, 38, 40, 41, 50, 53 nn.10, 12, 57, 58, 61, 62, 66, 67, 68, 69, 71, 93, 95, 96-97, 114-15, 117, 121, 122 n.1
Juvenile and Family Court Journal, 53 n.8, 66, 98

Kandel, Denise B., 67, 69, 75
Kaplan, M.S., 39, 69, 75
Kappeler, Victor E., 38
Katz, Jack, 107
Kawchuk, Karman B., 6, 10
Kelling, George L., 37, 45, 50, 83, 84, 89, 90 n.8, 101 n.1, 117, 118
Kennedy, Leslie W., 45
Kilpatrick, Dean G., 69, 70, 76
Klein, Malcolm W., 69, 73, 75
Klockars, Carl B., 107, 110
Kobrin, Solomon, 83
Kohlberg, Lawrence, 38

Korn, Richard R., 83
Koss, Mary P., 36, 40
Krisberg, B., 69
Kroes, William H., 38
Krohn, Marvin D., 14, 28, 30, 32, 34, 35, 50, 52, 83, 101 n.1, 119, 120
Kvaraceus, William C., 83

LaFave, Wayne R., 84, 101 n.1, 117, 118
Land, Kenneth C., 29, 30, 32, 34, 38, 120
Lander, Bernard, 83
Langworthy, Robert J., 35
LaPrairie, Carol P., 45
Latent content analysis, 112 n.1. *See also* Content analysis
Latessa, E.J., 69
Laub, John H., 28, 30, 120
Law and Human Behavior, 53 n.6, 66
Law and Society Review, 53 n.5, 66, 96, 97, 99-100
Laws, D. Richard, 39
Lazarus, Richard S., 37
Lea, John, 43, 47
LeBlanc, Marc, 45
Lee, Robert S., 83
Lemert, Edwin M., 84, 90 n.9, 101 n.1, 106, 109, 118
Length of coverage, as measure of influence: inches of print, 104-5, 111, 112 n.3; page coverage, 21, 103-6, 108, 109, 110-11, 112 n.3
Leschied, Alan W., 45, 48
Lewis, Orlando F., 83
Lilly, J.R., 69
Lind, N. C., 11
Linden, Rick, 45
Lindesmith, Alfred R., 83
Link, Bruce G., 37, 39
Lizotte, Alan J., 31
Loeber, Rolf, 29, 31, 32, 35, 44, 45, 50, 74, 78, 83, 120
Lombroso, Cesare, 106, 108, 110, 112 n.8
Long, J. Scott, 5
"The Long-Term Evaluation of a Behavioral Treatment Program for Child Molesters" (Marshall and Barbaree), 38
Luminaries. *See* Journals, ranking of
Lutzker, J.R., 39

MacKinnon, Cahterine, 69, 73

Maguire, Kathleen F., 107
Maguire, Mike, 43
Maltz, Michael D., 31
Manifest content analysis, 104-5, 112 n.1. *See also* Content analysis
Manning, Peter K., 38, 44, 47
Marenin, Otwin, 19
Markwart, Alan E., 45, 48
Marshall, William L., 38, 29, 40, 41, 50, 83, 120
Martinson, Robert M., 37, 51, 69, 71, 75, 76, 77, 78, 101 n.1, 108, 119, 120
Marx, Karl, 106, 108, 110, 112, n.8
Maslach, Christine, 37
Matsueda, Ross, 29
Matthews, Roger, 44
Matza, David, 47, 83, 84, 87, 89 n.5, 90 nn.9, 10, 101 n.1, 106, 109, 118
Maurer, David W., 83
Maxfield, Michael G., 36, 44, 46
Mayhew, Patricia M., 43, 48, 51, 52, 72, 74, 77, 78
McCaghy, Charles H., 108
McCarthy, Belinda R., 38
McCleary, Richard B., 31
McConnell, James V., 12
McConville, Michael, 43
McCord, Joan, 36, 40, 83
McCord, William, 83
McCorkle, Lloyd W., 83
McDermott, Eugene, 83
McDermott, Kathleen, 44
McDowall, David, 31
McElrath, Karen, 92
McGinnis, Robert, 5
McGlothlin, William H., 31
McIntyre, Jennie, 83
McKay, Henry D., 106, 108, 110, 112 n.8
McShane, Marilyn D., 26, 92-93, 95, 98-99, 100, 115, 122 n.2
Meadows, A. J., 2
Mean citation index, 11
The Measurement of Delinquency (Sellin and Wolfgang), 88
Measuring Delinquency (Hindelang, Hirschi, and Weis), 23-24, 29, 42
Mednick, Sarnoff A., 69, 70, 74, 77, 78, 84, 101n.1, 107, 109, 118
Megargee, Edwin L., 38, 29
Meier, Robert F., 5, 89 n.1

Mendel syndrome, 7
Merton, Robert K., 7, 83, 88, 90 n.7, 106, 108, 110
Messner, Steven F., 31, 33
Mijares, Tomas, 3
Miller, Walter B., 83, 84, 88, 90 n.7, 106, 110
Miracle, Andrew W., Jr., 25, 92
Mitchell, Michelle, 9, 65
Mittelman, M.S., 40
Monahan, John T., 39
Morgan, Rod, 43
Morris, Allison M., 69, 72, 77
Motiuk, Larry L., 39
Moyer, Sharon, 45
Mugford, Stephen K., 47
Mukherjee, Satyanshu K., 47
Mullens, Nicholas C., 2
Murphy, Chris, 45
Murphy, D.L., 32
Murphy, W.D., 40
Myers, C. R., 2, 3
Myers, Martha A., 35, 37, 41, 50, 83, 120

Naffine, Ngaire, 47
Nagin, Daniel S., 28, 30, 32, 33, 34, 50, 83, 120
National Academy of Science, 2, 17
National Institute of Justice, 27, 67
The National Survey of Crime Severity (Wolfgang et al.), 88
Neal, David J., 47
The New Criminology (Taylor, Walton, and Young), 48
New York University, 18
Newbold, Greg, 47
Niederhoffer, Arthur, 83
The 1988 British Crime Survey (Mayhew, Elliott, and Dowds), 43
Normandeau, Andre, 45
North, Robert C., 89 n.3
Nurco, David N., 31

Objective techniques. *See* Journals, ranking of
Obliteration by incorporation, 8
O'Brien, Robert M., 16, 25-26
O'Connor, Ian, 47
Ohlin, Lloyd E., 7, 29, 32, 50, 52, 69, 75, 78, 83, 84, 85, 89 n.5, 90 nn.6, 7, 8, 10,

101 n.1, 106, 109, 118
O'Malley, Patrick M., 33, 46, 48
Oreland, L., 32
Oxford University, 9

Page coverage. *See* Length of coverage, as measure of influence
Pardeck, John T., 11-12
Parker, James D. A., 10
Parker, L. Craig, Jr., 25
"Participation in and Frequency of Delinquent Behavior" (Nagin and Smith), 42
Paternoster, Raymond, 28, 30, 31, 32, 33, 34, 36, 50, 52, 83, 120
Patterns in Criminal Homicide (Wolfgang), 24, 42, 72, 88
Patterson, Amy L., 18-19, 20, 26, 93, 96-97, 98-99, 100, 102 nn. 9, 11
Patterson, Gerald R., 29
Pearson, Geoffrey, 43
Pease, Kenneth, 43, 48, 69, 72
Peer evaluation, 92; rankings, 2-3, 16, 17; recognition, 8; review, 3, 65, 94
Peritz, B. C., 7
Petersilia, Joan, 30, 32, 35, 37, 41, 42, 49, 52, 69, 70, 71, 75, 76, 78, 83, 84, 89, 90 n.8, 101 n.1, 107, 109, 118, 120
Polansky, N.A., 39
"Police Cynicism and Professionalism" (Lotz and Regoli), 36
Police Journal, 66, 98
Police Studies, 66, 97
Policing, 66, 98
Policing Domestic Violence (Sherman), 42
Polk, Kenneth, 47
Poole, Eric D., 15-16, 25, 26, 36, 37, 40, 49, 51, 67, 69, 71, 75, 76, 78, 92, 93, 101 n.1, 119
Porporino, Frank J., 39
Porterfield, Austin L., 83
Portland State University, 18
Pratt, John, 47
"Predicting Child Molesters' Response to Treatment" (Abel et al.), 38
Prestige of journals. *See* Journals, ranking of
Principles of Criminology (Sutherland), 88
The Prison Journal, 66, 96, 97
Proctor, W.C., 39

Producer-consumer index, 9

Qualitative content analysis. *See* Latent content analysis
Quantitative content analysis. *See* Manifest content analysis
Quay, Herbert C., 39
Quetelet, Adolphe, 107, 108, 110, 112 n.8
Quinney, Richard, 14, 36, 46, 51, 69, 72, 74, 77, 78, 84, 90 n.9, 101 n.1, 106, 109, 118
Quinsey, Vernon L., 39, 40, 41, 60, 83, 120

Radzinowicz, Leon, 47, 83
Reaffirming Rehabilitation (Cullen and Gilbert), 34, 36
Reckless, Walter C., 83, 84, 87, 89 n.5, 90 nn.6, 7, 10, 101 n.1, 106, 109, 118
Reductionism, 18
Regoli, Robert M., 15-16, 25, 26, 36, 37, 40, 50, 51, 69, 71, 76, 83, 92, 93, 101 n.1, 119
Reiner, Robert, 44
Reiss, Albert J., Jr., 29, 32, 35, 38, 50, 52, 83, 84, 85, 88, 89 n.5, 90 nn.8, 10, 101 n.1, 107, 109, 118
Reputational techniques. *See* Journals, ranking of
Research on Sentencing (Blumstein et al.), 24
Rice, Marnie E., 39
Richards, J. M., Jr., 10-11
Roberts, Julian V., 45
Robins, Lee N., 29, 69, 73
Robinson, David D., 39
Roche, Thomas, 9
Roediger, H. L., III, 3, 4
Rogers, Joseph W., 80 n.3, 95
Rogers, Robert D., 39
Roland, Charles G., 5
Rosenbaum, Dennis P., 45, 69
Rosenberg, Milton J., 4
Rosenfield, Eva, 83
Rosenthal, Uriel, 69, 72, 77
Ross, Robert R., 38, 45, 52, 69, 72, 73, 74, 77, 78
Rossi, Peter H., 46, 49, 51
Roth, Jeffrey A., 31, 33
Royal Society of London, 2

Rushton, J. Philippe, 2, 3, 4, 9
Rutgers University-Newark, 19, 20

Sacco, Vincent F., 45
Samenow, Stanton E., 106, 108, 110
Sampson, Robert J., 14, 28, 29, 30, 31, 32, 33, 34, 35, 37, 41, 42, 44, 49, 50, 69, 70, 74, 76, 78, 83, 101 n.1, 119, 120
Saunders, Dean G., 69, 70, 74, 76
Scarpitti, Frank R., 114, 115-16, 121
Schmidt, Peter, 31
Schur, Edwin M., 109
Schwendinger, Herman, 107
Schwendinger, Julia, 107
SCI (Science Citation Index), 2, 4-6, 7, 10-11, 20
Scutt, Jocelynne A., 46
The Second Islington Crime Survey (Crawford et al.), 47-48
Self-citations, 6, 8, 9, 11, 12, 27, 67, 79 n.b, 124
Self-feeding index, 9
Sellin, Thorsten J., 14, 24, 30, 31, 32, 33, 51, 83, 84, 87, 89 n.5, 90 nn.6, 7, 10, 101 n.1, 106, 109, 118, 119
Sentencing (Doob and Roberts), 44, 46
Shapland, Joanna M., 44
Shaw, Clifford R., 83, 106, 108, 110, 112 n.8
Shearing, Clifford, 47
Sheldon, William H., 83, 106, 108, 110, 112 n.8
Sherman, Lawrence W., 31, 32, 34, 35, 36, 37, 40, 41, 42, 44, 46, 47, 48, 49, 50, 51, 69, 71, 75, 76, 78, 83, 84, 89, 90 n.8, 101 n.1, 107, 109, 118, 119, 120
Shichor, David, 14, 16, 25-26, 89 n.2
Short, James F., Jr., 29, 83, 84, 89 n.5, 90 nn.6, 7, 10, 101 n.1, 107, 109, 118
Shover, Neal, 107
Sigelman, Lee, 1
Silverman, Robert A., 45
Singer, Simon I., 107
Sirken, M.G., 69
Skogan, Wesley G., 49, 67, 101 n.1
Skolnick, Jerome H., 31, 35, 37, 41, 43, 45, 46, 48, 49, 52, 69, 71, 76, 83, 84, 90 n.9, 101 n.1, 106, 109, 118, 119, 120
Smart, Carol, 47, 69, 73, 75, 77
Smith, Adrian, 5-6, 7

Smith, David J., 43
Smith, David Lewis, 9
Smith, Douglas A., 28, 31, 32, 34, 35, 37, 41, 42, 49, 69, 70, 83, 120
Smith, Michael D., 45
"Social Change and Crime Rate Trends: A Routine Activity Approach" (Cohen and Felson), 41
"The Social Dimensions of Correctional Officer Stress" (Cullen et al.), 36, 40
Social Forces, 13, 101 n.4, 102 n.9, 114
Social Justice (SJ), 53 n.4, 66, 68, 69, 73
Social Problems, 53 n.4, 66, 101 n.4, 102 n.9
"Social Structure and Anomie" (Merton), 7, 108, 110
The Society of Captives (Sykes), 117
Soma, Colette, 2, 13, 14-15, 81, 82, 83, 85, 87-88, 89 n.2
Sorensen, Jonathan R., 18-19, 20, 26, 93, 96-97, 98-99, 100, 102 nn.9, 11, 114, 115-16, 121
South, Nigel, 44
Spafford, Duff, 6, 10
Specialization, 8, 24, 29, 34, 36, 44
"The Specific Deterrent Effects of Arrest for Domestic Assault" (Sherman and Berk), 42
Spielberger, Charles D., 40
SSCI (Social Science Citation Index), 2, 4-6, 9, 10-11, 12, 16, 17-18, 19, 20, 24, 26, 55-56, 93-94, 99
Stack, Steven, 16, 26, 93, 99, 100, 102 n.11
Stanko, Elizabeth A., 46
Steadman, Henry J., 52
Steffensmeier, Darrell J., 30, 36, 84, 101 n.1, 106, 109, 118
Steinmetz, Susan K., 69, 70, 74, 76, 79
Straus, Murray A., 32, 35, 39, 41, 44, 45, 48, 49, 51, 69, 70, 71, 74, 76, 78, 79, 83, 84, 89, 90 n.8, 101 n.1, 107, 109, 118, 120
Streifel, Cathy, 31
Strodtbeck, Fred L., 83
The Subculture of Violence (Wolfgang and Ferracuti), 24, 99
Subjective techniques. *See* Journals, ranking of
SUNY-Albany, 18, 20

Sutherland, Edwin H., 14, 29, 32, 34, 52, 83, 84, 87, 88, 89 n.5, 90 nn.6, 7, 9, 10, 101 n.1, 105-106, 109, 112 nn.8, 9, 118, 119, 120, 122 n.6
Sutton, Adam, 47
Sweetland, James H., 5
Sykes, Gresham M., 14, 83, 84, 87, 89 n.5, 90 nn.6, 7, 10, 101 n.1, 106, 109, 117, 118

Taggart, William A., 115, 121, 122 n.1
Taking Account of Crime (Hough and Mayhew), 43
Tappan, Paul W., 83, 108
Tarde, Gabriel, 107, 108, 110, 112 n.8
Taylor, Ian R., 47
"Techniques of Neutralization" (Sykes and Matza), 87
Teeters, Negley K., 83
Thomas, Charles W., 18-19, 37
Thornberry, Terence P., 1, 4, 5, 13, 30, 37, 50, 81, 82, 83, 85, 89 n.1
Tittle, Charles R., 28, 29, 32, 34, 38, 52, 84, 101 n.1, 107, 109, 118, 119, 120
Toch, Hans, 37, 38, 39, 41, 50, 52, 69, 83, 101 n.1, 119, 120
Tompkins, William F., 83
Tonry, Michael H., 35, 37, 41, 50, 69, 83, 120
Tracy, Paul E., 107
Travis, Lawrence F., III, 18
"Trends in the Use of Custodial Dispositions for Young Offenders" (Doob), 44
Turk, Austin T., 84, 90 n.9, 101 n.1, 106, 109, 118
Turner, Susan F., 37
Twentyman, C.T., 39

University departments, citations and, 3, 9, 12-13, 18-20, 91. *See also individual universities*
University of California-Berkeley, 18, 19
University of Cincinnati, 20
University of London, 9
University of Maryland, 18, 19, 20
University of Missouri-St. Louis, 20
University of Pennsylvania, 18, 19
"Urban Black Violence: The Effect of Male Joblessness and Family Disruption" (Sampson), 42

Vanderbilt University, 18
Varieties of Police Behavior (Wilson), 34, 40, 42
Vaughn, Michael, 53 n.3, 80 n.3, 95
Veronen, L.J., 69
Versatility, 8, 24, 29, 34, 36, 38, 44
Vicari, Pamela J., 2, 12
Victimology, 66
Violence and Victims (VV), 53 n.8, 66, 68, 69, 70, 98
Visher, Christy A., 29, 30, 31, 33, 34, 36, 37, 50, 83, 120
Visions of Social Control (S. Cohen), 43, 48
Vold, George B., 14, 83, 84, 87, 89 n.5, 90 nn.6, 7, 9, 10, 101 n.1, 107, 109, 118
Von Hirsch, Andrew, 49, 51, 101 n.1, 119

Wagoner, Carl P. 26, 92-93, 95, 98-99, 100, 115, 122 n.2
Waldo, Gordon P., 29, 33
Walker, John, 46, 48
Walker, Nigel D., 44, 47, 48
Walker, Samuel, 37, 84, 101 n.1, 118
Ward, Richard H., 115
Wardlaw, Grant, 47
Washington State University, 19
Webb, Vincent J., 115
Weber, Max, 100
Weinrott, Mark R., 40
Weir, Adrianne, 83
Weis, Joseph G., 31, 33, 52, 53 n.11, 69, 73, 75, 84, 101 n.1, 110, 118, 119
Weisbrod, Burton A., 2
Welljams-Dorof, Alfred, 10
Wells, Gary L., 39
Werner, Mary A., 11-12
West, Donald J., 29, 43, 52, 75
Whitehead, John T., 37
Who Becomes Delinquent? (West and Farrington), 42
Wice, Paul B., 84, 101 n.1, 117, 118
Widmayer, Alan G., 18-19, 20, 26, 93, 96-97, 98-99, 100, 102 nn.9,11, 114, 115-16, 121
Widom, Cathy S., 29
Wiles, Paul N.P., 44
Wilkins, Leslie T., 69
Williams, Frank P., 26, 92-93, 95, 98-99, 100, 115, 122 n.2

Williams, Kirk R., 32, 35, 50, 83
Wilson, James Q., 14, 17, 23, 28, 31, 32, 34, 35, 37, 40, 41, 42, 44, 46, 49, 50-51, 61, 69, 71, 72-73, 74, 75, 76, 77, 78, 79, 83, 84, 89, 90 n.8, 101 n.1, 106, 108, 109, 118, 119, 120
Wilson, Kathryn E., 11-12
Wilson, Paul R., 46, 48, 69
Wilson, William J., 29
Witte, Ann D., 30
Wolfe, David A., 39
Wolfgang, Marvin E., 1, 4, 5, 13, 14, 17, 23, 24, 28, 30, 31, 32, 34, 35, 37, 40, 41, 42, 44, 45, 47, 48, 49, 51, 69, 70, 71, 72, 73, 74, 75, 76, 77, 78, 79, 80, 82, 83, 84, 85, 88, 89 n.5, 90 nn.6, 7, 8, 10, 101 n.1, 106, 109, 118, 119, 120
Wormith, J. Stephen, 39
Wright, Richard A., 2, 13, 14-15, 80 n.3, 81, 82, 83-84, 85, 86, 87-88, 89 n.2, 94-95, 104-5, 109-10, 112 nn.1, 2, 116-17, 118, 120
Wundersitz, Joy, 47

Yale University, 18
Yeager, Peter C., 107
Yllo, K., 69, 70, 76
Yochelson, Samuel, 106, 108, 110
Yoels, William C., 12-13
Young, Jock, 43, 46, 47-48, 50, 51, 69, 73, 75, 77, 83, 84, 89, 90 n.8, 101 n.1, 107, 109, 118

Zdenkowski, George, 47
Zimring, Franklin E., 36, 75
Zola, Irving K., 83

About the Authors

ELLEN G. COHN is Assistant Professor of Criminal Justice in the School of Policy and Management at Florida International University. She has published extensively in both criminology and psychology journals in both the United States and the United Kingdom. Her primary research interest involves the examination of the relationships between weather and criminal behavior.

DAVID P. FARRINGTON is Professor of Psychological Criminology at Cambridge University and President-elect of the American Society of Criminology. He is the author of numerous articles and books, including the award-winning *Understanding and Controlling Crime* (1986).

RICHARD A. WRIGHT is Assistant Professor in the Department of Criminology, Sociology, Social Work, and Geography at Arkansas State University. His previous works include *In Defense of Prisons* (Greenwood Press, 1994).

ISBN 0-313-30153-0

90000>

EAN

9 780313 301537

HARDCOVER BAR CODE